LOCAL AUTHORITIES AND THE CREATION OF EMPLOYMENT

Local Authorities and the Creation of Employment

J. A. CHANDLER
and
PAUL LAWLESS
Department of Public Administration
Sheffield City Polytechnic

Gower

© J.A.Chandler and P.Lawless 1985

Published by
Gower Publishing Company Limited,
Gower House, Croft Road,
Aldershot, Hampshire GU11 3HR, England

and

Gower Publishing Company,
Old Post Road, Brookfield,
Vermont 05036, U.S.A.

British Library Cataloguing in Publication Data
_____

Chandler, J.A.
   Local authorities and the creation of employment.
   1. Labor supply---Great Britain   2. Local government---
   Great Britain
   I. Title   II. Lawless, P.
   331.12'042   HD5765.A6

ISBN 0 566 00765 7

Printed in Great Britain

Contents

Preface

This book is intended to be of value to the practitioner in
local government and to students of the British local
government system. We hope that local authority officers
and councillors who are interested in developing the
economy of their community may find in this work many
valuable ideas and examples of good practice to aid the
promotion of this policy. The book is however intended to
be not only a critique of schemes to create employment
practiced by local authorities. It also aims to locate
employment creation strategies within the context of
economic and local government policy within Britain.

A particular problem in writing this study is to determine
what should be omitted since so much of the activities of a
local authority can indirectly relate to levels of employment.
We have kept the analysis strictly to a study of schemes
aimed at creating new jobs or better conditions of work
within Counties and Districts. The book does not therefore
consider in detail the development of commercial centres in
cities since this task is not intended to primarily create
further employment. We have also excluded studies of local
authority projects aimed at improving the lot of the
unemployed, by means other than creating employment, and
therefore do not consider the valuable work of centres for
the unemployed or claimants advice groups. As a study of
local authority initiatives the book also omits schemes to
alleviate unemployment initiated by government, such as
assisted area programmes, or by industry, such as business
enterprise agencies, that may involve local authority
co-operation but which are not under the control of local
government. Despite these omissions there remains a large
and varied pool of projects that have been developed by local
authorities to create employment despite indifference and,
on occasion, hostility from central government. We hope the
study will suggest that within local government in Britain
there is much ingenuity and competence that deserves to be
encouraged rather than constrained.

This study began in 1979 and was aided by a three year local authority research grant from Sheffield Metropolitan District Council, although the study itself was conducted independently of that Authority. Much of the research was conducted between 1979 and 1982 by Mrs Jaqueline Yates in addition to the two authors and we particularly wish to acknowledge her contribution to the work.

The book could not have been written without the co-operation of many councillors and local government officers whom we have interviewed during the last few years. It would be impossible here to list them all but we wish to express our thanks to everyone who has assisted the project. We cannot recall any occasion when workers in local government have refused, despite other commitments, to find time to talk or to correspond with us. Particular thanks is however due to Councillor Helen Jackson the Chairman of Sheffield City Employment Committee, Dr Andrew Coulson, until recently an officer in Sheffield City Employment Department, and Mrs Judy Chandler who have read and commented on parts of this book. We would also like to thank colleagues in our departments who have shown an interest in this work and particularly Bob Haigh who initially encouraged us to write this book and Roger Ottewill who helped initiate the original research project.

J A Chandler write chapters 1, 2, 3, 4, 8, 9, 10 and 15. Paul Lawless wrote chapters 5, 6, 7, 12 and 14. Chapters 11 and 13 were joint efforts.

Part I
The evolution, justification and scope of local authority economic activity

1 The development of employment creation

Local Authorities have always had a significant role as employers and made decisions that have had a major impact on the development of local economies. The subject of this book is not concerned, solely, with an area of innovation as it describes an activity that is intrinsic to the work of any local authority. The provision of education, roads and housing as well as many other local government services clearly have an important impact on the local economy although policies may not be developed primarily with economic consequences in mind.

The conscious creation of new employment by local authorities does however have the appearance of being a new departure for many councils. Many authorities are creating new initiatives in order to decrease local unemployment and it may well be the area of greatest expansion within local authorities during the 1980s. The extent of interest in employment creation has prompted the conclusion following a survey of local authority intervention by the Association of District Councils (1980) that:- 'support and development of the local economy is now a top priority for almost every local authority.' Although there is clearly a renewed enthusiasm for employment creation it is certainly not a new departure but rather a reawakened interest. Alleviation of high levels of unemployment was given considerable prominance by a number of local authorities in the 1930s and economic intervention was an important factor motivating policies of many large municipalities in the late 19th Century. This chapter will set recently developed interventionist policies in the context of the mainstream traditions of local authority activity. It will outline the decline of interventionist attitudes current in the late 19th Century and their revival in a different guise during the years of economic depression.

The modern structure of local government in Britain emerged
as a consequence of industrialisation and the growth of
cities. The formation of overcrowded, insanitary urban
conurbations alongside the heightened affluence of newly
enriched entrepreneurs created such obvious contrasts and
injustice that there were constant demands for social
regulation of the worst features of urban life. Behind many
of these demands lay fears that violence would follow in the
wake of squalor and degradation. Fear and concern over the
social conditions of cities was however assuaged by the
knowledge that the alleviation of these problems would cost
the wealthier citizens within these communities higher rates
on both their commercial and domestic interests (Hennock
1973). It required the business skills of industrialist
politicians such as Joseph Chamberlain to find an answer in
municipal enterprise to the problem that faced affluent city
rate payers.

Local government as opposed to local control by the courts
and landed gentry evolved during the 19th Century through a
process of piecemeal legislation to regulate pressing social
problems. In 1835 the Municipal Corporations Act allowed a
number of cities to establish town councils that were empowered
to raise a rate and have limited powers in dealing with items
such as drainage and street lighting. Not all towns leapt at
the opportunity and fears of increased local taxation led some
cities, such as Sheffield, to delay creating for themselves
a municipal corporation (Hampton 1970). Apart from those
areas controlled by town councils most areas of England were
increasingly subject to control by ad-hoc local organisations
formed to meet specific problems. The reform of the Poor Law
in 1834 established locally elected Boards to deal with the
increasing problems of poverty and destitution within the
context of laissez-faire economic beliefs. A passion for
creating Boards characterised local administration throughout
the mid-Century. In 1862 the Highways Act created district
committees to take care of many major roads. Local school
boards were established in 1871 to provide compulsory
elementary education. The need for better sanitation and
public health care was met by the formation of local health
boards under the Public Health Acts of 1848 and 1875. These
ad-hoc developments bequeathed to local government a confused
collection of powers administered in frequently overlapping
areas that were superimposed on the remaining administrative
interests of the Justice of the Peace and the Quarter
Sessions. Some of the confusion and administrative disorder

was rectified by the Local Government Act of 1888, which established the county councils and county boroughs, and the Local Government Act of 1894, which transformed local health boards into urban and rural district councils. These Acts established the basic framework of local government in Britain until 1972. It was a design with many defects that were further exacerbated by continued urban growth. The establishment of five types of major local government unit created a complex pattern of frequently overlapping powers. Administration of urban areas was hindered by the widely differing sizes of local government units which were confined to boundaries that were based on traditional divisions that had ceased to reflect the economic unity within communities established as a consequence of industrial growth.

The Local Government Act of 1972 was a none too successful attempt to modernise the local administrative system. It has created a two tier system of local government in which the greatest responsibility is given to the county councils whose boundaries were partially redrawn. The counties spend approximately $\frac{2}{3}$ of the local government expenditure in their areas and are responsible for most major services, including education, social services, police, highways and strategic planning. The district authorities which form the lower tier of the system have, as major responsibilities, housing and jointly with the county councils certain planning decisions. The balance of powers between county and district is however reversed within six Metropolitan Counties which have the more reduced portfolio of highways, transport, the police and strategic planning. At the time of writing the future of these counties is in doubt given proposed legislation for their abolition. The metropolitan districts have major responsibility for education, social services, housing and planning. A two tiered system of local government was also established in Wales whilst Scotland was divided into nine large regional councils which have powers similar to the non-metropolitan counties and have a second tier of district councils whose main interest is in the provision of housing. London had been subject to local government reform in 1963 which established a pattern similar to the metropolitan councils in which a Greater London Council had powers over strategic planning and transport whilst smaller London boroughs held the responsibility for social services and housing and outside the inner city, education.

LOCAL GOVERNMENT POWERS AND ECONOMIC INTERVENTION

Although there has been a major enquiry into the structure of
local government and a subsequent major overhaul of the
boundaries and functions of each tier there has never been
a systematic attempt to define the powers of local as
opposed to central government. The responsibilities assigned
to local authorities have been acquired through piecemeal
legislation to meet specific needs of localities as perceived
by governments during the last two centuries and to a lesser
extent through initiatives raised by the local authorities
themselves. Many of the powers that were acquired have
important economic repercussions but few were allocated with
the intention that they allow councils positively to shape
the local economy.

The most important duties assigned to local authorities
during the first half of the 19th Century were concerned with
regulating public health. The Municipal Corporations Act of
1835 provided town councils with powers to improve health,
sanitation and safety within urban areas. The municipal
corporations were however able to expand their powers through
the promotion of private bills in parliament and, as shall be
discussed later, gained in certain cities considerable
interests within the local economy. The county councils
were originally provided with an ill assorted set of powers
that they took over from the courts of quarter sessions.
They had responsibilities for major roads and police at the
most significant level and many minor duties such as the
management of asylums or prevention of infection among farm
animals. Not until 1903 were the county councils able to
promote legislation that enabled them to expand their powers
on their own initiative (Keith Lucas and Richards 1978).

The Local Government Act of 1894 was primarily designed to
break down a confused pattern of local boards established on
an ad-hoc basis to deal with specific problems. Urban and
rural district councils took over the powers and the areas
designated to the health boards and in addition they acquired
the responsibilities previously administered by highways and
burial boards. In 1902 the school boards were abolished and
their powers distributed among the various tiers of local
authorities. The poor law boards were however left as a
separate organisation until 1932 when they were also incorporated into the local government system with their powers over
health care, social services and the relief of poverty being
transferred to the county councils and county boroughs.
Many of these powers were not held for long since central

6

government took over the duty of providing national
assistance to the poor two years later and with the establishment of the National Health Service in 1949 transferred many
hospitals under local authority control to the new service.
Local authorities were however left with responsibilities
for individual social welfare which were expanded by post war
legislation and in 1970, following the Seebohm Report,
brought together through the Local Authorities Social Services
Act which forms the basis of the present social service
responsibilities held by local authorities.

An important range of powers in terms of economic impact
that are held by local authorities concern the provision of
housing and the regulation of planning. The Artisans
Dwelling Act of 1868 permitted municipal corporations to
replace houses considered on grounds of sanitation to be
unfit for habitation. The Act was further enlarged in the
1870s but could not form the basis of large scale housing
schemes as all revenue for building had to be provided by the
local authority. It was not until 1919 that the era of
council housing estates came into being, through the Housing
and Town Planning Act which made provision for government
subsidies and local borrowing powers. In 1925 the Housing
Act consolidated preceding legislation into provisions that
form the basis of the present housing services provided by
local authorities.

Effective planning powers are one of the later acquisitions
of local government and were obtained through a lengthy and
rather tortuous process of legislation. The Housing and
Town Planning Act of 1909 first gave local authorities
responsibility for planning although this was confined solely
to allowing them to submit to parliament provisions for lay-
ing out housing estates. In 1919 a Housing and Town Planning
Act obliged joint planning committees to devise plans to
deal with housing needs although the cumbersome procedures
connected with the parliamentary approval of these schemes
made it almost impossible for even the most enthusiastic
council to comply with the law. Planning powers were further
extended in 1932 to all types of land but local authorities
were relieved of the obligation to submit plans and any
scheme that was put forward remained subject to acceptance
by parliament which had the undesired effect of making plans
once approved totally inflexible (Cullingworth 1976).

By the 1930s the impact of garden city projects, the
increasing difficulties of commuting especially in London,
and the depression gave greater impetus to advocates of

planning as a means not only of regulating environmental
problems but of creating conditions for more effective social
and economic development. In 1934 the Special Areas Act
initiated under central government control schemes to
alleviate unemployment in the most depressed areas. The
problem of serious unemployment in Northern cities led to the
establishment in 1938 of a Royal Commission to investigate the
economic and social problems created by the growth of large
industrial conurbations. The Barlow Report which was the
outcome of the investigation was published just after the
outbreak of the Second World War and could not immediately be
put into effect. Its proposals which included suggestions
for dispersing industrial development and creating a national
mechanism for planning had considerable influence on the
1945 Labour Government. The Report paved the way for the
1947 Town and Country Planning Act which imposed on county
and county borough councils a duty to devise development
plans for their communities and gave them powers to regulate
all forms of building development within their areas.

By 1947 local authorities had gained considerable powers
to influence their local economies through planning regulations although these were essentially negative and restictive
powers. They could arrange the location of industry or
housing and prevent many forms of social and environmental
dangers and disasters but they could not through these
powers do much positively to encourage the establishment of
new sources of employment within their areas. The following
two sections of this chapter will trace the principal
movements which have enabled local authorities up to 1945
positively to intervene in local economic development.

MUNICIPALISATION

The main task of the Municipal Corporations Act of 1835 was
to establish councils that would remove some of the most
socially unpleasant excesses of rapid urban and industrial
development. These aims had clear economic repercussions by
providing a better environment in which to establish new
business and, at least for the more farsighted employers, a
healthier and more capable workforce. In addition to their
powers granted by government sponsored legislation the new
corporations were able to seek additional powers through
bills privately sponsored in parliament. The potential for
expanding local powers through such means was considerable.
Parliament allocated much of its time to the scrutiny of
private bills and many politicians were not opposed to

limited extensions of local powers. The most important field for expansion during the second half of the 19th Century was the municipalisation of public utilities such as gas and electricity which normally could only be operated by either public or private organisations as a result of legislation. The major restraint on expansion of local schemes for economic intervention was not at this time government or parliament but the local councils themselves.

For most of the 19th Century candidates for local office had to comply with property qualifications which ensured that most municipal councils were governed by men of some means. The growing industrial cities for the most part attracted business and tradesmen to their councils. Commercial sectors affected by local authority activity, such as publicans eager to keep an eye on the licensing committees, formed groups of vested interest on councils to ensure that the local authority did not curtail their business activities. Small businessmen regardless of political affiliation tended to be hostile to local authority spending and rejected all but the most essential projects in order to keep rates at as low a level as possible (Hennock 1973). The capital involved in major improvement schemes was moreover beyond the dreams of the average city innkeeper or workshop master so that few wished to risk ratepayers' involvement in such grand projects (Hennock 1973). The growth of town councils into prestigious municipal corporations with considerable involvement in their local economies was predominantly fostered by large scale manufacturers who were attracted in considerable numbers to local government during the second half of the 19th Century. Successful industrialists such as Joseph Chamberlain in Birmingham had the business experience and acumen to handle the large sums of money that were necessary to develop municipal enterprise and were also able to appreciate the value of municipal reforms to the growth of industry and commerce.

Prior to the accession of a number of wealthy businessmen to Birmingham City Council, long overdue schemes to improve sewage disposal and drainage had been advanced in the city in a very limited form through fear of overburdening the rates. Joseph Chamberlain solved the economic and development problems of the corporation by following the example of a number of other cities which had bought their local gas companies. Chamberlain was able to demonstrate that a single municipal gas undertaking in the city would not only end the hazards connected with competition between two rival privately owned gas companies but also produce a considerable source

of revenue for the Corporation (Hennock 1973). His scheme
was as profitable as his expectations and was soon followed
by the municipalisation of the water company and an ambitious
and successful scheme to remove slum property from the centre
of the city in order to develop a major commercial thorough-
fare, aptly named Corporation Street, which would ensure
Birmingham's place as the major shopping centre in the
Midlands. The success of Chamberlain's schemes showed that
a local authority was able to buy local monopolies which if
properly managed could provide not only a service but profits
that could be used to pay for other improvements within the
city. In Birmingham it was possible by this means not only
to improve local services but also decrease rates and even
the price of gas (Hennock 1973). Despite the success of
Chamberlain's schemes he saw strict limits to the extent of
municipilisation. He believed that it was necessary to take
over services that were established by an Act of Parliament
to hold a monopoly position within a particular area but was
not in favour of extending local public ownership to businesses sponsored on a competitive basis by private capital
(Hennock 1973). The interest among businessmen to promote
municipal enterprise will in part have been motivated by
commercial reasons since privately held monoplies for the
distribution of services and raw materials could lead to
profiteering at the expense of manufacturers of private
goods. They were not however willing to face the municipalisation of their own business interests.

The municipalisation of local services was nevertheless a
major area of expansion in local government between 1870 and
1914 and it involved a direct commitment to intervention in
the local economy. By 1914 local authorities held 37% of
the gas services within the country, 66% of electricity
companies, and many water companies (Robson 1954). In
addition to these concerns they had also taken control in
many areas of local public transport services and a range of
trading ventures such as abattoirs, markets and public wash
houses. Towards the end of the era of municipalisation it
was possible to develop a number of very adventurous schemes
such as the Birmingham municipal bank founded in 1915 and
Hull City's management of telephone services.

The extension of local authority powers through municipalisation came to an end during the 1920s as it became
increasingly difficult to pass through parliament legislation
necessary to establish local enterprise. The growth in the
time given to government as opposed to private bills within
parliament in part contributed to this trend. There was more

seriously an increasing aversion among Members of Parliament and in particular those within the Conservatives to approve legislation that appeared to move towards greater collective ownership as favoured by the Labour Party. Throughout the preceding years the wealthy businessmen who had promoted schemes involving municipalisation were becoming less interested in city politics partly as a result of the emergence of the Labour Party as an important political force in the industrial cities.

Given the support for municipalisation by Labour Party theorists such as George Bernard Shaw and the Webbs it is surprising that once in power, either in local authorities or after 1945 in government, the Party made little attempt to foster public ownership through local councils. During the pre-1945 period many local Labour Party supporters may have been suspicious of a movement promoted largely by local businessmen. Robert Tressell depicted these doubts in his portrayal of the tradesmen councillors of Mugsborough Borough Council debating how to cut their losses in an electric company in which they held personal shares.

> 'I've tried to sell my little lot several times already' said Didlum 'but nobody won't buy 'em' 'Whose to buy?' repeated Sweater ... 'the municipality of course, the ratepayers. Why shouldn't Mugsborough go in for socialism?' (Tressell 1965, p.306)

After 1945 the implications of Keynsian economic planning made local economic solutions to unemployment unfashionable. Thus by 1930 many cities owned municipal enterprises but there was little capacity for any great extension of these powers.

THE DEVELOPMENT MOVEMENT

The end of expansion in the field of municipalisation coincided with the growth in interest and awareness in the possibilities of planning. Regulations in this area were largely negative in character and could only be implemented by following some highly cumbersome procedures. The work of pioneers in planning such as Ebeneezer Howard had however brought to the attention of more far sighted city fathers the possibility of using their powers to redesign their communities in order to provide full employment and attractive living conditions. The depression of the 1930s gave further impetus to many urban councils seriously to consider how they could plan their areas in order to alleviate the high level

of unemployment and resultant social depression that had
settled like smog on industrial Britain. Unemployment in the
1930s, just as in the 1970s, was a major stimulus to local
authority intervention in the economy.

Government reaction to the depression was to exercise
traditional deflationary policies which tended to exacerbate
rather than alleviate economic decline. Ministers did not
in general appreciate the possibilities of positive
encouragement of industry let alone see any role for local
authorities in expanding production and activity. A very
limited response to the problems of the areas of highest
unemployment was the Special Areas Act of 1934 which
appointed commissioners with some funds at their disposal to
establish new industry in four designated areas of serious
economic hardship. Many local organisations were by this
time using the limited powers and funds available to establish
their own agencies for redeveloping the economies of their
areas.

The development associations established through local
initiative in the 1930s were usually set up on an area basis
and covered territory administered by a number of authorities
which had similar economic problems. On occasion development
associations were formed to cover a single authority such as
Bristol or the task of development was taken over solely by
the borough itself as in the case of Birmingham. The
organisations were in many cases brought together through the
initiative of local businessmen rather than local councillors
and, in the case of the special areas designated by government,
by the special commissioners. Local authorities were however
invariably represented on the committees that controlled the
development agencies although they did not always hold the
majority of seats. (Fogarty 1947)

The development associations were almost wholly voluntary
organisations that had no legal foundation and therefore
varied greatly in respect to their size, effectiveness and
composition. A few associations such as the Medway Towns
District Full Employment Committee put forward highly
ambitious aims:-

> 'The District Community Group is the basic governing
> unit of a modern industrial democracy ... full employ-
> ment combined with a full and satisfactory life can
> be obtained only by taking account of people's
> 'homes' and other strong social group ties.'
> (Fogarty 1947 p.11)

12

Certain associations such as the West Cumberland Development Council, situated in a special area, could attract sufficient government funds to become powerful self regulating bureaucracies administering highly ambitious projects. At the other extreme many councils were little more than occasional discussion groups for local authorities and businessmen that did little or more than publish an occasional leaflet advertising the merits of their area.

Many of the activities that were initiated by the development movement form an important part of the interventionist policies of present day local authorities and in certain fields there has been a continuity of action from the 1930s until the present. The most widely practised function of the committees apart from their role as a discussion forum was the attraction of new industry into their communities through publicity campaigns. This activity which has now become a well accepted function of local government is considered in detail in Chapter 3 had its origins in schemes to promote tourism.

An organisation was established as early as 1917 by spa towns to promote their attractions and after the First World War seaside resorts also began to promote their delights for holidaymakers. Belatedly legal recognition of these efforts was provided in the Health and Watering Places Act of 1921 which permitted local authorities to spend up to a penny rate in promoting tourism. The Act was further extended in 1936 and by this time certain major resorts such as Blackpool were spending considerable sums of money through their publicity committees in order to boost the major source of income for the town. (Fogarty 1947)

A development arising from publicity aimed at attracting tourists was efforts to attract industrialists to the cities. The Local Authorities (Publicity) Act of 1931 gave such an activity an ill defined legality by providing the Travel Association of Great Britain with the responsibility for attracting new industry into the country in addition to tourists. The apparent simplicity of the principle of solving local unemployment by attracting new industry has led to a considerable emphasis being placed on publicity by local authorities wishing to develop their economies. Advertising is however expensive and was within most development agencies the most costly item of their budget. The merits of particular towns were nevertheless promoted widely through press adverts, brochures, posters and exhibitions during the 1930s and many of the larger development committees employed full time publicity and information officers (Fogarty 1947).

An equally significant and certainly more valuable activity promoted by the development associations was the establishment of industrial estates. The idea of planned industrial sites was by no means new and had been a major part of early planning philosophies. The concept of trading estates was made a reality in the development of Letchworth and Welwyn Garden City. The construction of factory units in well planned and serviced estates was an obvious method of creating and maintaining employment within the depressed areas but it was an exercise only open to the largest authorities or to the Special Areas which could build the estates with the aid of government grants. Within Special Development Areas such as West Cumberland the development committee established a subsidiary company to manage the construction and operation of these estates which proved in some of the most depressed parts of industrial Britain to be capable of attracting new employers (Fogarty 1947).

In addition to publicity and the provision of factory space the development associations attempted to establish many of the activities aimed at alleviating unemployment that are discussed within this book. The associations frequently commissioned surveys of their areas that foreshadow the compulsory structure planning of the present day. Efforts were made to convince local authorities, the government and private industry to improve local infra-structure. The West Cumberland Development Council for example successfully pressed for major improvements to the railway line serving the Cumbrian coast. (Fogarty 1947) Schemes were established by a number of associations to train the local workforce for the new industries although many of these ventures received little encouragement from the government. A joint scheme between local authorities and new local industries promoted by the Development Council in West Cumberland is reported by Fogarty as providing the County with one of the best facilities for technical training within the country (Fogarty 1967).

Apart from the practical efforts to regenerate employment within depressed areas during the 1930s a number of local authorities also attempted to alleviate their problems through more dramatic protests. The most spectacular but not the only example of such action was the Jarrow Hunger march to London which was organised in part by the local urban council in order to protest at the closure of shipyards which were the main employers in the town. It is impossible to assess the exact impact of this protest but its position within the tradition of labour protest suggests that it has had a lasting impact in shaping attitudes towards local unemployment.

The inter-war years had witnessed the ending of expansion of local authority intervention in their economies through municipalisation of services but had with the depression produced a strong development movement that could be linked to planning powers. The progress of the development associations was greatly altered by the war which by 1942 brought to an end the immediate problems of unemployment in all areas of the country and produced much greater government direction of economic development which was geared almost exclusively to the exigencies of total war. The post 1945 governments were not inclined to return to the 1930s in respect to central government and local relations

POST WAR DECLINE

Since the second world war local authorities have enjoyed a considerable expansion in terms of their expenditure in real terms and in the numbers of their employees. Local authority revenue expenditure increased threefold in real terms between 1952 and 1972 (Keith Lucas and Richards 1978) and the number of individuals employed by local authorities increased by 78% during this period. (Poole 1978) The expansion is not so much a result of new tasks being imposed on local authorities but rather an increase in the scale of activity in their traditional service duties. During the 1960s local authorities with government aid were encouraged to build large council estates. Schools and colleges received larger numbers of pupils and benefited from a reduction in the pupil staff ratios. The elements of social and health care left to the authorities and in particular the area of social work were greatly expanded. Although local government increased in size it did not increase in scope. The 1947 Town and Country Planning Act and the 1947 Childrens Act provided local councils with significantly expanded duties in the area of planning and social services but outside these areas central government removed rather than increased the range of local authority powers.

A major casuality in the post 1945 tendency to place local administration in the hands of central or regional organisa- tions has been the demise of municipal enterprise. The 1945 Labour Government's conception of the ownership of the means of production extended only to national ownership rather than municipal or co-operative control. The nationalisation of the gas and electricity services took over many companies

administered by locally elected councils and placed them in
the hands of appointed national boards. The responsibility
of local authorities for water supply and drainage was
gradually taken from local control by the amalgamation of
council water and drainage committees and finally in the
Water Act of 1973 which established 10 huge, non-elected
water authorities to serve Britain. Municipally operated
bus services were for a time placed in the hands of non-
elected transport executives although they were returned
to local authority control by the 1972 Local Government Act.
Recent Conservative Governments have also passed legislation
to restrict the powers and operation of direct works
departments. Outside the sphere of economic intervention the
process of nationalisation and amalgamation has removed wholly
or in part from local authorities services such as hospital
provision and the police service.

The lack of enthusiasm for local authorities as a major
element of government is also shown in the attempts of post
war governments to stimulate industrial development. Although
local authorities were given a measure of planning control,
subject to appeals to the Minister, by the 1947 Act, the
Labour Government excluded local authority participation from
many other aspects of their planning strategy. Central
government held the power to designate particular parts of
the country as development areas without any need for formal
consultation with the local authorities concerned. The 1947
Town and Country Planning Act permitted government to
determine the location of industries through the award of
industrial development certificates which again did not
require for their award consultation with local authorities.
One of the most marked demonstrations of government disdain
for local authorities was the New Town Act of 1946 which set
up corporations appointed by central government to establish
the new centres. The process was not left to either locally
elected councils or the county councils.

The post-war decline in the interventionist powers of local
authorities cannot be regarded as solely the result of
legislation passed by governments which were either oblivious
or contemptuous of the potential economic role of local
authorities. Although many parliamentarians had little
experience or interest in local government their indifference
could not persist if pressure for greater economic powers had
been resolutely pressed upon them by the leaders of large
authorities or through the ranks of the major political
parties. Local politicians during the 1950s and 1960s showed
little interest in gaining further controls over their local

economies. During these two decades the Labour Party Annual
Conference debated the need for a reform of the rating system
on several occasions but it was not until debates took place
in the 1970s on the reform of local government boundaries
that any serious concern was expressed by conference delegates
on the loss of local economic powers to central government.
The lack of interest in local economic intervention was
reflected in a decline of the development movement. The role
of these groups had been considerably modified by war and the
end of unemployment. Many smaller development councils disappeared by 1945 or became little more than discussion groups.
Larger development councils such as the West Cumberland
organisation were often content to administer schemes established in the 1930s or in the immediate post war years.
Although some councils disappeared others however were to be
formed in the post war years although within this fluctuating
pattern of development organisations there were few if any
major innovations in the employment creation practices
established in the 1930s. The development movement did not
disappear but became stagnant.

A number of factors led to the retreat from municipalisation
and the decline of the development movement. It has been
indicated earlier in this chapter that Conservatives and
Liberals objected to public control of profitable services
when this became associated with socialist ideas of
collective ownership. Conservative idealogy in all its forms
ascribes at most a limited role to public ownership and in
general holds that economic development should stem largely
from the activities of independent entrepreneurs. Despite
a theoretical commitment to the ownership of the means of
production the Labour Party has done as much since 1945 to
prevent municipalisation as the Conservative Party. A
number of Labour councillors in the late 1940s may still have
held the view suggested by Tressell that municipalisation
would aid rich councillors at the expense of poor workers.
A further factor was the lack of interest in collective
socialist policies among many members of the party and the
deferential attitudes of some members who believed that in
capitalist society businessmen are better fitted to operate
a successful enterprise than manual workers. These
attitudes also permeated Labour cabinets. Few post 1945
Labour M.Ps believed as did Shaw that socialist controlled
local authorities free to intervene in the local economy
would be so successful that their example would be accepted
by electors throughout the country.

The stagnation of the development movement after the Second
World War owes much to the acceptance by both major parties

of Keynsian economics which demands central rather than local
economic controls. Governments cannot manipulate the economy
if local authorities are able to determine prevailing levels
of public expenditure. It is probable that this factor will
for some time dissuade governments from permitting local
authorities to raise large sums of money outside the close
surveillance and regulation of the Treasury. Probably the
most important factor prompting the decline in the development
movement was however full employment and the relative
prosperity of the 1950s and 60s. The expansion of the
economy was sufficient to alleviate many of the problems of
long term unemployment that had been a mark of the 1930s.
The most pressing problem facing conurbations was not seen to
be the creation of employment but the management of environmental problems created by growth. The Buchanan Report on
traffic in towns was very much a document of this age,
concentrating not on planning transport systems to aid
industrial efficiency or improve labour mobility but to
resolve the environmental hazards that would accompany the
creation of a society in which every family owned at least
one car.

THE END OF INDUSTRIAL DEVELOPMENT

Although it has been indicated that after 1945 there was
relatively little enthusiasm for employment creation by
local authorities within central government or among
councillors and their officers it would be misleading to
suggest that there was little or no activity in this area.
The post war years certainly witnessed the virtual elimination
of whatever had remained of the ideal of municipalisation but
they marked a consolidation of the economic development
movement. Camina shows that the more widely practised
elements of the development movement were well established
by 1972 in the larger authorities. In that year 62% of
county boroughs employed an industrial relations officer,
72% had land available for industrial use, and 47%
advertised their area to promote industrial development
(Camina 1974). In addition to these activities many
holiday resorts continued to promote their attractions in
order to secure greater numbers of visitors to their towns.

   The predominant form of local employment promotion had
however reached by 1970 a static if accepted pattern.
Authorities offered land and premises for incoming or
expanding industries, on occasion provided rent concessions
or key worker housing, and often advertised the values of
their territory to secure relocating firms. These packages

18

were administered by the now well recognised post of
Industrial Development Officer or in smaller or less
interested authorities through officials in Planning or
Estates Departments. Given this pattern very few authorities
were offering schemes that were any advance on the methods
used in the 1930s to overcome local unemployment. The now
established nature of the scheme had however moved the role
of employment promotion to a backwater of local authority
innovation. Councillors were not in general enthusiastic
about a policy that had become routine, professionalised and
at a time of relatively high employment not of immediate
value to the authority. The Industrial Development Officer
was housed in obscure offices as a forgotten element of
Planning and Estates Departments. The office although in
receipt of a regular budget in many cases received as much
interest from councillors or senior officers as they gave
to the local authorities function of providing burial grounds.

2 The revival of economic intervention

Although the three decades following the end of the Second World War can be described as at best a consolidation of a land, premises and publicity package developed in the 1930s the succeeding years have seen a major revival in employment creation strategies. A larger proportion of local authorities have taken an interest in directly influencing their local economies following the reform of local government boundaries and the reemergence of higher levels of unemployment. Many authorities are now pursuing schemes pioneered in the 1930s development movement of making land and premises available to expanding industries, improving industrial infrastructure, and publicising the attractions of their areas for businessmen and tourists. In addition to these established techniques there has also been a growth in innovations aimed at securing greater local authority influence within local economies among a relatively small number of larger authorities. Alongside the provision of land, premises and publicity these innovatory councils have for example developed schemes to fund local industry, promote and buy local products, advise and shelter new businesses and encourage differing forms of industrial ownership. This chapter will outline the extent of employment creation activity among local authorities during the first half of the 1980s and also discuss some of the motives that have led local authorities to renew their interest in local economic intervention.

THE EXTENT OF LOCAL AUTHORITY ECONOMIC ACTIVITY

Although there has been an increasing awareness within local government of their potential for developing local economies this movement has not been taken up with equal degrees of enthusiasm by local politicians. It is not intended here to provide a detailed analysis of the extent of employment creation activity within local authorities or the social and demographic factors that may be associated with such policies. The growth in new techniques of employment creation has made it difficult to compare levels of activity between local

20

authorities given that there is more to politics of local
economic intervention than simply appointing an industrial
development officer with the task of administering a land
and attraction package.   It is nevertheless possible to make
some generalisations about the extent of employment creation
based largely on data relating to the appointment of staff to
deal with this policy area.

The study of local authority interest in the attraction of
industry by M.M. Camina (1974) showed that among the pre-1974
local authorities, county councils and county boroughs were
much more active than the less powerful tiers of local
government.   This pattern has persisted within the new
structures of local government.   Metropolitan county councils
have all developed an active interest in employment creation
and among all types of authority are the most consistently
involved in such activities.   They have all established well
staffed industrial development units and many have pioneered
new techniques, such as providing industrial finance through
enterprise boards.   The high level of interest in employment
creation within the metropolitan counties is paralleled by the
Greater London Council which has become particularly active
through the creation of the Greater London Enterprise Board
following the Labour Party acquisition of control over the
authority in 1981.   Should these authorities be abolished
by 1986 it is as yet unclear as to the fate of many of their
economic initiatives but the proposed legislation would
certainly break up important concentrations of interest and
initiative within the arena of employment creation.

In general the metropolitan district councils are active in
the field of economic intervention and all but three of these
authorities designate an officer who can be contacted about
industrial development.   The extent of enthusiasm however
varies considerably.   Several metropolitan district
authorities are in the forefront of innovation and their
activities will be frequently mentioned within this study.
Sheffield Metropolitan District Council is the first
authority to establish an employment committee at the same
level as other major committees of the council.   Bradford
Metropolitan District Council has established an employment
development unit that links both industrial and tourist
promotion.   Not all metropolitan districts are however
equally active in creating employment.   Within South
Yorkshire despite the considerable work of Sheffield two
other district authorities, Doncaster and Rotherham which
have considerably higher rates of unemployment than Sheffield,
have promoted few economic initiatives other than appointing
an industrial development officer and establishing factory

units. A similarly mixed pattern of economic activity is to
be found within the London boroughs where a number of councils
are highly active whilst others take little or no interest in
economic development. The pattern of activity in London
tends to correlate with levels of employment. The most
active authorities such as Southwark and Hackney are within
inner city areas whereas many of the least interested councils
such as Bromley are in the affluent suburbs. (London
Industry and Research Group 1981.)

Among the non-metropolitan counties 18 out of 47 reported
to the 1983 Municipal Yearbook that they had appointed an
industrial development officer whilst a further 18 designated
an officer to receive enquiries about industrial development.
Five counties situated in the South East have however
indicated within their structure plans that they wish to
restrict rather than promote industrial development within
their areas. A few non-metropolitan counties, particularly
those within development areas, show considerable interest
in employment creation. Cleveland County Council has for
example sponsored private legislation to extend their powers
over the creation of industrial estates and Mid Glamorgan was
probably the first authority to establish a local products
register. In general however non-metropolitan county
councils have demonstrated less enthusiasm for generating
employment than either the metropolitan counties or many metropolitan districts. Much of the activity within those
counties that have appointed industrial development officers
is confined to the traditional functions formed during the
1930s development movement. The Scottish regions demonstrate
a somewhat greater interest than the non-metropolitan counties
of England and Wales and all but one of these authorities
have appointed industrial development officers.

The extent of interventionist activity among the non-
metropolitan district councils in England was surveyed by
the Association of District Councils in 1980. They concluded
that they were:-

   'actively engaged in encouraging and assisting
   industry both in urban and rural areas, especially
   where the economic and employment base is
   declining or is not sufficiently diversified...'
   (Association of District Councils, 1980, p1.)

The survey showed that 70% of the responding councils were
particularly active in acquiring and servicing sites for new
industry. This level of apparent enthusiasm must however
be set against the low proportion of these authorities, 17%,
that, according to the survey, designated an officer to be

concerned with industrial development. The Municipal Year Book for 1983 records only 14% of district councils in England and Wales with industrial development officers although 74% provide the name of an officer who can be contacted on development questions. A survey by Chandler and Yates (1980) also suggests that non-metropolitan district councils in England and Wales are much less likely than other authorities to appoint joint consultative committees between the authority and local business interests. There appears to be no greater readiness among Scottish district councils to establish an industrial development officer and only seven of these authorities have made such an appointment. Several Scottish district councils consider that the task of employment creation is a regional rather than district responsibility. In general most of the non-metropolitan and Scottish district authorities that have appointed industrial development officers appear to pursue long established patterns of employment creation, designating land for industrial development, building or maintaining factory units and attracting industry or tourists through publicity. Some of the larger districts based around major industrial cities such as Glasgow and Kingston upon Hull have nevertheless used resources in pursuit of the more conventional techniques of employment creation and have also begun to divert funds into attracting tourists.

A final class of local government organisation that has an important impact on employment creation techniques are the new town corporations. Although these non-elected government quangos are excluded from detailed consideration in this book, recognition of the scale of their employment creation activity is necessary. The responsibility of these corporations to build new towns around industries imported into largely green field sites has given these organisations legislative and financial resources for attracting new industry that are greatly envied by many industrial development officers in local authorities. The methods used to attract firms to the new towns are however little more than those used by the development movement writ large. The new towns can offer custom built factories at initially low rent and can in addition provide housing for all required labour. The package is backed up by advertising and publicity budgets that few local authorities can match.

Analyses of employment creation in terms of the characteristics of the local authority area rather than the type of authority all suggest that the prevailing levels of employment within an area are an important factor underlying levels of activity (Camina 1974, Falk 1978, Middleton 1981) among county councils and Scottish Regions in 1983, three out of 13 authorities with less than 10% unemployment had according to the Municipal Year Book appointed industrial development officers although 14 out of the 29 with between 10% and 15% unemployment, and 13 out of the 19 with more than 15% unemployed had such an officer. Authorities in assisted areas are also much more likely to have appointed industrial development officers. Middleton (1981) found in a sample of authorities with populations exceeding 150,000 that 92% in assisted areas had appointed full time officers concerned with industrial development as opposed to 56% of these authorities in non-assisted areas.

It would however be premature to attribute high levels of interest in employment creation solely to rates of employment. Organisational and resource factors may have some bearing on employment creation. The innovatory techniques devised by metropolitan counties may be a reflection of the recent creation of these organisations as much as their responsibility for areas of economic decline. These counties possess considerable resources and were formed alongside the publication of initiatives such as the Bains Report arguing for a more corporate approach to policy making. The metropolitan counties were much better placed than more established larger authorities to incorporate these ideas into their organisational structures and as a result created administrative machinery that was more able to handle the multi-disciplinary demands of employment creation policies. Metropolitan counties may also have moved readily into the field of employment creation because of their relatively few powers in comparison with the large populations for which they had responsibility. Responsibility for economic development was a means of further substantiating their raison d'être.

Camina shows that in the pre-reorganisation authorities the resources available to the local authority had little or no bearing on the extent of its interest in employment creation (Camina 1974). Table 2:1 indicates that in the reformed system of local government the larger non-metropolitan district authorities are somewhat more likely to have appointed an industrial relations officer but little distinction can be made between those authorities with no interest in employment creation in relation to the resources, as measured by population, that they can command. (Municipal Year Book, 1983.)

Table 2:1
Officers concerned with Industrial development
in non-metropolitan districts by population

Population	Over 100,000	100,000 - 50,000	Less than 50,000
I.D.O.	22%	12%	2%
Non I.D.O. designated	56%	62%	70%
No officer designated	23%	26%	28%
Number in survey	108	187	36

The political control of an authority is a further and important variable that on occasion can be seen to have a direct impact on the extent of employment creation activity. A change in the political control of a council has had in some cases a dramatic effect on its economic policies. The Greater London Council became a leading innovator in employment creation only after the Labour Party gained control of the authority in 1981 whilst enthusiasm for employment creation has declined within Metropolitan Districts such as Birmingham and Calderdale when the Conservative Party took control within these authorities. Table 2:2 indicates that Labour controlled councils are more likely to report to the Municipal Year Book that they have an industrial development officer or at least someone who can be approached on developmental matters than do Conservative controlled councils.

Table 2:2
Non-metropolitan districts with I.D.Os and other officers
concerned with development enquiries by
Labour and Conservative control

	Labour	Conservative
I.D.O.	34%	9%
Non-I.D.O. designated	46%	65%
No designated officer	22%	26%
Number in survey	69	150

It cannot however be inferred from Table 22 that all
Conservative controlled councils are less interested in
employment creation than those under Labour control. Within
many authorities employment creation initiatives may be
determined by officers rather than elected councillors and
as will be shown in the next section both major parties
encompass a range of attitudes towards economic intervention
within local communities.

ECONOMIC MOTIVES

High employment levels in the decades immediately following
the Second World War created a climate in which most local
authorities had little need for interventionist policies.
Even in the more depressed areas of the country most local
authorities considered that the government's regional
economic policies along with a publicity and land package
was sufficient to overcome their problems. The growth of
unemployment in the 1970s resulting in over 3 million of
the workforce being without work by 1981 has reversed the
economic complacencies of the previous years and made the
creation of employment a central political issue at both
local and national levels. The extent of the economic
decline ought not to be underestimated. As Gudgin, Moore
and Rhodes (1982) point out the growth of unemployment has
occurred throughout extensive areas of the United Kingdom and
has characterised most sectors of the economy. It is true
that manufacturing decline has been especially marked in the
inner cities in particular but the outer suburban areas are
also beginning to encounter a contraction in employment not
just in manufacturing but in construction, distribution and
public utilities.

   The relative contraction of the British economy has
moreover created pockets of depression outside the major
conurbations. Small towns such as Consett or Corby which
lose their major employer face serious economic depression
whilst districts of small villages dependent on industries
such as mining as in the Durham coalfield may face complete
dereliction if the sole source of jobs within the area is
closed. Less obvious but nevertheless significant in terms
of numbers is the growth of unemployment in rural areas which
due to a generally higher than average standard of living
within their communities retain an outwardly more prosperous
image but nevertheless enclose an increasing number of
families suffering from both the economic and social
deprivations associated with unemployment.

Local councillors, regardless of their political
persuasion, and local government officers are just as likely
to be concerned at the effects of economic depression and
unemployment as Ministers, M.Ps and civil servants.   Although
local politicians may not have the powers of central government they are nevertheless likely to be motivated to use
whatever means are open to them to remedy the economic decline
within their communities.   An expression of this general
concern prefaces many local authority statements on their
economy strategy.   In its structure plan South Yorkshire
County Council wishes to ensure that there should be
sufficient jobs in the County to meet all needs up to 1986
and that there is a 'need for some 39,000 new jobs between
1976 and 1986 to reduce unemployment to 5%.   (South
Yorkshire MCC 1978, p2.)   The Greater London Council is
concerned in the 1981 Labour Party manifesto that 'over the
past 20 years the capital has lost some 500,000 jobs, a pace
of decline that outstrips any other region in the country'
(Greater London Council 1981, p7), whilst a more prosperous
city, York, with an interest in its economic future states
within an Economic Development Strategy Report that

> 'the face of industry is changing at a rapid rate,
> new growth industries are emerging and it is vitally
> important that we are able to attract them to York
> and to adapt to the requirements of modern electronic
> technological advances'   (City of York, 1983, p6.)

Underlying many general statements about local economic
decline and the need to retain future prosperity is a
realisation by many councils that the ability of their
organisation to fulfil adequately their statutory duties or
to have any significant impact on their communities is
dependent on a flourishing local economy.   A number of local
authorities realise that in the existing economic system the
strength of their organisation, the well being of their local
community and the viability of local industry are all
interdependent.   Sheffield City Council for example demonstrates a clear recognition of such links in a widely circulated leaflet replying to accusations that high rates harm
local business.

> 'Sheffield City Council and local industry are
> interdependent and the good health of each is
> important.   The Council provides services needed
> by industry and buys goods and services from local
> firms.   This is why we are concerned at the
> impact on the economy of the Government's monetary
> policy and why industry should be concerned at

Central Government's attack on local authorities'
(Sheffield City Council, 1981a, p1)

Closure of industries will have both immediate and long term
effects on the capacity of local authorities to influence
the development of their communities. Approximately 40% of
the revenue raised in rates by local authorities covering an
industrial area come from the commercial and industrial
sectors and this can amount to around 15% of the total
revenue for the authority. In addition to the loss of
revenue occasioned by industrial decline unemployment creates
greater demands on local services especially in the sectors
of personal social services and housing. The London
Borough of Hammersmith and Fulham for example justified, in
part, its employment creation policies on the grounds that:-

> 'Since the middle 60s there has been a rapid decline
> in the number and range of jobs available in the
> Borough which was creating severe hardship among
> certain groups such as manual workers, young
> coloureds, and non-manual female workers.....
> if solutions could not be found quickly then a
> large and rapidly increasing proportion of the
> Borough's population would require supportive
> services of one kind or another.'
> (Hammersmith and Fulham, 1980, p1)

In addition to the direct demands on local authority
services the downward spiral creates indirect pressures
through the deterioration of the physical environment
especially as a result of industrial dereliction and the
decline of the private housing stock. At its worst poor
environment, and poverty of these areas along with high
unemployment among the residual population can lead to
increases in crime and occasional outbreaks of collective
violence as occurred in Brixton or Liverpool which in their
turn require higher expenditure in law enforcement. An
additional problem facing local authorities is the progress-
ive reduction in grant from central government as a
consequence of Conservative policies since 1979. In these
circumstances some local authorities such as Liverpool are
facing the unpleasant alternatives that confronted, a decade
previously, a number of cities in the United States. They
must either face bankruptcy which would mean direct control
from central government and later the election of a
completely new council or a major reduction in the level of
social provision by the authority which would further
heighten the social crises that their councils wish to avoid.

In these circumstances local authorities may be desperately concerned to improve the local economy whilst they still have some capacity to make significant developments within their communities.

POLITICAL MOTIVES

Economic policy cannot be divorced from ideology.   The motives that determine local authority policy on employment creation are founded on prevailing ideological attitudes among political activists concerned with local government. During the 1960s it was fashionable to analyse party politics in Britain within an 'end of ideology' framework. The Atlee government had established a welfare state that provided safeguards for those who could not benefit from the predominant mode of production that remained securely in private hands.   A measured policy of nationalisation and Keynsian economics allowed the state to intervene in the management of the economy so as to uphold and maintain the largely private economic sector.   This 'Butskellist' consensus between the Conservative and Labour parties during the 1950s and 60s was reflected in the style of inter-party competition with both groups seeking to convince the electorate that they were the better managers of the mixed economy.   The ideological consensus was also reflected in a widely held view of the correct function of local authorities within the state.   Debate over the system of local government rarely touched on the question of the powers of local units but on their size, management structure and efficiency.   Local government formed an integral element of the welfare state and was largely concerned with dispensing a range of social services that could, under the tutelage of central government, be adapted to suit local conditions.

Although local councils had an important role in providing welfare services they did not replicate the role of the state in respect to economic intervention.   This was not however due to any ideological objection to their assuming such a role within their sphere of jurisdiction.   As we have indicated earlier, full employment through the operation of a centrally controlled economy ensured that there was little need for local authorities to have a predominant interest in economic regulation.   This role did however exist on the margins of local government through the work of industrial development officers who continued in the more depressed regions a tradition based on the rather different economic

29

circumstances of the 1930s.   The reemergence of unemployment
as a serious political issue has however created much
greater interest among local authorities in economic
intervention and for the many local politicians who are still
imbued with the political ideology that dominated the 1950s
and 1960s there is little that is anomalous in local authority
involvement with the local economy provided that it follows
the pattern as established by the 1945 Labour government of
being supportive of private capital and not an attempt to
supplant the predominant role of the private entrepreneur.

In local authorities in which the ideology of a mixed
economy welfare state is not seriously questioned the
principal aim of any interventionist strategies is to ensure
that the existing economic system is made to work
sufficiently well to secure full employment and local
prosperity.   The aims of the 1980 Wandsworth Borough Plan
in relation to employment clearly indicated an unquestioned
reliance on public aid to ensure private development.

> 'The present and future prosperity of the Borough
> depends on employment.   It is vital that existing
> employment is conserved and that local firms are
> encouraged to expand, and that new enterprises of
> all types are promoted.   Private sector invest-
> ment is crucial and the Council will do all it can
> do to encourage it.   The emphasis is on industrial
> and office employment and investment is being
> promoted on sites which could mean at least 15,000
> jobs more than half of these in industry.   The
> extension of training opportunities is crucial for
> local people to benefit fully from the new jobs
> created and for the prospects of future school
> leavers to be improved.'
> (Wandsworth Borough Council, 1980, p8)

Economic decline and a fall in support for the two major
parties has prompted many, although by no means all,
national political activists to reconsider their ideology.
Within the Conservative Party, Tory paternalism has been
overshadowed by a laissez-faire neo-liberal ideology which
has made the governments of Mrs Thatcher the most radical
in Britain since 1945 and done much to demolish the machinery
of the mixed economy welfare state.   In reaction the Labour
Party has become less accommodating towards private capital.
Although most Labour politicians fall short of adopting
a strictly Marxist approach to economic problems there is a
much greater demand within the Party that the balance of

power between capital and labour should be seriously altered rather than simply ensuring that capitalism has a human face. The re-assertion of these ideologies on the right and left have had considerable consequences for policies of employment creation.

The Conservative neo-Liberal stance is wholly inimical to local authority involvement in the economy. According to neo-liberals the economy will only expand if private individuals and groups are allowed to pursue their own interests given the incentive that they will hold on to what they gain by their enterprise. The principal barrier to private enterprise is government intervention and if the country is to be regenerated by reducing public interference in private enterprise then little value can be obtained from local authority attempts to solve the problems of unemployment. In line with this philosophy Conservative policies for overcoming the problems of acute economic depression have removed rather than increased local authority controls over industries. The establishment of enterprise zones for example ensures that firms can operate within estates that are free from many restrictions that can be placed on them by local authorities. Rather than emphasise a need for public employment Conservative councils imbued with a neo-Liberal philosophy have enthusiastically privatised local authority services which in many cases has resulted in a loss of jobs.

In contrast to these views the more radical philosophies current within the Labour Party provide motives for local economic intervention that add to their interest in alleviating the problems of local unemployment. These authorities which have been led by Sheffield District Council and the G.L.C. have concluded that the problems of unemployment cannot be solved by getting the existing economic system to work properly but by changing the system altogether. High levels of unemployment is a consequence of the capitalist system which must be modified if there is to be any permanent solution to the problem. The 1981 manifesto of the Labour Party group now controlling the Greater London Council states that:-

'We have shown that London's economic problems are the direct result of the largely uncontrolled operations of the free market.'
'The decline is now so serious that only a large scale investment programme aimed at key sectors of London's industry will rescue the

capital's manufacturing economy from almost total
annihilation. The public sector will have to
take an active role in such a strategy'.
(Greater London Council, 1981, p12.)

Public sector involvement within the economy should not,
according to socialist councillors, simply result in the
replacement of private capital by public capital. Local
authority intervention provides opportunities to create a
more equitable distribution of wealth and to ensure that
industry and commerce is more sensitive to local needs.
Sheffield City Council (1981) has justified establishing an
employment committee on account of:-

'the rapid rise in unemployment and the crisis facing
Sheffield's traditional industries. However the
longer term aim is to try to gain more direct, local
democratic control over employment and to impose a
greater degree of social planning on the structural
and technological changes taking place in Sheffield.
(Sheffield District Council, 1981b, p1.)

The 1981 Labour Party manifesto for the Greater London
Council was even more explicit on the opportunities that
local economic intervention could provide for changing
patterns of industrial control and ownership.

'The aim of the Strategy will be to strengthen the
economic base of Greater London.....In pursuit of
this aim we shall set out to increase the element
of democratic control over industrial decisions:
control by elected authorities so that investment
decisions are taken with regard to the wider
interests of the community, and control by work-
people in the workplace.

We shall encourage new forms of social ownership:
independent public ownership, and municipal
enterprise, as well as employment by the G.L.C.
itself. We shall use the position of the G.L.C.
to attempt to influence the manner in which
technological change is implemented, so that the
consequences of change are not increased by
lay-offs and redundancies, but a shorter working
week and more fulfilling working opportunities.

Particular attention will be paid to the development of producer cooperatives: not because we expect
the principles of cooperation to transform the London

economy overnight, but because we regard the
creation of new jobs under the control of working
people as a distinct advance.'
(Greater London Council, 1981, P 15.)

The desire to foster more equitable economic relationships
have led these councils to develop schemes for industrial aid
that place conditions on the recipients of help or favour
more disadvantaged groups. A number of Labour authorities
demand as a condition of financial aid that a company con-
forms to planning agreements that establish minimum standards
of working conditions for employees. Preference has been
given by many councils to funding cooperative commercial and
industrial enterprise and organisations such as the Greater
London Enterprise Board will provide preferential support
to minority groups wishing to set up a business.

The motive behind these schemes is a challenging attempt to
change prevailing economic relationships within Britain
although, as the extract from the G.L.C Labour Party manifesto suggests, one that most practically minded socialist
policy makers perceive as a distant goal. The extent to
which their policies are in practice more supportive of the
present system of private ownership than a means of fostering
new economic relationships will be questioned in later
chapters. The most enthusiastic municipal entrepreneurs are
faced with an economic structure which quickly forces them
into a position in which they can only support with public
funds industries that will be profitable within the existing
market place. Local government does not have the facility
of central government to support loss making industries.
Despite the doubts and limitations facing the socialist
authorities their activities nevertheless suggest the possibility of establishing new roles and functions for local
authorities which may have a major bearing on current theories of intergovernmental relations.

Part II
Local authority economic initiatives

3 Attraction of industry and commerce

City fathers beset with the problems of industrial decay may dream that the following morning they will awake to be inundated by requests from large employers wishing to establish non-polluting factories within their communities. Making such dreams a reality has exercised the minds of city councillors since the 1930s. 'Bring in new jobs to replace those that have been lost' appears to be an obvious solution to local employment problems but, as will be argued later, may also be one of the least effective means of creating new jobs.

Despite doubts surrounding policies to attract industry, until recently if an authority did nothing else to boost local employment it adopted strategies for attracting employers or tourists into its area. Fogarty observed in 1948 that:-

> 'publicity, lobbying and advisory services provide the core of the (development) movements work, whatever other functions may have become attached to it.' (Fogarty 1948, p.15)

On the basis of lists published in 1939 by The Travel Association and The Municipal Year Book he estimated that 85% of county boroughs and 35% of borough and urban district councils were in some way engaged in development work. This level of activity was greatly diminished during the war years and took some time to recover after 1945. Camina (1974) nevertheless found that in 1971 72% of county boroughs had land immediately available for industrial use whilst 48% of lower tier authorities could provide such a facility. The survey conducted in 1980 by the Association of District Councils shows that at least 57% of the responding lower tier authorities had land available for incoming industries and that 73% were engaged in publicising their facilities to attract employers.

STRATEGIES

In the earliest years of the development movement the methods of attracting industry concentrated on publicity and the task was regarded as having a similar role to that of attracting tourists. The similarity of interest was shown in 1932 when the Association of Publicity and Development Officers was established to represent the common interests of officers promoting industrial towns or tourist resorts. The organisation was however soon to develop a federal structure with separate sections representing tourist promotion and industrial development (Fogarty 1947) and in 1948 divided into two bodies with the members from the holiday towns forming what is now the British Association of Tourist Officers.

Advertising and public relations nevertheless remains a major element of the industrial development officer's work related to the attraction of industry although it is widely recognised that publicity is of little value unless the community has features worthy of promotion. The local councils and development associations of the 1930s developed their publicity campaigns around a package of benefits that they could offer incoming firms. The practice of attraction adopts today a similar pattern. The principal elements include the provision of land for industrial development, factory premises, suitable infra-structure provisions in the form of good communications, key worker housing and on occasion educational provisions. Considerable attention may now be paid to the cultural amenities of a town in its advertising and this has prompted some authorities to provide recreational facilities with at least a partial interest in attracting employment. The establishment of development areas, new towns and inner city funding has given certain authorities enhanced government incentives to incoming firms with the result that many councils have petitioned Whitehall to be given a favourable grant status. Some authorities have also organised their own methods of giving a measure of financial aid to incoming firms through rent allowances on municipally owned factory space. In addition to the management of a package of attractions, much of the work of an industrial development officer is devoted to processing enquiries from companies considering expansion or relocation of their businesses and smoothing over difficulties such as obtaining planning permission.

Many of the policies employed by local authorities to attract industry have a variety of functions that benefit other areas of the local economy or generally improve the social and cultural life of a community. The provision of

land for new factories will for example aid both incoming
firms and local businesses wishing to expand into better
premises. Improved road links with a motorway will not only
help to attract new employers but provide economic advantages
to existing industries and also enable families with cars to
increase their range of recreational opportunities. Detailed
analysis of local authority strategies that help ensure an
improvement in the local economy will be provided in later
chapters and discussion of these areas will be confined in
this section solely to their role in securing the location of
business into a particular authority's territory. There are
however areas of local policy that are for the most part concerned with attracting new employment. Publicity and the
accommodation of the demands of firms seriously considering
relocation are the most important of these strategies. These
tasks will be considered in detail within this chapter which
will also conclude with a general review of the success and
value of schemes to attract industry.

Publicity

It has already been indicated that the majority of local
authorities have in recent years produced some form of publicity aimed at attracting industry. The Association of District
Council's survey (1980) shows that if all non-respondents were
assumed to have no interest in advertising their potential for
industrial development over 50% of these lower tier authorities
would nevertheless be engaged in promotional work. In a study
of local authority advertising material Jaqueline Burgess
(1982) received examples of promotional material from 158 out
of a sample of 250 local authorities. Powers to advertise
facilities in order to attract industry were originally
obtained by local authorities through the 1931 Local
Authorities (Publicity) Act which permitted them to spend the
product of up to a 3d rate on such activity. This Act was
repealed by the 1972 Local Government Act but it is presumed
that the publicity functions of local authorities may be dis-
charged under section 142 of this Act which permits them to
provide information on their services and, for many purposes,
by section 111 which allows local authorities to carry out any
actions that facilitate the discharge of their statutory
functions.

Many means are available to local government officers
wishing to dispose of their council's advertising budget
although the costs involved in the most widespread and
elaborate campaigns are generally beyond the means of most
local authorities. Television advertising is for this reason

rarely if ever used and the medium would also be unsuitable in terms of its audience. Local radio would similarly have little impact in comparison with costs since its programmes would be unlikely to reach employers outside the confines of a particular local authority area. Advertising in the press although relatively easy to organise is also expensive. Since decisions on industrial relocation are normally made by the affluent and well educated, most employment creation adverts are confined to the quality press at a national level. These newspapers have developed an occasional symbiotic relationship with local authorities through the production of special supplements on particular cities or regions that combine articles, usually favourable to the area, along with adverts from local organisations. More modest local authority budgets may permit advertising in local weekly newspapers covering areas of the country thought to be full of potentially migrant industry and publicity may also be placed in trade magazines which are read by employers in particular industrial sectors.

Industrial development and publicity officers attempt to use the services of the media free of charge by seeking local newsworthy events that will provide a favourable item in press or television news reports. Completion of an industrial estate may for example be publicised by inviting a prestigious politician to open the premises. A science park developed largely through the initiative of the West Midlands County Council sited at Warwick University was, to the annoyance of the Labour controlled Council, opened by Mrs Thatcher whose presence gained the attention of the media as much on account of the possibility of hostile student demonstrations. Media attention may also be manufactured by those with an eye for the absurd. Sheffield City Council publicity department drew attention to the clean air in the city which many still associated with Orwell's observation that 'if at rare moments you stop smelling sulphur you have begun smelling gas' (Orwell 1974, p 95) by canning the local air and dispatching Sheffield atmosphere to impressible employers. More prosaic publicity departments scan the press for adverse comments on their cities and supply information to correct unfavourable impressions.

Most authorities engaged in advertising their localities produce their own publicity in the form of town guides, leaflets, information packs and occasional newspapers. It is not difficult for a researcher in this field to amass a large library of different forms of promotional material. Town guides represent one of the earlier forms of publicity and are still favoured on account of their low cost and range of users.

These booklets usually contain information on the vital statistics of the town and often list established local firms. They cost the authority little or nothing to publish since they are paid for by adverts from local businesses which are normally assembled by specialised publicity companies. Burgess found that 62 Councils out of a sample of 240 published a town guide (Burgess 1982). Most authorities with a developed interest in securing new industries will however rely on more sophisticated techniques of promotion and publish brochures or folders of information to suit a variety of needs.

The range of available promotional material reflects attempts by local authorities to gain the attention of differing groups of employers with a variety of beliefs and misconceptions about a particular area. Small leaflets can be produced in some quantity to catch the attention of large numbers of people in the hope that a few may be manufacturers with an interest in relocating their factories. Inexpensive brochures can be freely distributed to visitors at trade fairs, posted to large samples of businesses or deposited in hotels or first class railway carriages. A number of specialist publicity agencies can provide the names and addresses of firms that form the target of a publicity campaign and a mailing service. Posters may also be used to catch the interest of the passing businessman. In 1984 Glasgow placed a considerable number of simply designed posters in London Underground stations in the hope of convincing weary executives commuting within London that life might be much better in the largest city in Scotland.

More elaborate packages of publicity material are frequently published to impress employers who show some serious interest in opening new premises. These may be given for example to employers enquiring about the availability of sites within the local authority or distributed at promotional seminars. In addition to printed pages, publicity officers now construct audio-visual material to aid city promotion. Films and tapes are a frequent component of local authority displays at trade fairs, and promotional meetings and may even be mailed to selected firms.

Much of the publicity assembled by local authorities is designed for events that bring industrialists in contact with local government representatives. Most industrial development officers expect to travel beyond their local boundaries in order to meet businessmen. Trade fairs frequently feature stands sponsored and staffed by local authority personnel and a number of councils, such as Sheffield, have used these displays to feature the products of local industries in order to demonstrate that businesses can flourish within the area and cooperate with the local authority. A well used technique is the organisation of seminars for businessmen in regions of Britain or abroad where industry is thought to be expanding. Local government officers and on occasion councillors explain with the help of visual aids and sufficiently lavish entertainments the advantages their cities offer to incoming business. Attempts to attract foreign companies have led larger authorities to dispatch trade delegations abroad. These visits, particularly when they involve councillors, are likely to attract adverse comments from local electors who may see the excursions as little more than holidays at the ratepayers' expense. A number of authorities such as Doncaster which promoted visits to Switzerland, have abandoned the policy after finding that their excursions created considerable amicable interest but no new jobs. A related development was the establishment of offices abroad to process enquiries which were usually operated by agencies specialised in public relations work. Favoured areas were the United States and Switzerland but as with the case of foreign tours the lack of any substantial gains in employment through the use of such offices has led to their abandonment by most authorities.

The content of local authority publicity normally places considerable emphasis on the location of the district in relation to centres of population and the means of communication. Reference is also frequently made to the availability of industrial sites and premises and to the splendours of the adjoining countryside or the liveliness of local arts, entertainments or sporting provisions. The area is therefore shown to provide not only the facilities needed by industry but the conditions for a full social life for resident business executives.

Burgess (1982) argues that much of the copy is written in an amateurish style particularly when it is attempting to build a pleasant social image for the area. It is however only too easy to criticise purple prose aimed at dispelling images of smoke, grime and tripe. Academics may not have the same perceptions of northern cities as the businessmen for whom most of the copy is written. The industrial development officers who provide the copy are generally recruited from outside the established local government services and many have a background in public relations within private industry. These officers do not so much lack experience of publicity but rather an understanding of local government. A number of local authorities rely on advertising agencies to supply copy although Burgess found that only a few of the authorities surveyed used this facility and went on to point out that their 'copywriters are often unfamiliar with the needs of the market and may well tend to produce text more appropriate to the tourist than the executive'. (Burgess 1982, p 15) The value of local authority publicity to attract industry should however not revolve around the question of whether those involved in the task know what they are doing but whether the exercise can or should be relocating jobs from one part of the country to another.

Responding to enquiries

An important task for local authorities wishing to secure new industrial developments is to respond quickly and effectively to enquiries from firms considering moving into their area and to follow up any signs of interest by providing as much assistance as possible to facilitate a move. Local authorities receive a considerable number of approaches by or on behalf of industries thinking of moving premises or opening new trading units. The number of enquiries will however vary considerably depending not only on the location of the authority but the extent to which its industrial development officers consider that advising local businesses is part of their function. Doncaster Metropolitan District receives for example between 50 to 75 enquiries per month many of which are from small local businesses whilst Cleveland County Council had 124 requests for information in the two years of 1975 and 1976 of which the majority came from companies located outside the local authority area (Storey and Robinson).

A considerable number of requests for information do not come directly from the firms concerned but through agencies working on their behalf. These may be private estate agents, regional development agencies or the regional offices of the Department of Industry. It was found that in Cleveland nearly 50% of enquiries came from an indirect source (Storey and Robinson) although it is probable that district authorities have in recent years been getting many fewer enquiries through government departments or the development agencies. Bradford District Council received last year only a very small proportion of their enquiries from such bodies although their development unit considered that keeping close relations with personnel in the regional offices of the Department of Industry was of importance since enquiries emanating from this source often involved large overseas companies seriously considering building new plants.

Information needed by businesses can range over many subjects and in the case of authorities which perform an advisory task for local firms will often involve requests for help in obtaining loans from banks or information on basic accountancy or law relating to small firms. Industries which are established outside the local authority area and are considering setting up a new branch will be more concerned to find out about the facilities such as land or grants that can be offered within the local authority. Probably the most frequent request for information concerns sites and premises. In order to meet this interest many local authorities maintain a list of vacant industrial sites and factories which can be sent along with other promotional material to prospecting industrialists. These lists are however of value not only to firms outside the local authority but to local companies considering expansion. A survey of five inner city London Boroughs showed that they all supplied lists of sites and premises available to industry and that 40% of companies establishing new premises in these areas had used this information although many firms complained that the lists provided were out of date (London Industry and Employment Research Group 1981).

Local authorities not only provide answers to firms prospecting for new sites they may also keep in close contact with businesses during the period in which they are implementing their decision to move. In smaller or less active authorities industrial development officers act as a channel of contact between a firm and other local authority departments whilst in some cities and counties arrangements are made for the economic development unit or its equivalent to solve many of the difficulties faced by an incoming business. An important source of potential difficulty between a council and a new firm concerns planning consent and close liaison between employers and the authority may be able to prevent misunderstandings and delays in this process. The Economic Development Unit of Bradford Metropolitan District Council has acquired some delegation of powers concerning planning from the appropriate committee of the Council and through discussions with business managers is able rapidly to ensure agreements over industrial and commercial planning applications that are acceptable to both the needs of employers and the local environment. Close liaison between relocating firms and local authorities may also facilitate mutually beneficial developments in other areas of local authority competence such as the provision of roads or public transport services to link up with incoming firms.

Premises, infra-structure and environment

Publicity alone will attract few industries if the local
authority cannot provide sites to house incoming firms or
provide infra-structure and an environment that interests
either employers or workers. The provision of these resources
has a value that transcends the attraction of firms and most
of the developments in these areas will be considered in
detail later in this book. It is however necessary to
indicate the extent to which developments in these areas are
used primarily to attract businesses.

It has been recognised since the 1930s that any serious
schemes to attract firms must involve the development of sites
or premises to house incoming employers. The first industrial
estates such as Trafford Park were established largely with a
view to bringing new companies into areas of high unemployment
although it is now widely recognised that land for industrial
purposes is also necessary to allow local industries a chance
to expand without having to move elsewhere. The attraction
of industrial sites may be enhanced if the local authority
can either directly or indirectly ensure that financial
incentives are made available to incoming firms. Many
authorities therefore provide lower than normal rents to
firms occupying their premises for the first few months of a
tenancy. More effective incentives are subsidies available
through central government within the assisted areas or
enterprise zones. Many authorities attempt to convince
central government that they should receive some form of grant
aided status in order to strengthen their competitive edge
over other authorities seeking to attract new firms.

Improvements in infra-structure are as likely to help
established firms as incoming industries but on occasion
major public works projects may be undertaken in order to
attract new industry. A number of road building schemes have
been initiated largely on account of this motive. The Humber
Bridge was constructed in order to ensure the development of
the south bank of the Humber Estuary and British Leyland only
agreed to the siting of a bus factory in West Cumberland on
condition that major improvements were made to the road
connections between the Cumbrian coast and the M.6.

Local authorities eager to attract new industry and commerce
will frequently be prepared to adapt their policies concerning
the provision of services to this interest. It has already
been observed that many local authorities will work closely
with incoming firms in order to iron out any difficulties that

may hinder their obtaining planning permission. An important and widespread activity during times of labour scarcity is the allocation of council housing to key workers to enable firms to become rapidly established. Camina (1974) found that a majority of County Boroughs and Boroughs could provide key worker accommodation. Transport authorities will adapt bus services to the needs of new industrial sites and South Yorkshire County Council has assiduously pointed out the advantages of its cheap fares policy to industry and office development within the County. A more unusual adaptation to service provision was suggested by Clwyd County Council which offered to arrange school lessons in Japanese for the benefit of the children of Nissan managers should the company have decided to locate its car plant within North Wales.

Improvements to the local environment and cultural provisions within local authorities are usually motivated by social and aesthetic values rather than a desire to attract employment although this interest may also serve as a justification for some cultural and environmental provisions. Bradford City Council has created a number of attractions for tourists as part of its policy to develop the city as a holiday centre and as a related advantage create a better image for the area in order to aid the attraction of employment. West Yorkshire County Council made a more direct connection between environmental improvement and the ability to interest businessmen through an application for a grant to remove spoil heaps close to the M1 on the grounds that their presence would deter travelling captains of industry from locating their factories in such an unsightly County (Wallwork 1974).

THE VALUE OF ATTRACTING EMPLOYERS

The attraction of industry has been a major element in employment creation strategies since the 1930s and is still widely practised. It is however a strategy that is increasingly the subject of criticism and a number of authorities, including the G.L.C., have ceased to place any reliance on this policy. The objections to policies of attraction are made on two fronts. It is argued that the strategy is inefficient as a means of enhancing local employment since it brings relatively few jobs into a local authority in comparison with funds it absorbs. The policy is also criticised as being a self defeating competitive exercise which only redistributes the jobs nationally available but does not actually create new employment.

a) The effectiveness of strategies of attraction

A number of studies, written largely in the 1970s, have
attempted to evaluate the impact of economic and political
factors on industrial relocation in Britain. Much of this
research recognises that there are a number of separate stages
in the decision making process that ends in the removal or
expansion of a business on a new site. A company must first
decide whether it is worth moving or expanding its premises
and is then faced with the problem of where and how to move.

    There is considerable evidence to suggest that local
authorities play little or no part in determining the basic
decision of a firm to either relocate or establish a new
branch. A survey undertaken on behalf of the Department of
Trade and Industry by its Inquiry into Local Attitudes Group
(I.L.A.G.), (House of Commons 1972-73, p 533) found that a
sample of 531 firms gave reasons listed in Table 3.1 for their
decision to relocate. Among positive factors for relocation
cited in Table 3.1 'inducements and facilities made available
by official bodies' is the most important that could be
provided by local authorities but a more detailed breakdown
to responses mentioning this point shows that only 13% of
firms considered that inducements by local government or
new town corporations were a major reason for relocation and
none gave this as an outstanding factor. It is also the case
that few firms appear to move because of negative pressures
induced by local government. Difficulties over planning
permission is the most important in this category and it is
interesting to note that although firms could indicate this
in the survey none appear to have been concerned at the levels
of local authority rates.

    The findings of the I.L.A.G. survey are also substantiated
by Cooper who states that 'internal problems are given much
more weight than external prospects in promoting location
decisions'. (Cooper 1975, p 82) Both he and Townroe (1971)
conclude that the desire for growth within a company is the
most important factor determining relocation. In respect to
overseas companies it is suggested by Forsyth (1972) that
American firms were motivated to move to Scotland on account
of a desire to expand their market. In his survey however no
analysis is made of the impact of local policies on the
decision to establish new plant in Britain.

    If local authority influence has any impact on relocation it
is at the stage of company decision making when the firm has
already decided to move and is now looking for a suitable site.

47

Table 3.1

Factors in the decision to move

Percentage of all respondent firms	Major reason	Minor reason	Outstanding single reason
To permit an expansion of output	83	8	20
Inadequate existing premises or site	50	11	8
Unsatisfactory labour supply at existing location	40	11	15
Inducements and facilities made available by official bodies	27	14	2
Opportunity to purchase or rent premises or site at new location	20	8	3
Too far from established or potential markets	19	1	9
Refusal or expected refusal of IDC	12	4	5
Town Planning difficulties	11	3	4
Lease of former premises fell in, or good offer received	5	2	3
Desire to be in more attractive surroundings	4	8	1
Too far from supplies, actual or prospective, of materials or services	3	2	1
More profitable to operate elsewhere, no other postulated reason being major	1	–	1
No one outstanding reason	–	–	28
			100

The I.L.A.G. survey (House of Commons 1972-73 p 573) found some evidence of local authority impact as shown in Table 3.2. Over half of the responding firms suggest that local authorities had some influence over their location although the proportion given in Table 3.2 is approximately 10% higher than would be the case if the question directly asked for the influence local authorities had in attracting firms to their area. A number of respondents had been persuaded by regional development associations and others had been prompted by the G.L.C. to move out of London. The survey however also includes as a separate category factors such as the provision of factory space and 'good amenities and environment' over which local authorities can have influence. These findings are substantiated by the Cameron and Clarke (1966) study of industrial location which found that 58% of mobile companies

cited local authority cooperation as a major reason
determining their choice of site although as in the case of
the ILAG study a much smaller number, only 6%, thought the
factor was one of the most important.

Table 3.2
Factors inflencing the location of a site

Percentage of all respondent firms	Major reason	Minor reason	Outstanding single factor
Availability of labour at new location	72	20	20
Knowledge or expectation that IDC obtainable immediately or in future	48	18	2
Accessibility to markets or supplies	39	21	9
Availability of government inducements	39	7	7
Assistance or encouragement from LAs or promotional bodies	36	30	3
Accessibility to one of firm's plants or to location from which moving	32	18	7
Access to specified transport facilities	31	20	2
Good amenities and environment	29	41	1
Availability of suitable non-government factory	28	5	6
Special characteristics of site	20	17	3
Other factors	12	2	3
No outstanding single factor	—	—	38
			100

A number of econometric studies of industrial location have
arrived at broadly similar conclusions to the surveys cited
above (Henderson 1980, Keeble 1976, Keeble and Hauser
1971 and 1972).   The studies that are based on data collected
in the 1960s stress the importance of a satisfactory labour
supply as a foremost factor determining industrial relocation.
The much higher levels of unemployment in the 1980s have
however probably greatly diminished the relative differences
between many regions in respect to the supply of labour.   A
number of factors over which local authorities have more
control have therefore become more important determinants

49

of industrial location. Both Henderson and Keeble cite the availability of factory space as an important factor and one which is much more significant than simply the supply of building land (Henderson 1980, Keeble 1976). Henderson also considered that the image held by managers and workers of a particular locality was a contributory although not a major factor determining the choice of a particular site (Henderson 1980).

Although studies of industrial relocation rarely provide precise data on the impact of particular local authority strategies to attract employment they do suggest that certain strategies have greater value than others. The availability of factory space is clearly an important consideration determining the choice of a site and those authorities that can provide either through their own powers or through stimulating the private sector a number of modern factory premises for immediate occupation have a much greater chance of attracting employers. Inasmuch as the function of an industrial development officer concerns the provision of factory sites and buildings they retain a valuable role even if considerable doubts can be raised about their publicity function.

Analyses of industrial location also suggest that there is some advantage, even if it is not an overwhelming one, of developing a favourable image of the local environment. In areas where factory sites, labour, and government grants are equally plentiful the local environment may be a determining factor. Henderson (1980) for example suggests that in the 1970s a poor image has deterred many firms from relocating in Glasgow rather than other areas of Scotland. The local environment is not wholly under the control of its local authority but can be enhanced by public provision of better infra-structure, entertainments and attractions and through a constructive process of image building through publicity. Creating a better environment is a process that has many advantages in addition to the attraction of employment and the merits of schemes of improvement must be considered by councils in a wider context than solely their impact on employment.

There has been considerable criticism of the publicity function of local authorities (Middleton 1981, Greater London Council 1981, Burgess 1982) although this does not make any distinction between publicity material that is distributed to firms which deliberately make enquiries about the facilities the local authority can offer and material that is sent unsolicited to businesses with the hope of attracting their attention. It has been observed that many local authorities will receive a considerable number of enquiries from firms considering the possibility of building new premises and that an important function of industrial development officers is to process these enquiries. It is possible that local authorities are a valuable source of information for industries considering expansion. Cooper (1974) found that although many relocating firms in his survey did not seek information from public bodies, a larger proportion contacted local authorities than any other government organisation.

Storey and Robinson in a study of industrial relocation in Cleveland not only indicate that the County Council dealt with a considerable number of enquiries from industry but were relatively successful in turning these enquiries into firm decisions to relocate in the area. They show that 23% of firms that contacted the County Council and actually relocated, chose Cleveland as their site.

Although publicity material aimed at responding to enquiries from firms may be of some value to businesses and help a local authority to attract employment there is little evidence to suggest that this is the case in respect to unsolicited information distributed by local authorities. Studies of industrial relocation provide no evidence to suggest that advertising by local authorities had any influence over their decision to move or expand premises but the nature of many advertising campaigns would make it difficult to ascertain the exact influence of unsolicited publicity. Successful image building should ensure that clients are unaware that there was ever anything amiss with a particular location. A number of local authorities seem however to be finding that they attract little serious attention from expanding companies solely as a result of widely distributed publicity. Doncaster Metropolitan District Council concluded that the results achieved from a series of imaginative advertising campaigns were insufficient to warrant continuing to publicise the District in general rather than drawing attention from time to time to newly developed factory sites. Bradford District Council has reduced its budget for publicising the industrial attractions of the area on the grounds that economic conditions in the 1980s were not generating sufficient interest in relocation to justify the expense involved in trying to attract the few firms that were on the move. The Council has consequently diverted some of its publicity budget to the attraction of tourists.

b) Problems of competition

Although it is possible to argue that certain elements in

51

strategies to attract industry are effective in achieving
their goals it can still be maintained that there is little
to be gained from pursuing policies to locate mobile firms in
a particular local authority area. In itself the strategy of
persuading a business to settle in one part of the country
rather than another does not create jobs but only
redistributes employment. Indeed it may be the case that a
firm will relocate into new premises and close older and less
efficient plant with an overall loss in jobs.

The objection that the strategy does not create new jobs
must however be considered in relation to the various elements
of the package of policies that may be used to induce
industries to settle in a particular locality. A local
authority that hopes to attract employment through the
development of better roads or the provision of modern factory
premises will be creating conditions that will help ensure
the success of incoming firms and may also be of value to
industry already established in the area. Reliance on the
persuasive powers of an advertising campaign will on the other
hand be of no direct benefit to an incoming firm, unless it is
an advertising company, apart from the rather marginal value
of providing information about a particular locality.

An objection to strategies for the attraction of industry
concerns the essentially competitive nature of the exercise.
If all local authorities seeking new sources of employment
are equally involved in promoting their areas then the
inducements offered by each authority will tend to cancel
each other out with the result that no area gains any
advantage despite its considerable effort and expense.
Local authorities may also be forced to publicise the
attractions of their communities simply in order to avoid
being ignored in favour of those councils which actively
promote themselves. Competition among local authorities for
jobs may not however be a wholly sterile and self defeating
exercise since the process may induce them to produce
innovative schemes that are of value to incoming industries
and established firms. Many of the strategies described later
in this work were developed by local authorities that were
prominent in the race to attract firms and had as a result
developed an organisation within the authority that could
devise and establish more innovative schemes.

There is however little to be gained from a situation in
which local authorities are producing large quantities of
publicity in order to compete with one another for relocating
firms. Publicity does not create jobs in itself and when
widely practised the efforts of one area are cancelled out by

its competitors. Competitive advertising also cuts across the aims of regional policies directing new jobs to the most depressed areas of the country. The problem of competitive advertising has prompted widespread comment and at least one writer has suggested that the government should regulate the advertising policies of councils in relation to the attraction of industry (Middleton 1981). Government intervention in this area may not however be wholly beneficial since it would be necessary clearly to differentiate between publicity which conveys valuable information such as the availability of land or grants and publicity that is largely concerned with placing the name and image of the authority in the minds of company directors. A more effective approach than creating further limits to local discretion would be the development of a more positive and cooperative relationship among local authorities through establishing a code of practice fostered by local authority associations or the regional development agencies.

A growing realisation among local authorities that competitive advertising is self defeating may also lead individual councils to decrease or even terminate this form of activity. The 1981 Labour Party manifesto for the Greater London Council which became the policy of the Council when the Party took control of the authority in that year observes that:-

> 'An economic development programme for London based on the public sector does not mean that we are competing with other areas of industrial decline in the assisted areas. Our strategy is aimed at the region's particular problems and would take its place in a national strategy for Britain's economic revival.' (Greater London County Council, 1981, pp.13-14).

The practical consequence of these sentiments has been a deliberate policy within the Greater London Council not to attract industry through glossy advertising packages but to concentrate on aiding existing industry and establishing new businesses within London.

4 Attraction of visitors

Tourist promotion has been regarded as a predecessor of the industrial development movement but this view is perhaps misconceived given 19th century policies of municipalisation. Whilst Chamberlain was buying gas works in Birmingham on behalf of industrial interests, Blackpool was becoming a major tourist resort through private initiative.

The holiday industry began in the early 18th century with the gravitation of aristocrats and 'persons of good breeding' to inland spa towns during the summer months. The development of Bath as a fashionable resort was initially achieved without any encouragement from the town's existing self-appointed corporation (Neale 1981). In the late 18th century fashion and entrepreneurs moved down to the sea and villages such as Brighton were enlarged through royal and aristocratic patronage and property developers' wealth. As railways brought opportunities for relatively inexpensive travel the rich fled overseas to find resorts less accessible to the common English throng and their places were filled at first by the rising middle class and towards the end of the 19th century by working class families using their recently acquired holidays. The new demands for mass tourism prompted the growth of a number of coastal villages close to industrial centres into major seaside resorts such as Blackpool and Southend largely through private develop- ment.

As villages grew into towns with economies based on tourism the entrepreneurs who profited from these developments came to have an interest in the government of their resorts. In many of these towns local businessmen became local council- lors. The Chairman of the private company that built Blackpool Tower was also a mayor of the Borough (Parry 1983). The coincidence of private and public interest led to projects carried out by the local authority aimed at attracting greater numbers of tourists. In 1917 Blackpool obtained through a private act the powers to construct the promenade (Parry 1983) and by 1939 the borough's publicity committee was outspending all rivals with a budget of £20,000 devoted to advertising (Fogarty 1947).

Tourism is not the only means of bringing paying visitors into a town. During the last fifty years the conference trade has become increasingly important and enables many resorts to supplement the seasonal nature of their character- istic industry by keeping hotels and entertainments open for a longer season. Efforts have also been made to attract visitors to exhibition halls and in a few cases shopping centres. Promotion of tourism and conferences, although a recognised specialist role of local authorities has remained until recent years the province of a relatively small number of resort and spa towns. In the days before smoke abatement the leaders of Wigan and Bradford did not, for all their civic pride, see that the future of their town lay in the tourist industry. Pollution controls, slum clearance and town centre redevelopments have however considerably improved the attractiveness of industrial cities. Local government reorganisation has also given many local authorities an extensive rural hinterland which can on occasion include areas of considerable natural beauty. These factors have provided new opportunities for industrial cities to develop the tourist and conference trades which can have a further indirect value towards employment promotion by creating a better image for areas usually identified with 'dark satanic mills'. A city that can attract tourists may be a city in which business executives would care to establish themselves and their factories.

THE EXTENT OF TOURIST AND CONFERENCE PROMOTION

The authorities that are most involved in tourist promotion not surprisingly encompass established coastal resorts and historic cities but, somewhat less predictably are generally district rather than county councils. The 1983 Municipal Year Book lists 128 district authorities giving the name of an officer who can be contacted in relation to enquiries about tourism and of these 56 were in coastal areas and a further 21 covered old cathedral cities. If we add to these areas a further 13 districts that include Spa Towns such as Harrogate or areas of scenic beauty such as South Lakeland it can be suggested that 70% of districts with tourist officers encompass well established tourist centres.

A survey of tourism in the pre-local government re-organisation West Midlands indicated that the rural authorities were more concerned with tourism than urban authorities (Veal, 1975), but in the last decade a number of city based authorities have shown considerable interest in attracting visitors. Among the metropolitan districts 13 out of the 36 designate officers concerned with tourism and of these only 4 cover established holiday resorts. A few cities such as Bradford, Manchester and Glasgow that have never been considered as holiday centres have relatively large tourist offices. Despite the interest shown by some metropolitan districts and Scottish cities only one London Borough, Hillingdon, has appointed a tourist officer. London is nevertheless the premier tourist attraction within the country despite any serious promotional efforts being made by its local authorities which may believe that their interests are adequately met by the work of the London Tourist Board.

The county councils of England and Wales similarly show little interest in the tourist industry with only Devon and Cornwall employing tourist officers although 5 of the Scottish Regions have appointed such officers and the Isle of Wight has established a county wide Tourist Board which involves the district councils and private tourist interests. The lack of county tourist officers may however like the London boroughs be a reflection of the work of the Regional Tourist Boards. A survey of structure plans in the context of tourism indicated however that the counties had a very varied concern for the industry with coastal counties showing a much more developed interest than inland areas (White 1981).

It is difficult to provide any clear estimate of the extent of enthusiasm for developing a conference trade within particular areas of the country as this activity does not figure as an element within structure plans or produce an established group of professional officers. The business is moreover varied in its demands. Most authorities have facilities to accommodate small unplanned conferences whilst the largest gatherings become the concern of the very few cities and resorts that can accommodate them. The large conferences were until recently largely confined to major seaside resorts such as Blackpool and Brighton but the monopoly on the trade by these coastal towns is in some danger from inland cities such as Harrogate, Nottingham and Sheffield which are assiduously building or developing city halls to handle large conferences.

STRATEGIES FOR ATTRACTING VISITORS

Visitors can be attracted into a local community through a wide range of strategies that to be effective must be related to one another through a coherent plan for tourism and conferences. The council can make the most of its existing attractions through schemes for conservation and reclamation. Where existing sources of interest are limited they may be enhanced through the foundation of museums, pleasure domes stately or otherwise, and the organisation of entertainments. Visitors must be able to get to the area through a network of reasonably accessible communications and can also be brought into the district through packaged holiday schemes that can be promoted by the local authority. The attractions of a resort must be made known to the public through the arts of public relations and the glossy brochure. The marvels to be seen and experienced within a district are however of little value to the community if the area does not have appropriate accommodation. Tourism and conferences aid the economy through the establishment of hotels, catering facilities and entertainments.

(a) Conservation

Who would visit Wells were it not for its Cathedral or Keswick were it not for the Lake District? Many centres of tourism are dependent on the conservation of historic buildings or areas of great natural beauty in order to sustain their economies. A survey conducted by the City Planning Department of Canterbury found that in 1975 58% of recreational visitors to the city came specifically to see the Cathedral and suggested that the building brought some £5 million of spending into the area of which £1.5 million contributed directly to the local economy (Binney and Hanna 1978). A growing interest in industrial history and the progress of industrial decay has extended the range of buildings thought worthy of preservation beyond Cathedrals and half timbered houses. Cities such as Bradford and Manchester preserve old factories and warehouses that can serve as tourist attractions. Few if any local authorities would today claim that they encompass neither buildings nor landscapes worthy of preservation.

Conservation of buildings and the landscape has benefits other than simply the generation of tourist revenue. Historic, scientific and aesthetic values are factors that also underlie the need for preservation and in many instances prompt the public to visit particular sites. The coincidence

of these values with the economic gains from visitors has
led during the last hundred years to the creation of a
powerful lobby concerned with conservation that has
succeeded in creating extensive legislation to protect
buildings and land.

Pressures for conservation were sufficiently powerful to
promote legislation (The Ancient Monuments Act 1882) giving
some protection to ancient buildings before the county
councils were created. The laws protecting buildings have
evolved since 1882 into a complex body of regulations which
give powers to central government to preserve buildings and
archæological sites but permit local authorities to ensure
that buildings within their boundaries are considered worthy
of becoming protected species. Local authorities can refuse
permission for alterations or demolition of any building for
a six month period during which time the Minister must
decide whether the property deserves protection. Compulsory
purchase powers are also available to acquire listed
buildings that are being neglected by their owners. In
addition to legislation concerning individual buildings or
archaeological sites it is also possible to protect urban
areas through the Civic Amenities Act of 1967 which instructs
local authorities to 'identify areas of special architectural
or historic interest' (Cullingworth 1982, p.129) and ensure
their preservation as conservation areas in which requests
for planning permission can only be accepted if they do not
damage the existing character of the area (Cullingworth 1982).

Conservation of rural and coastal landscape is largely
secured through the National Parks and Access to the
Countryside Act of 1949 which led to the creation of
National Parks and Areas of Outstanding Natural Beauty.
Planning in these areas must be primarily concerned with
protecting and enhancing the existing landscape and remains,
often through joint boards in the case of the National Parks,
largely in the hands of local authorities. In 1972 this
policy was further extended by the designation of Heritage
Coasts to protect large stretches of sea shore. The 1962
and 1968 Countryside Acts gave local authorities powers to
establish nature reserves, country parks and picnic areas
(Cullingworth 1982). Responsibility for maintaining rights
of way footpaths and ensuring that they remained open was
assigned in the 1949 National Parks Act to the County Councils.
Trees find shelter from developers through powers granted
to planning authorities which gives them authority to
prevent felling of trees and they can also compel a developer
to plant trees on a new building site (Cullingworth 1982).

Conservation may be an expensive process although considerable financial aid is effectively given to local authorities through planning acts that in general place the responsibility for repairing listed buildings on their owners. Problems may nevertheless arise if owners of buildings refuse to maintain their historic white elephants and the local authority has no wish to purchase the property and become itself responsible for finding the maintenance costs. A small district council that sees little tourist potential in a listed building may find that its powers of conservation are more an embarrassment than an asset. Authorities that wish financially to promote conservation are however able to provide grants to private owners through the Local Authorities (Historic Buildings) Act of 1962 in addition to their powers of compulsory purchase. Grants are also available to local authorities from a number of sources which include the Department of the Environment, the National Tourist Boards and the Historic Buildings Councils. A number of private charities such as the Architectural Heritage Fund and the Civic Trust may also aid conservation whilst the Countryside Commission can provide grants and loans to protect rural landscape.

One of the authorities most concerned with conservation is the City of York where nearly £1 million has been given since 1966 to owners of property within the historic central preservation area of the town to aid renovation schemes. The grants have been provided under the auspices of the Historic Buildings and Monuments Council which provides half of a contribution which is matched by equal sums raised by the district and county councils covering the area eligible for receiving funds. Since the owners of property must provide at least as great a contribution as they receive in grant it is estimated by the York City Planning Department that since 1966 up to £3 million has been put into repair work for private buildings within the city centre which not only maintains the tourist potential of the city but provides an important stimulus to local building contractors and craftsmen. In addition to these grants York City Council can also attract conservation grants directly from the Department of the Environment and through the work of its Engineering Department directly maintains monuments and buildings such as the city walls that are owned by the Council.

The scale of conservation work conducted by York will be matched by few if any other councils although some 180 district councils participate in the town centre conservation schemes operated by the Historic Buildings and Monuments

Council. Many local authorities will however attract grants
or directly spend funds on projects to convert older buildings into tourist attractions. The Greater London Council
for example initiated the project, that cost overall around
£4 million, to restore the Covent Garden area of the city
following the departure of the fruit and flower market.
Halifax Borough Council now part of Calderdale Metropolitan
District based much of its ability to attract tourists around
the renovation of the Piece Hall within the town as a museum,
crafts centre and market place.

(b) Reclamation

It may be an unnecessary academic exercise clearly to
differentiate reclamation from conservation but such a
distinction has relevance to local authority powers for
acquiring land and obtaining grants for its development.
Derelict land suitable for reclamation is not defined in
statute but has been described as 'land so damaged by
industrial or other development that it is likely to remain
out of use unless subject to special treatment'(Cullingworth
1982, p.138). Such land can be purchased and rehabilitated
by local authorities under a wide selection of powers. A
number of planning acts and the 1949 National Parks and
Access to the Countryside Act allow local authorities to
remove depressing abandoned blots on the landscape and make
derelict land available for later private use. Few
authorities made much of these powers until the Industrial
Development and Local Government Acts of 1966 and later the
Inner Urban Areas Act of 1978 ensured that generous government grants were available to reinstate derelict land. The
largest grants are available in development areas and are
designed to clear land for industrial use although it is
possible to argue that the provision of a tourist attraction
would be acceptable for grants aimed at increasing industrial
employment. Within the National Parks and Areas of Outstanding Natural Beauty government grants of 75% of the cost of
rehabilitation are available to reinstate landscape to blend
with the surrounding countryside.

Since 1945 attempts to reclaim land for tourist attraction
initially centred around a discovery that it was far cheaper
to clear up the margins of flooded gravel tips and use them
for recreational purposes or nature conservation than
laboriously fill in the abandoned workings. During the 1960s
a number of authorities established water sports and angling
centres around flooded workings. The Cotswold Water Park
provides over 1,500 ha of lakes for tourist purposes. With

the greater availability of grant aid for reclamation a
number of important tourist developments constructed on
reclaimed land were opened during the 1970s. One of the
largest schemes is the Black Country Museum at Dudley in the
West Midlands which is built on a site cleared by the County
Council that was

'riddled with filled in mine shafts and the remains
of lime kilns' (English Tourist Board, p.10).

A scheme planned eventually to cost up to £11 million has
been initiated by Cumbria County Council to reclaim a coast
line at Workington which has been submerged under a steel
works slag bank. The project which incorporates, among
other attractions, an artificial ski-slope illustrates the
possibilities of using reclamation to attract both visitors
and industry and was justified by the Chairman of the County
Council on the grounds that:-

'We will be improving the environment for the people
of Workington as well as encouraging industry to
come here' (Cumberland Times and Star 19.4.84).

(c)   The creation of attractions

The Fylde coast in its wild untutored state would be no more
distinguished than many other stretches of British shore-
line. Blackpool's Golden Mile is a major tourist attraction
largely on account of man made structures. Industrial towns
once distinguished for gloom and grit can similarly build
museums or provide entertainments that transform them into
visitor centres. Local authorities have several powers that
enable them to construct and maintain tourist attractions.
They are able to operate museums and art galleries under the
Public Libraries and Museums Acts of 1964. The 1972 Local
Government Act, section 145, permits local authorities to
provide entertainments, maintain orchestras and bands and
generally foster and encourage the arts. They may also
construct halls and theatres to accommodate these activities
and to provide parks and recreational facilities that can
range from golf courses or sports stadia to trampolines,
swings and deck chairs.

Although local authorities have powers to operate a
considerable number of attractions they have not used these
very extensively. Resort towns tend to confine their role
to supplying unspectactular infra-structure and items such
as sea front walks, parks or sporting facilities that are for
the most part taken for granted by holidaymakers. The more
spectacular attractions such as fun fairs, piers, and theatres

are usually maintained by private initiative although in many cases, as with Blackpool's Tower, the facility was constructed through municipal encouragement. A few resort towns have now bought theatres and cinemas in order to maintain a formerly private resource which has ceased to be profitable and in some tourist centres, such as Harrogate, theatre and entertainment facilities have recently been built which also accommodate conferences and exhibitions. In provincial cities such as Manchester and Bradford efforts are being made to develop municipally controlled theatres as part of their attempts to create a tourist industry.

In the larger provincial cities local authorities usually maintain a museum and on occasion an art gallery although these normally cater for local interests and only a few, such as the Walker Art Gallery in Liverpool or the Castle Museum at York, could be said to serve as tourist attractions. In the last decade there has however been a revival of interest in establishing museums and this movement has been closely connected with tourist promotion. Many of these museums illustrate the development of industry and help to generate an interest in cities once dismissed as unattractive legacies of an age best forgotten. A consortium of the counties of Durham, Northumberland, Tyne and Wear and Cleveland have, for example, established the North of England Open Air Museum which depicts rural and industrial life in the North East in the late 19th century.

Museums can also be established as a result of co-operation between local authorities and other public or private sector organisations. Bradford became the home of the National Museum of Photography when the District Council persuaded the Director of the National Science Museum to consider basing the project in an uncompleted theatre that had been half heartedly constructed by an earlier Council. The District offered the museum the use of the building at a peppercorn rent and also provided a grant of £1.8 million towards the scheme. The initiative not only secured the location of the museum in Bradford but also brought forward the opening of the National Photography Museum.

Local authorities may also attract visitors by sponsoring special events which can range from arts festivals, traditional fairs and customs, to sporting events. In 1984 the British Arts Festival Association publicised 24 arts festivals in Britain and many of these received considerable aid from local authorities. The most renowned, the Edinburgh International Festival, was founded shortly after the Second

World War with a view to stimulating tourism in the city.
The Edinburgh District Council gave £560,000 to the organisers
of the festival in 1984 and were the most generous public
sponsor of the event although they leave almost all aspects
of its organisation to the Edinburgh Festival Society. On
a less regular basis cities may attract large numbers of
visitors if they host major sporting events such as the
Commonwealth Games which have taken place in Cardiff and
Edinburgh using municipally owned facilities.

(d)   Tourist infra-structure

Much of the economic value of tourism will be lost to a
community that lacks facilities to cater for the demands of
visitors. Attractions such as Stonehenge for example may
receive many visitors but in itself employs few workers and
in the absence of hotels, restaurants or shops in the area,
little holiday money will be spent in its vicinity. Money
and employment from tourism is largely acquired through the
accommodation, catering and retail trades, and the proportion
of revenue that can be obtained by a locality will be
increased if visitors can be induced to stay overnight. A
number of studies of income generated from tourism showed
that day trippers spend much less per person per day than
staying visitors and as a result generate less employment
(English Tourist Board 1981a).

   A local authority that wished to benefit from tourism must
therefore ensure that a wide range of services are available
to tourists within reasonable proximity to centres of
attraction. Local authorities are however not nearly as well
placed to establish facilities that generate most revenue as
they are to supply facilities that bring in visitors in the
first instance. They cannot build or operate hotels or
guest houses unless these are for the use of council
employees or tied to the authority's recreational functions.
It may be possible to exploit these opportunities but in
practice council provision of accommodation runs to little
more than camp sites and caravan parks. Local authorities
rely on the private sector to maintain hotels although they
may facilitate their construction through suitable planning
strategies. Land can be earmarked for hotel construction
and it is even possible to renovate and lease buildings to
serve as accommodation. Bradford District Council has for
example encouraged an international hotel company to build
within the city. The process of attracting the hotel
operator followed the techniques used to attract industry into
the city with a package consisting of a fully serviced site

63

with sufficient land for recreational facilities and close co-operation with the company in solving planning problems raised by the development.

It is possible for local authorities to operate catering facilities under the 1947 Civic Restaurants Act as discussed in greater detail later in this book. Few municipalities make much of this provision apart from setting up cafes in museums, art galleries and theatres and in many cases these facilities are operated by private contractors. For the most part the provision of catering services in tourist resorts is left to the private sector and since these services tend to be offered on a much smaller scale than hotels there is frequently little thought given through planning controls to the balanced provision of restaurant facilities.

A major source of revenue from tourism is the retail trade which may vary from small confectionery stalls purveying seaside rock to expensive antique shops or the sale of food to self catering holiday makers. Local authorities are unable to establish or maintain retail services except when these are developed in close connection with their own services. The major role of local authorities is therefore in the provision of sites and the grant of planning permission. Most publicly owned museums and art galleries will however generate a small income from the sale of guides and souvenirs and a few authorities have developed museum workshops to enable craftsmen to continue a skilled trade and make a living by selling their produce to visitors. The industrial museum established in Sheffield has a number of small workshops where 'little mesters' can continue to manufacture hand made cutlery under the gaze of visitors.

Although inkeeping with the capitalist basis of British local government, municipalities can at most facilitate the establishment of those services that bring in tourist money, they have a duty to supply many services that are frequently taken for granted. The attraction of a town is much enhanced if it is clean and well maintained, provides pleasant parks and gardens, constructs shelters for the not infrequent occasions when it may rain and has a suitable supply of sanitary public conveniences. In most cases these facilities are provided at little or no cost to the tourist and their expense is met by government block grant and the ratepayers of a resort. Provisions such as parks may be developed into major attractions in their own right. Exeter and Torbay for example have established major reputations for their parks and floral decorations.

Since items such as street cleaning, roads and provisions of toilets fall under the direct control of local authorities many established resorts pay considerable attention to the role of these facilities in ensuring the continued attraction of their towns. A study of tourism in Stratford upon Avon by the District Council is for example largely concerned with making recommendations for improvements in these often mundane but important areas (Stratford on Avon District Council, 1978). The report highlights the need for a country park to be developed in the vicinity of the town, pedestrianisation of shopping streets, the establishment of larger car parks and the provision of new public toilets.

One of the few facilities to improve tourist infra-structure that attracts grants from other public bodies is the provision of information centres for visitors. Most major tourist centres and many large and even middle sized industrial towns have at least one tourist information office. Many of these centres are set up and operated by local authorities but considerable help and encouragement towards establishing these services has been provided by the National Tourist Boards.

County councils have an important role in providing infra-structure for the tourist industry through their highways responsibilities. Good communications are essential for major entertainment based resorts such as Blackpool although it may be a mixed blessing for areas such as the Lake District where preservation of landscape is important not only for tourist purposes but also aesthetic and ecological reasons. Decisions concerning major roads will usually involve central as well as local government and can have a major impact on tourist patterns. The Lake District has for example greatly increased its intake of visitors following the building of the M6. The continuation of rail services may also be important to some communities dependent on tourism and the location of major international airports close to London has certainly promoted the tendency of foreign tourists to venture no further than the capital city. Provision of communications is not however important solely for tourism. It also has an impact on industrial and residential location. Tourist resorts that demand better road or rail connections must therefore lobby for these needs alongside industrial areas requiring new factories or office developments.

(e) Packaging holidays

Many holidays are arranged and promoted by packaged holiday
companies. Local authorities will increase the traffic of
visitors to their towns if they can induce tour operators
to include their attractions in appropriate schemes. Since
most of these packaged holidays include accommodation in
hotels they have an added advantage to the local community of
bringing more money into the area than most other forms of
holiday.

  Tour organisers will frequently arrange holidays in well
known resorts without any approach being made by the local
authority to help or encourage the tourist company. Local
authorities can however advertise the delights of their
resorts for the benefit of tour operators at trade fairs
organised for the holiday industry or through direct contacts.
Such activity is essential for a city such as Bradford which
is establishing itself as a tourist centre and is unlikely
to be uppermost in the minds of those who package holidays.
Bradford District Council plans, in consultation with local
hotels and attractions, detailed programmes and costs for
holiday packages within the area. The schemes are then
published in a booklet and circulated directly or through
trade shows to the tourist industry. The City has succeeded
through this strategy in convincing a number of tour companies
to include Bradford in some of their holiday packages.

  In 1981 Bradford District Council began organising its own
weekend holidays and gained immediate media attention given
the novelty of vacations spent in industrial Yorkshire. The
Economic Development Unit of the Council arranges tours which
include both industrial monuments such as the village of
Saltaire, the Worth Valley steam railway, and rural and
literary excursions to the 'Wuthering Heights' of the Bronte's
Haworth. These itineries are arranged by council officers
with local hotels and managers of the attractions. The day
to day management of the scheme is entrusted to a private
travel agency based in York which distributes publicity for
the holidays, largely in the South of England, and receives
bookings and payments. The agency then pays the District
Council approximately half the revenue it receives although
the proceeds are insufficient for the Council to cover its
initial costs in setting up the Scheme. The programme is
not however intended to supplement local authority revenue
but to promote the local tourist industry and as a result
secure greater employment within the City.

A packaged holiday scheme operated by the Borough of East
Yorkshire based on Bridlington is almost wholly operated and
maintained by the Local Authority. The Borough invites local
hotels and guest houses to accept, at prices set by the
Authority, guests who subscribe to the scheme. The holiday
package includes not only a wide choice of accommodation
but free admission to the Borough's theatres, cinema and
other attractions. It is also possible to book, through the
Council, coach travel to the resort from the industrial
centre of Scotland. The Local Authority receives bookings
and payment for the package which is mostly passed on to the
participating hotels. The scheme is subsidised by the Council
at a cost of approximately £5000 in 1983 and can be justified
on the basis of its success in attracting 2,500 bookings in
that year which ensured a considerable boost to the local
tourist trade at a comparatively low cost to the Borough.
Scarborough District Council has also organised a package
scheme based on local hotels and guest houses to attract
conference bookings. The scheme not only includes accommodation and meeting places but free entertainments (Yates, 1982).

(f)   Publicity

If tourists are to visit locally provided attractions they
must know what delights exist and where they are located.
The need to publicise resorts and spa towns was recognised
as early as 1921 through the Health Resorts and Watering
Places Act which was probably the first statute nationally
to acknowledge the role of local authorities within the
tourist industry. The passage of this act was symptomatic
of the precedence given to publicity as a means of attracting
visitors. By 1938 several larger resorts were spending over
£10,000 on advertising (Fogarty, 1947).

It has been shown that the activities of coastal resorts'
publicity officers in attracting tourists was soon
paralleled by industrial cities which began in the 1930s to
use advertising to attract new employers. The techniques for
attracting industry which have been discussed in chapter 3
are not dissimilar in respect to publicity from those used to
gain the attention of tourists and conference organisers and
need not therefore be developed in this section.

It is however argued in Chapter 3 that large budgets spent
on publicising the advantages of a local authority for
industrial relocation is in general one of the most inefficient, even if one of the most widely practised, means by
which local authorities try to increase employment. These
strictures are not however so easily applied to publicity

aimed at attracting visitors. Tourists do not base their
decision on where to spend their holidays on sophisticated
analyses of labour markets, transport costs and availability
of subsidies. Publicity put out by local authorities may
be greatly welcomed by tourists as a means of widening their
knowledge of possible attractions. Cities may also find
publicity a valuable means of restructuring traditional
images of their communities which can have advantages
transcending those of tourist promotion. Bradford has in
recent years begun to dispel the image of industrial
depression by presenting the area as being closely connected
to the Yorkshire Dales and steeped in the history of
industrial development. The presentation of this new image
although primarily designed to attract tourists may also
change the attitudes of industrialists and perhaps more
importantly give local people an enhanced enthusiasm for
their area. The relatively small number of expanding
industries in the early 1980s has prompted the city to spend
more of its advertising budget on attracting tourists than
on attracting industry.

Publicity is nevertheless expensive and money invested in
this process can arguably be put to more effective and
positive use by building new museums, parks or other
facilities that will generate their own publicity. The most
effective attractions need little advertising. It is possible
that Canterbury Cathedral is sufficient to bring visitors into
the city and that Blackpool illuminations are so well known
they require little further promotion. Indeed certain tourist
centres such as Stratford on Avon have become so overwhelmed
with visitors in the summer that further advertising, if it
brought more people, would only bring greater problems and
pressure on existing services (Stratford on Avon District
Council, 1978).

CONFERENCES AND EXHIBITIONS

A significant number of visitors to resorts and large cities
now arrive for conferences. The conference trade has two
major advantages for a tourist resort. Meetings are usually
held in the Spring or Autumn rather than the peak Summer
tourist months and therefore may help hotels and restaurants
remain open for a longer season than would otherwise be the
case and the conference delegate who is frequently spending
someone else's money on average contributes more revenue to
a city than the average tourist.

The trade has until recently been associated with resort towns which could provide large enough halls for meetings and sufficient accommodation for delegates. The attractions offered by these resorts also aided their selection by conference organisers. A developed sea front, or historic buildings are not however essential for the success of a conference. In recent years large cities have begun to adapt and promote their halls and hotels as conference centres and many local authorities in industrial centres have become involved in publicising their potential for hosting large meetings.

Most large cities and many tourist resorts can offer suitable facilities for small or medium sized conferences. Hotels are frequently able to house modestly proportioned business gatherings and, outside academic terms, University and Polytechnic halls of residence provide ideal situations for conferences requiring a considerable number of small meeting rooms. Local authorities can often let accommodation under their direct control to house conference meetings. A major role of local authorities in aiding smaller conferences has been to publicise facilities available within their areas. A number of authorities provide a booklet on request listing all available meetings rooms within the city and major hotels and halls of residence.

The largest conferences which involve over 2000 delegates have until recently been the province of a relatively few specialised centres. During the 1960s the major political party and Trade Union conferences seemed to be concentrating on a small number of resorts which had facilities to accommodate large delegate meetings and many overnight visitors. Blackpool, Brighton and Scarborough were by 1960 appearing to monopolise the major conferences and of these three Scarborough was beginning to drop out of the race by 1970. Brighton District Council ensured a position of pre-eminence when it opened in the mid 1970s a new Conference Hall with associated exhibition and sporting facilities, at a cost of £10 million. Scarborough has subsequently refurbished its conference centre with a £3 million investment. There has however been an upsurge in potential competitors for the large conference market. A number of major cities such as Sheffield are beginning to use their 2000 plus seater City Halls for this purpose. Cardiff and Nottingham opened new major conference halls in 1982.

The most ambitious project to capture the conference trade has been undertaken by Harrogate which opened a large

conference and exhibition centre in January 1982. Prior to
the development of this complex the town could house
conferences of up to 1,300 delegates in a converted
Edwardian theatre. The District Council decided early in the
1970s to revive their role as a tourist centre not by polish-
ing their image as an upmarket northern spa-town but by
becoming a leading conference centre. It was calculated that
their existing conference trade brought approximately £25
million into the city and a new meeting complex would repay
its capital costs if it increased conference revenues by
no more than a quarter of the existing levels. The District
Council entered into a partnership with a private contractor
to develop a 2,500 seater conference hall and exhibition
complex for which it would provide £3 million in capital.
When the original contractor withdrew from the scheme the
Council decided to take on the whole project. At the cost
of an extra 6 pence in the pound on the rates the Authority
built a £25 million complex in time to stage a Young
Conservatives Conference and the Eurovision Song contest.

PLANNING AND IMPLEMENTATION

It has earlier been indicated that tourist and conference
promotion, at least in England and Wales, has become largely
a district rather than county council interest. Within the
district authorities there is however a wide variation in
their capacity to implement and co-ordinate the many
strategies open to them for attracting visitors. A number
of authorities have established specialist committees which
may operate on the basis of a well researched plan for
tourism whilst the majority muddle through diverse ideas
which are usually implemented by a variety of committees.
Not surprisingly the larger resort towns are more likely
to have a coherent plan and the organisational structure for
implementing a tourist or conference policy.

   The lack of interest in tourism shown by many counties
within their structure plans has been criticised by the
English Tourist Board which has observed that:-

    'the absence of strategic policies within a county
    is likely to hinder the development of integrated
    local tourism policies' (English Tourist Board,
    1981a, p.80).

The Tourist Boards offer to aid local authorities conduct
surveys and construct plans to co-ordinate tourist promotion
policies and have had a positive response from a number of
districts. The City of York and Scarborough District Council

have for example sponsored studies of tourism by the English
Tourist Board (English Tourist Board 1972; English Tourist
Board 1981b). Other districts such as Stratford on Avon
have conducted their own surveys into the needs and demands
of visitors to the authority (Stratford on Avon District
Council 1978). Few authorities have however developed
extensive studies of tourism as an industry to be placed
alongside other methods of employment creation within a
locality. Among the most active councils concerned with
creating employment such as the Greater London Council or
Sheffield Metropolitan District there has been virtually no
attempts to integrate tourist and conference promotion into
their wider strategies of economic intervention. An
exception among these authorities is Bradford Metropolitan
District Council where the Economic Development Unit has
control over the planning and implementation of tourist and
conference promotion policies alongside its responsibilities
for other aspects of employment creation. It has already
been shown that the Development Unit perceives important
links between their ability to attract tourists and create
conditions for generating employment not only directly
within the tourist industry but in other manufacturing and
commercial enterprises.

The implementation of tourist policies in most district
authorities that are highly dependent on the industry is
placed in the hands of tourist or publicity officers who
usually head a small staff of subordinate officers. Many
personnel engaged in this work have considered themselves to
be members of a distinct profession since the formation of
what is now the British Association of Tourist Officers in
1932, although the background of its members may be relatively
diverse in comparison with most local government officers.
They can be recruited from the hotel and catering industries,
public relations work or be promoted from junior positions
in local authority tourist or publicity offices. In a few
authorities covering the larger resorts the officers are
responsible to a sub-committee of the council specifically
concerned with tourism although in many cases this function
is administered along with wider powers concerning recreation.
In 1983 23 district councils in England and Wales had a
major sub-committee whose title indicated that it was
concerned with tourism (Municipal Year Book, 1983). Among
authorities that are less enthusiastic about attracting
tourists a designated officer, if appointed, may be subject
to a wide variety of superior officers and committees and in
most cases will ensure the implementation of most of his
responsibilities through a number of appropriate service
committees.

Since many tourist facilities can only be provided through private enterprise no effective plan for attracting visitors can ignore local business interests. Certain strategies such as the organisation of package holidays can only be successful if close liaison takes place with the managers of local hotels and attractions. A few authorities have established committees to provide a permanent forum for consultation between the private sector and councillors. Scarborough District Council for example has a committee that includes representatives of the local Hotels Association and the Chamber of Commerce which among other tasks co-ordinates the advertising programmes of the District Council and the Hoteliers Association (Yates, 1982). The number of such consultative committees is probably small. A survey conducted in 1980 by J A Chandler and J M Yates which asked local authorities if they had set up any system of regular consultation with local economic interests found that only one of the respondents from district authorities that included resorts maintained that it had a consultative committee.

Links between the private and public sectors concerning tourist promotion are also achieved through the workings of the Regional Tourist Boards. These organisations were set up by the Development of Tourism Act 1969 to bring together representatives of local authorities and private businesses interested in tourism. The ten Regional Boards are however assigned large areas and will provide only limited opportunities for the representation of small businesses. On a more local and day to day level links between the private sector and local authorities may be achieved through the membership of hoteliers and tradesmen on district councils in resort areas. Small businessmen form a significant element of the councils of many Conservative held authorities and it is possible that in many areas further links between the local authority and local business interests are secured through the medium of that party.

THE VALUE OF TOURISM FOR EMPLOYMENT CREATION

A number of studies, several sponsored by the Tourist Boards, have attempted to demonstrate the value of tourism to local economies. Particular interest has been directed towards the multiplier effect of tourist spending on local incomes and employment. It has for example been demonstrated that within the Woodspring and Eastbourne District Authorities £49 is retained within the community for every £100 of

tourist money spent in local hotels or boarding houses. It
has also been calculated in a study of Tayside that 0.39
jobs are created for every £1000 of resident tourist
spending (English Tourist Board, 1976).

This research has some value for the industry since it can
be used to evaluate which forms of tourist provision generate
the greatest financial benefits for an area. The Tayside
study for example showed that visitors staying overnight in
hotels and guest houses generate greater levels of employment for every £1000 of spending than day trippers or self
catering holidaymakers. The research does not however give
much guidance to local authorities wishing to evaluate the
comparative advantages of putting resources into tourism
rather than efforts to create jobs in manufacturing
industries. The multiplier effects of tourism cannot,
without the development and use of comparative techniques to
evaluate the multiplier effects of investment in other forms
of industry in a particular area, tell us much about the
relative merits of the tourist industry in solving
unemployment (Adams, 1977 Bryden, 1973).

Although no one could deny that tourist and conference
delegates put money into the economies of the area in which
they stay it may be argued that their presence creates
unseen but major financial and social costs. The amenities
of an area popular with visitors may be destroyed by their
enthusiasm. The tramp of many feet is wearing away parts
of the Lake District and Snowdonia. Few individuals find
quiet and solace whilst worshiping the sun on a bank
holiday beach. A frequent complaint of residents in tourist
centres is that visitors create overcrowding, delays and
congestion on roads and in shops.

Much of the damage to the environment caused by tourism
along with the problems of congestion can be solved but
only at a price paid largely by local authorities. A
resort town will also incur expenditure to meet the needs of
a greater number of people using its services: such as highways, recreation facilities and refuse collection. The
visitors who create these extra demands do not directly
contribute to their provision as rate payers.

The net cost of tourism on local authority services is
however probably not very high and certainly not so onerous
that it undermines the value of the industry as an aid to the
local economy. Tourists will indirectly contribute to local
authority services through the rates collected from hotels,

restaurants and other properties created to meet tourist demands. It has been estimated in a study of the costs imposed on local authorities in the South West that in 1972/73 tourists added £4 millions to expenditure by Councils but over £3 million was raised in extra rates from these visitors (Jackson, 1977). Expenditure to meet tourist demands will also be of benefit to local residents who may often use the parks, entertainments or roads that have been provided for holiday traffic.

A more serious objection to tourism as a means of creating employment concerns its structure and conditions of work. Unlike most manufacturing industries which produce seasonal goods the service sector that forms the bulk of the industry cannot stockpile its product. The industry therefore generates a high proportion of seasonal and part-time employment. A study of tourism in East Anglia showed that at best only 20% of jobs generated by the industry along the region's coast were full-time permanent occupations whilst 44% of all jobs were part-time seasonal posts for women. (Archer, de Vare, Moore 1976). Similar findings have been found in the Tayside study (English Tourist Board, 1981a). The majority of the jobs created are also unskilled and the trade in general does little to produce an educated work force.

The seasonal and unskilled characteristics of employment in tourism may be of considerable advantage to students wishing to supplement low grants in the vacations and perhaps more importantly can provide, for some of the year, suitable part-time work for women who have family respons- ibilities and require flexible work schedules. The structure does not however provide a firm base of employment within an authority that is attempting to find alternative forms of employment to replace jobs lost in manufacturing. At its best tourism will generate a relatively small number of skilled and semi skilled full-time posts and be a useful source of employment to those requiring flexible part-time work.

A further characteristic of the tourist industry is that it is one of if not, the, lowest paid sector of employment. The 1983 New Earning Survey shows that the average weekly earnings for manual male employees over the age of 21 within hotels and catering is, at £98, the lowest within the standard industrial classifications and compares with an average weekly wage for manual male employees of £134. The rate of pay for non-manual male workers in the hotel and catering industries is also the lowest in the standard

industrial classifications and although not quite the poorest
rate for women in manual and non-manual occupations is much
below the average. It can be concluded that almost any
other industry that a local authority would wish to promote
would provide a better income for its employees.

The economic problems of the tourist industry in terms of
structure, pay, and conditions does not rule out other ways
in which tourism can benefit the local economy. One issue
here that has received little analysis is the extent to which
tourism may provide opportunities to individuals with little
capital to become self employed. This may be achieved by a
resident willing to open up his house to paying guests or to
craftsmen who are sufficiently skilled to be able to make
and sell goods such as pottery and jewellery to the visiting
hoards.

A little researched economic consequence of tourism is the
migration of elderly families to resorts. The extent to
which these immigrants create wealth and jobs within the
community has yet to be determined. The retiring couple
will bring with them pensions and savings although they will
be unlikely directly to employ anyone themselves. They will
also generate few demands on certain services such as
education and a major demand on others such as social
services and public sector health care. The settlers may
also create some problems for incoming industry since they
will increase housing costs thus creating problems for
housing younger industrial workers let alone the seasonally
employed worker within the tourist industry. The economic
gains and losses from this element of tourist attraction is
however a phenomenon of established resort towns that is
unlikely as yet to trouble cities such as Bradford.

It can be concluded that the promotion of tourism is at
best a complement to other forms of economic development
within a local authority. This factor is clearly recognised
by an industrial city, such as Bradford. Any community
that relies on only one industry is economically vulnerable
and when like tourism that industry can be subject to major
fluctuations due to cycles of depression and boom the town
is likely to face periodic bouts of economic decline. A
number of towns dependent on tourism such as Blackpool or
Scarborough are therefore interested in attracting industry
to ease their dependence on the holiday and conference trades.

5 Allied policy areas: housing, transport and environmental improvements

Many local authorities have made major efforts in recent years to orientate more closely housing, transport and environmental improvement policies to the overall objective of employment generation. Central government has also suggested that many local authority policies ought to be more closely tailored to the needs of industry. (Department of the Environment 1977). Such advice is not mandatory, although it is nevertheless apparent that many local administrations are becoming increasingly aware that the local economy can benefit through policy modifications in areas such as housing and transport. Policy changes in these areas might not necessarily prove expensive, and might have a significant impact in terms of attracting and sustaining employment, and increasing labour mobility. Considerable direct employment gains may also accrue from, for instance, enhanced local programmes of residential rehabilitation. There is too the additional point that expenditure in areas such as housing and transport whilst subject to substantial cuts imposed by central government since the mid-seventies, might nevertheless amount in global terms to sums of an altogether different dimension to those specifically available for economic development. Bearing these issues in mind it is not therefore surprising to find comprehensive approaches to local economic expansion placing increasing emphasis on the role of policy modifications in areas allied to, and closely inter-related with, employment generation. The rest of this chapter will be concerned with these issues. Briefly however, two organisational points should be made. Firstly the emphasis within this chapter will be placed on the three most important allied policy areas of housing, transport and environmental improvements. It should of course be remembered that intervention in policy arenas such as, say, education and social services will obviously too have employment implications. More interventionist authorities for example will employ more people in these services. Housing, transport and environmental improvements nevertheless represent the most relevant policy areas in terms of any direct impact on economic development and employment creation. And secondly there is inevitably some overlap between issues discussed in this chapter and elsewhere. This is minimal in scope. Certainly there is every justification for a separate consideration of the allied policy areas raised in this chapter. Their impact in terms of job creation might prove as important as will more specifically employment orientated interventions.

HOUSING

Housing can be seen to enhance local economic prospects in at least three ways: key housing can be provided for labour required by incoming or expanding firms; labour mobility can be enhanced through a variety of mechanisms; and local programmes designed particularly to improve older areas of housing can provide additional jobs.

The provision of local authority housing for key workers has been particularly well developed in London no doubt because of the problems of an expensive and difficult to enter owner-occupied market. Southwark, for example, has operated a scheme whereby the authority will provide public housing to assist both workers already employed within the borough encountering accommodation problems and also skilled employees moving into London. Clearly bearing in mind local authority waiting lists and the substantial cut-back in new starts in the public sector in recent years many councils may find it increasingly difficult to provide very much in the way of key housing for incoming employees. There seems anyway to be evidence that certainly many district councils whilst accepting the principle of key worker housing have been traditionally inclined to impose certain constraints and reservations on this policy. (Association of District Councils 1980). There may be limitations imposed, for instance, on the numbers of units provided for a particular company. Allocations for local authorities might well be vetted by local Chambers of Commerce, and where housing is provided for those coming from outside the area the relevant job may often have to be advertised locally first and only in the event of an unsatisfactory response will housing be made available for non-local employees.

For many authorities the provision of key housing is merely one aspect of the overall objective of improving mobility in the labour market. Such an aim can in particular help to smooth mismatches which can occur between the location of specific jobs within a particular sector and the presence of suitable labour to the benefit of both employer and employee. Sometimes this mismatch will be intra-urban in scale but more probably it will be regional in its impact. The extent to which individual authorities will be able to intervene in the latter case is limited, and indeed many policies which might improve spatial and tenurial mobility, such as for instance a national allocations pool for local authority lettings, will depend on central government. Nevertheless some policies designed to improve mobility within and between tenures might be mentioned.

The most obvious instance of where immobilities within a tenure have tended to reduce geographical mobility is usually held to be in the local authority sector. Attempts to reduce these constraints are likely to depend to a large extent on centrally imposed initiatives such as amending housing allocation procedures in order to remove the residential qualification requirement, as implemented in the 1980 Housing Act, or in the introduction of intra-county and inter-county procedures designed to widen mobility within the public sector as was implemented in the National Mobility Scheme begun in 1981. Nevertheless it is worth pointing out the efforts made at different times by the Greater London Council to create an inter-borough nomination scheme which would allow the transfer of tenants from one part of the city to another within public accommodation. Working parties have for example, indicated the potential value of a Co-ordinated Allocation System that would be mandatory on all boroughs (London Boroughs Association 1977). In general such a system would provide for the allocation of a certain percentage of each housing authority's accommodation being given to a central pool and that pool would in turn be made available to applicants according to some common method of assessment. Political circumstances within London have militated against the full implementation of such a scheme particularly because of the determination on the part of some Conservative Greater London Councils to reduce the strategic role of that administration. Early in 1984 it appears that all the functions of the Greater London Council are to disappear. Certainly in terms of the role a strategic authority might play in easing labour mobility that must be seen as unfortunate.

Much of the effort undertaken by local authorities on the housing front has however been concerned not so much with widening mobility within individual tenures as with attempting to ease access into certain tenures, notably into the owner-occupied sector. · This, it is often argued, is a generally desirable policy because, amongst other apparent advantages, it improves mobility in that buying and selling houses normally imposes relatively few problems and hence allows a more efficient match between job opportunities and appropriate accommodation. Whether this is the case in times of national recession is debatable. Nevertheless many local authorities have developed policies designed to ease access into owner-occupation. Clearly there may be many and varied motives on the part of administrations wishing to promote this policy but improving economic opportunities for house buyers and facilitating labour supply for employers usually figure prominently.

A number of initiatives adopted by local councils should be mentioned in this context. Although imposed as a national policy by the Conservative government in 1980, a number of administrations had been eager to sell public sector accommodation, especially to sitting tenants. Birmingham, for instance, sold over 1,000 houses between 1976 and 1978 at a discount of up to 30% of the sale price (Birmingham Metropolitan District Council 1979). That authority too has attempted to boost owner-occupation in inner city areas by offering improved pre-1919 properties for sale to either existing tenants or other first time buyers at an all-in-cost which is discounted by the equivalent of the improvement grant that would have been available had the improvement taken place in the private sector. Other policy developments worthy of mention in this context include efforts by authorities such as Coventry to provide areas of land for executive housing in the inner areas, and the more or less standard provision by local authorities, subject to adequate financial resources, of mortgages for potential purchasers often under more preferential circumstances than would apply through normal building society regulations.

Two final policy directives designed to increase owner-occupations ought to be outlined. The Greater London Council, and other authorities have instigated homesteading programmes where vacant property is purchased through mortgages available from the council (Goodchild 1981). For the first three years interest payments may be waived on condition that the property is improved. Evidence from London would indicate however that the impact of the policy has been relatively small partly because of the areas selected for the introduction of the scheme. Probably of greater long-term significance for authorities wishing to widen the owner-occupied sector within their administrations are the efforts made by a variety of authorities notably perhaps Liverpool (Couch 1981) to approve private housing schemes in and around the central cores of cities (Swain 1979). Generally speaking land is acquired under relevant Housing Acts and resultant properties tended to be purchased by locally employed, older residents. For authorities wishing to adopt this approach it is quite apparent that enhanced owner-occupation within the urban core can assist in providing the varied socio-economic demographic structure that economic development will both require and in turn engender.

Of more direct assistance in the creation of local jobs through housing policies are enhanced programmes of residential rehabilitation. As with other aspects of housing policy the main legal and financial thrust will need to come from central government. Clearly too there would be a variety of objectives implicit in a strengthening of the improvement initiative. Most obviously unless older areas of housing are to be renovated through an expanded and simplified administrative process, the problems of decay and obsolescence will become ever more apparent, particularly within the major conurbations (The Royal Town Planning Institute 1981). On the other hand the employment implications of programmes of renewal ought not to be ignored. Between 1973 and 1981 unemployment within the construction industry almost quadrupled with a particularly marked increase in the early 1980's. Not surprisingly lobbyists have argued strongly for a determinedly expansionist programme of house construction and improvement, which, bearing in mind costs of unemployment to the Exchequer and employment multipliers inherent in any expansion of the building industry, would involve minimal net costs (Steller 1981).

In practice the implementation of any substantial expansion in new house construction will certainly depend on national political directives. The scope for local authorities to intervene in their housing markets is wider however with residential rehabilitation schemes. Here too the overall framework for action is provided nationally but local modifications at the margins are possible. Birmingham, for example, has initiated the 'envelope' scheme whereby extensive improvements are undertaken to the external fabric of dwellings on a block by block basis free of charge. This additional subsidy, largely financed out of urban aid, enables owners to complete internal improvement and hence in turn to provide additional jobs locally. Newcastle-upon-Tyne is another authority which has adopted an interventionist approach to housing renewal. Here older Tyneside flats can be improved using two grants on one property. Using this procedure the authority has ensured widespread improvement to a high standard in several areas with obvious benefits to both the local housing stock and to local employment prospects. It is clear too that, although of minimal importance at the moment, locally implemented programmes of domestic thermal insulation might in the future provide considerable gains in energy conservation whilst at the same time assist in the creation of employment (Barbier 1981). Quite evidently the potential interactions between locally designed programmes to improve and to insulate properties and the resultant jobs created, often of a semi-skilled and unskilled nature, has not been fully realised.

TRANSPORT

As with housing, many transport policies and programmes are to a large extent framed by national government's legal and financial directives. Local authorities may nevertheless be in a position to improve economic opportunities within their administrations in two broad ways: access to and within employment creating areas can be improved; and labour mobility can be eased. In both cases objectives other than the direct creation of new jobs may be of primary importance. Many modifications to transport infrastructure will, however, even if unintentionally, improve the economic efficiency of towns and cities.

A central aspect in any programme designed to ameliorate communications within cities is the construction of new, or upgrading old, highways. Such a policy can improve links with the national motorway and trunk road network, remove bottle-necks, and assist in the installation of a more efficient, faster and fuel efficient road system. Such developments can only help authorities in their efforts to attract new and retain existing firms. The provision of a better communications system is not in itself going to turn the tide of economic decline apparent in many cities and larger towns but by bettering links to markets and easing access for suppliers, some of the factors generally held responsible for economic decay might well be moderated.

The most obvious manner in which communications within cities and towns can be improved is through the implementation of major new road construction proposals. Liverpool, for instance, has given a high priority to the improvement of its strategic highway network through the creation of an Inner Ring Road (Liverpool Metropolitan District Council 1978). That authority and many others has also embarked on a variety of schemes designed to use more efficiently the existing road network. The annual Transport Policies and Programme submitted to central government by transport authorities reveal a multitude of proposals to by-pass bottlenecks, widen roads, improve junctions, and generally assist essential traffic movement. Many administrations would also wish to see direct improved access into older industrial areas scattered within residential districts. In Liverpool, a new access road is to be provided to the Garston industrial area which will assist in realising the full industrial potential of the area. Elsewhere local traffic management schemes can improve access to industrial areas through the introduction of one-way systems, parking bans on narrow access roads, the installation of off-street parking for industrial employees and the provision of commercial routes through residential areas. Initiatives such as these can often reduce delay and ease access at limited cost.

Other major infrastructural innovations are likely to prove, however, both more expensive and also much more difficult for local authorities to implement. Attempts for example by South Yorkshire authorities to persuade British Rail, and hence ultimately central government, to electrify the London line will be dependent on the prevailing position of British Rail's finances and the economic strategy devised by the government. Whatever the actual and psychological merits in improving communications between the area and the South-East, local government is here in a lobbying and not executive position. However efforts within the same region to improve the Sheffield and South Yorkshire Navigation proved successful in part because of lobbying institutions such as the EEC. This scheme is designed to improve the capacity of the canal so that barges of 400 tonnes will be able to reach Rotherham. South Yorkshire County Council has argued, in co-operation with the British Waterways Board, that substantial economic and environmental benefits will accrue to the area (British Waterways Board and South Yorkshire County Council 1977). These include suggestions that canal based industry will be attracted to the improved navigation, communications with Europe will be bettered to the benefit of both importers and exporters, and the County's general competitiveness will be enhanced through this provision of an alternative mode of transport.

Many transport policies which might benefit employment generation relate not so much to the creation of a new infrastructure designed to ease access for industrial and commercial companies, but rather to increasing labour mobility through the creation of a more cost efficient public transport system. The attainment of this objective has clearly been part of central government's planning for many years, partly because of its determination to reduce overall expenditure on transport. In the 1976 Transport Consultative Document for example the Labour administration of that period accepted that resources on transport were likely to suffer both an absolute decline, and, compared with health and housing, a relative one too (HMSO 1976). Hence many of the policies designed to improve the efficiency of public transport were to involve minimal additional expenditure. The potentially important role of policy developments such as bus priority lanes, the staggering of working hours and traffic management schemes was stressed in the 1976 report. Many transport authorities have introduced such initiatives in recent years. To some extent any subsequent increase in efficiency must assist in the economic development of the area concerned. On the other hand because of the complexity and

and variety of urban transport planning it would not be
appropriate here to enter into any comprehensive analysis of
policy innovation. It is anyway apparent that policy programmes designed to improve the functioning of public transport
do not always have as a primary aim the creation of employment
or the furthering of economic efficiency. Nevertheless one or
two approaches ought to be outlined.

The improvement of rail facilities has figured prominently
in the transport programmes of a number of authorities.
Liverpool, for instance, has concentrated on the improvement
of bus/rail and car/rail interchange at suburban stations.
The Glasgow Underground has been comprehensively modernised in
terms of stations, track and rolling stock (Strathclyde
Regional Council 1980). In Tyne and Wear a high proportion of
total local transport expenditure has been absorbed by the
construction of the Metro. Here by utilising redundant British
Rail lines and constructing new tracks an extensive rail
infrastructure has been provided. Such developments clearly
require the co-operation and financial support of central
government not least because they can represent a high
proportion of total central government assistance to public
transport throughout the country in any one year (Newcastle
and Gateshead Metropolitan District Councils 1978). Of more
immediate relevance for most authorities wishing to better
their rail system are the attempts made, for instance, by the
Greater London Council to improve rail communications in the
east and north-east of London. In Hackney new stations are
proposed on the North Woolwich Line and existing stations are
to be substantially renovated (Hackney and Islington London
Boroughs 1978). These sorts of relatively cheap schemes can
be of importance in that new employment areas can be opened
up to the mutual benefit of employees and employers.

This latter objective is most likely to be achieved however
through an interventionist approach to bus rather than rail
travel, simply because of the relative proportions of
commuters dependent on each of these modes. Virtually all
transport authorities have attempted to provide a more
efficient system for commuters subject, of course, to the
obvious proviso that their legal and financial operating
limits have been ever more circumscribed by central government.
This is particularly the case in terms of the ability
authorities may have to subsidise public transport facilities.
Financial support seems to be required for public transport
systems because of high capital costs, maintenance problems,
the peaking difficulty and fears that economic fares would
be counterproductive. If subsidies are available they can
clearly assist local authorities in the provision of a more
reliable, frequent, cheaper service which, if implemented with

a fares taper applied to longer journeys, can widen both job opportunities for local residents and job applicants for employers. This policy of subsidising public transport has been especially well developed in South Yorkshire.

In this county the controlling Labour group allowed a small overall increase in 1975 and marginal rises in 1976 to equalise fares throughout the county. From 1976 to 1983 however fares did not rise. Despite attempts made by both Labour and Conservative governments to force increases in fares the County resisted any changes in its policy. The objectives of this approach are clearly manifold, but one central aim has been to provide cheap transport in order to further the social and economic welfare of all in the area (Waugh 1980). In order to peg fares the County has had to provide a substantial subsidy which by 1980/81 amounted to £43.5m overall of which £23m was spent on direct bus fare subsidy, the rest being allocated to concessionary fares and a small element to British Rail. The overall impact of the policy has been profound. Between 1975 and 1980 passenger usage increased by $7\frac{1}{2}\%$ when in most other areas there was a marked decline. Moreover in efficiency terms using indicators such as miles run per bus year or passengers carried per bus then the system appears efficient compared with most other areas in the country (White 1980).

There have it is true been criticisms of the approach. The fares have been seen as too low. They could be increased arguably with minimal effects on usage rates. The subsidies obviously require high rate calls within the authority and this has been seen as a potential disadvantage in that employers may leave for other areas and new ones would be unlikely to arrive. But it should be pointed out that only about 8% of rate borne expenditure goes toward public transport, that rateable values in the area are low, that the policy has proved politically popular, and that in terms of easing mobility this must benefit both retailers and indeed all employers seeking labour. The degree to which cheap public transport actually reduces unemployment must nevertheless be held in some doubt. It might, because of rate calls, prove relatively unpopular to employers. In a largely self-contained economic sub-region such as South Yorkshire it must also be open to question as to whether there are genuine discrepancies between labour supply and demand which will be eradicated through a policy of cheap public transport. The approach in essence has more value in terms of social and welfare gains. than in alleviating unemployment. But for those employed in public transport and for those whose job opportunities are widened, the approach will be seen as eminently reasonable. Whether the cheap fares policy will survive rate-capping and

the demise of the metropolitan counties planned for 1985 is
however another matter.

ENVIRONMENTAL IMPROVEMENTS

A third major policy area open to local authorities which can
be utilised to further economic development is the whole
question of environmental improvements. As with housing and
transport it is apparent that most policy initiatives in this
area will have a number of mutually supporting objectives, of
which one may relate to economic issues. An additional problem
of definition is that in many administrations the substantial
thrust of environmental improvement has come in industrial
improvement areas which will be dealt with in the next chapter.

Some authorities, and especially those with major problems
of industrially derelict land and poor environmental standards
have made efforts to overcome these problems. In economic
terms such developments can improve the environmental percep-
tion of an area, can attract new investment, and can lever
funds from the private sector. Authorities may however have
to develop such policies under tight financial constraints.
A great deal of industrially derelict land is reclaimed using
derelict land grant issued by the Department of the Environment.
Despite a generally generous attitude to projects requiring
this grant aid, not all parts of the country have always been
eligible for the grant, and a great deal of waste land does
not fall within the definition of derelict land for grant
purposes. Not surprisingly some observers have suggested that
land reclamation may not be keeping pace with new land falling
into a state of dereliction (Association of Metropolitan
Authorities 1981).

Despite these constraints some authorities have made progress
in this area. Liverpool has recently launched a new initiative
in conjunction with the Department of the Environment to
improve the inner urban environment of the city (Liverpool
Metropolitan District Council 1978). This programme will
involve the Department allocating at least £2.5m to
environmental improvements, which when combined with urban aid
monies, should ensure some amelioration in the undoubtedly poor
environmental standards pertaining within the area. In some
places the authority is to declare environmental improvement
areas. In these localities it is intended to establish higher
environmental standards than would normally occur within inner
city areas. Four such areas are initially likely to be
designated varying in size from 55 to 104 hectares. Although
improvement undertaken within these localities is not
necessarily primarily concerned with enhancing economic
performance it is anticipated that the wide range of

environmental programmes will have an impact on local working conditions, local employment, and on the external image of the city.

Similar objectives lie behind the activities of South Yorkshire County Council's Environmental Department (South Yorkshire County Council 1978). A wide range of policies pursued by the Department, such as the preservation of historic buildings or the development of increasing accessibility to the countryside, might have an impact on the environmental image of the area and hence on the degree to which new firms might be attracted to the area and existing ones retained. But of more specific direct interest from the point of view of economic expansion are the policies contained within land reclamation and environmental improvement.

In terms of land reclamation the County has a long tradition of improving derelict, despoiled and degraded land. Derelict land, that is land incapable of beneficial use without further treatment, has been reclaimed at the rate of about 80 hectares per annum primarily using central government grants. Despoiled land where industrial activities are still being undertaken is more difficult to improve but certain modifications such as the screening of colliery sites has been undertaken. Degraded land consists of all forms of run-down industrial land, railway land and sites within the vicinity of highways. Each of these types of degraded land has been approached with a different policy perspective.

Industrial land for instance needing improvements is subject to a specific combined scheme between the County and relevant industrialists. In these schemes firms will be encouraged to look after their land by, for instance, the planting of trees, regrading and seeding waste areas, demolishing derelict buildings and improving perimeter fencing. The costs are shared between the County and the industrialist and the overall scheme is agreed between both participants. Although many of the individual schemes will not be expensive the investment can help create a mutual confidence out of all proportion to the sums invested.

The same would probably be true for railway line improvements. Here however the County faces, as indeed do many other authorities, a major task. There are over 300 miles of operational lines in the county and also considerable land owned by British Rail which by reason of its size, shape and position may be impossible, or difficult, to utilise. There are therefore two major problems when considering British Rail land within the County in environmental terms. First, long stretches of line are flanked by unattractive industrial development. And secondly, the increasing scale of the operational run-down of the rail system in recent decades has meant that British Rail has found itself with an ever-increasing amount of redundant land and buildings. In an attempt to overcome these problems the County signed an agreement with British Rail in 1977 allowing the former to carry out improvements on approved sites. The landscaping design is produced by the County, approved or modified by British Rail and ultimately implemented by the Council at its own cost. Most of the schemes are relatively simple partly to reduce costs and partly to ensure easy maintenance. In the last four years of the seventies work was carried out at a cost of £16,000. British Rail will benefit because of environmental improvements near to its stations and the County clearly gains in terms of the improved image of the region apparent to rail travellers. This latter point is important in that the authority believes that a high proportion of those using the rail services will be business-men whose impression of the County will be changed for the better as a result of environmental projects.

This latter point is clearly debatable. It might be argued that environmental improvements have only a marginal impact. Evidence however from some of the early industrial improvement areas indicates both that environmental issues are important to developers, industrialists and businessmen in that they help create confidence in an area and also that they can lever substantial supportive investment from the private sector in the way of additional environmental projects and in turn increased investment in plant and machinery. Since environmental improvements will remain an objective of public policy making in many of the major cities any spin-off effects in the way of economic development can only be of considerable benefit to the authorities involved.

CONCLUSION

As a concluding comment to this area of potential assistance that local authorities might provide through housing, transport and environmental policies to the overall objective of economic expansion, three issues are worth raising. First, all three policy fields have been well developed in the past, in many ways more so than has direct intervention in economic or employment issues. For this reason funds may be available more easily than are resources specifically allocated to economic planning. Secondly, it does appear to be the case that many administrations are becoming more aware of the potential economic impact of policy initiatives in these areas. Sometimes the impact will come through making an area more attractive to industrialists, or by improving accessibility, or by providing a more varied housing market. But equally so, and often neglected, are the direct employment implications of programmes for home insulation, the improvement of older dwellings, environmental schemes and the provision of a better infrastructure. Such projects will mean more jobs, often of a semi- or unskilled nature. But thirdly the overall influence of developments in these policy areas must not be exaggerated. In some circumstances, notably perhaps the creation of better communications, the impact might be considerable. In others, minor environmental schemes for instance, the overall influence of projects will be limited in many cases.

6 Commercial and industrial development and improvement

One area of economic and employment planning undertaken by local government that expanded rapidly throughout the 1970's was industrial development and rehabilitation. In the case of the former, authorities have become involved in wide variety of developmental functions including provision of land, installation of facilities, construction of units, selection of tenants and so on. From the mid 1970's too, many authorities in the older urban areas turned their attention to the improvement of older industrial infrastructure. These policies will form the focus of attention for this chapter.

It would initially be worth pointing out however that the increasing confidence with which authorities have entered the industrial development area, where many potential schemes involve close collaboration with the private sector, reflects in part the experience gained by local government in the extensive redevelopment of city centres which occurred throughout the United Kingdom in the post-war period (Ratcliffe 1978). The extent of city centre redevelopment has been considerable, boosted by the continued profitability of the retail sector, the willingness of institutions to invest in retail and commercial infrastructure, and the close co-operation between local government and the market. In terms of this last point extensive city centre redevelopment frequently involved the creation of partnerships between the public and private sectors. The details varied from scheme to scheme but local authorities might become involved in land acquisition and sale, planning permission, financial and tenancy arrangements and so on. By intervening in these areas local government often proved able to raise financial capital and expertise from the market, to spread development risks, to retain some control of land use, and to ensure that community benefits in the way of, say, the provision of community facilities were integrated into proposals as a whole.

Clearly for many authorities undertaking city centre redevelopment any employment spin-off from the project was

welcome but was not the major objective. Instead city centre
schemes were perceived as mechanisms through which authorities
could control and benefit from development that would also help
retain or enhance the commercial and retail status of the
city or town concerned. In retrospect however it seems
apparent that the joint development of city centres proved
useful when authorities turned their attention to the
industrial sector. In particular the joint creation of new
shopping centres gave authorities confidence and expertise in
dealing with the market and development problems, indicated
the extent to which astute councils could direct proposals,
and probably helped create a more entrepreneurial spirit in
many administrations. Certainly many have been more than
willing to enter into the industrial development process.

THE PROVISION OF INDUSTRIAL LAND AND DEVELOPMENT

(a) Industrial sites

Numerous powers exist allowing local authorities to acquire,
control and develop land. These include the 1963 Local
Authorities (Land) Act, the 1971 Town and Country Planning Act,
and the 1972 Local Government Land Act (Bramley et al 1979).
In planning terms most authorities would adopt a number of
measures with regard to the provision of industrial land.
These might include preparation and release of cleared sites,
allocation of sites in statutory plans, assembly of industrial
sites and release of surplus land (The Royal Town Planning
Institute 1979). In recent years too with the imposition of
land registers on local authorities there has been in general
a greater awareness of vacant public land and a greater
inclination to dispose of it to the market for a variety of
uses, including industrial and commercial development. Such
land may be released after servicing. In the past this has
been implemented by grant available through say, Section 250
of the Town and Country Planning Act 1971 and through derelict
land grant.

Although there is evidence from some parts of the country,
such as the West Midlands (Williams et al 1980), that there is
an adequate allocation of industrial land, there nevertheless
appear to be problems in the creation of industrial sites.
Land available may be in small relatively inaccessible pockets.
The market may increasingly wish to invest in sites beyond
built-up areas wherein much industrial land will be allocated.
Not all land allocated for industrial uses will in the event
be used for this purpose. Because too, of the reluctance of
the private sector to become involved in site preparation per
se, it proving largely unprofitable apart from on the

relatively small number of accessible, easily developed sites, the public sector must be seen as the primary agent in land assembly and preparation. This raises questions such as the continued availability of public finance and the costs of land acquisition compared with other forms of intervention (Smith 1980).

However, exactly because economic development will depend on the assured availability of industrial land, so authorities will continue to see it as a vital function for them to perform. Indeed restraint on local government spending on economic development and the increasing willingness of the private sector to invest in factory units may force local government to concentrate more on the particular problems of land acquisition and servicing rather than on industrial development per se.

In an extensive review of this area of local government activity Boddy (1983) points out that a number of authorities such as Derby and Bristol steadily acquired land throughout the postwar period for industrial purposes. In the 1950's and 1960's the main motive for such activity was to relocate industrial units displaced by redevelopment proposals. By the following decade however the main motive was to help retain, and if possible expand, local employment opportunities severely undermined by economic recession. In part changing motives towards intervention was paralleled by a growing awareness of the mechanics of land acquisition and development engendered by the 1975 Community Land Act. Although relatively little industrial land was acquired under this Act before its repeal in 1979 it encouraged, according to Boddy (1983), wider local government activity and interest in the industrial development process and helped instil more sophisticated development practices.

As has been expanded elsewhere (Boddy 1983; Boddy and Barrett 1980) authorities will often retain some control of development on land serviced by them. The actual mechanics of disposal frequently involves an authority in acquiring a freehold site, providing roads and sewers, and leasing plots to industrialists. A later section of this chapter will consider the sorts of legal arrangements which have come to characterise the construction and disposal of industrial units. Here some brief mention ought to be made, however, of the sorts of considerations which have governed the disposal of industrial land.

An authority even if disposing of land freehold will retain some control of development through relevant planning powers which may well cover development aspects such as design,

intensity, form and layout of the development and so on.
Increasingly however many authorities will adopt some form of
leasehold arrangement. These vary but typically may well
allow authorities to participate in rental growth through
reviews rather than them receiving an initial once and for all
premium. Alternatively authorities may well wish to issue
development briefs. These will be made available when
leasehold interests are offered for sale. Typically that
might indicate desired planning standards, the form of leasing,
financial arrangements sought and the way developers are to be
selected (Boddy 1983). Other arrangements whereby authorities
may wish to enter into agreements with the private sector,
such as leaseback measures are considered later.

(b)   Industrial units

As a number of commentators have established there was a
considerable expansion of industrial development undertaken by
local government in the 1970's (Boddy 1983; Chalkley and Perry
1984). In 1971 perhaps 5% of authorities were involved in
this policy area. By the end of the decade most authorities
had in some way or other intervened in the industrial
development process. The metropolitan districts might have
produced the most concentrated response but many shire counties
had undertaken some development. In some authorities the
programme of development had been considerable. Tyne and
Wear for instance built almost 200 units between 1976 and
1979 (Boddy 1983).

A great deal of local authority effort has been concentrated
on the small firm sector. Partly this reflects a traditional
reluctance on the part of the market to invest in this area
where risks may be considerable and management costs formidable (Robinson 1979). The emphasis on units of less than
5,000 sq ft may also reflect the determination of some
councils to assist as far as possible the creation of new
companies.

Frequently authorities have constructed new industrial
units on sites of less than three acres acquired through slum
clearance or the redevelopment of older industrial infra-
structure (Boddy 1983). The development may be undertaken by
the authority's own direct labour organisation, or, as through
tender, by using the market. Generally rents are set at
market rates. Rent and rate relief may be made available
especially in the assisted areas where any appropriate
development grant can be passed on in the form of initial rent
concession. Authorities may prefer to let to certain tenants,
industrialists for example, rather than service sector
employees, but the financial imperatives of ensuring total

92

leasing may force authorities ultimately to accept a wide
range of tenancies. Some encouragement for firms which an
authority may wish to assist can be provided however through
the granting of mortgages secured against industrial buildings.

Despite the rapid growth of local government activity in
the industrial development process in the 1970's several
factors suggest that other agencies may prove more important
in this policy field in the 1980's. Tax allowances created in
the 1980 budget for instance have dramatically increased private
sector interest in industrial development. The continued
activities moreover of the English Industrial Estates
Corporation and the Scottish and Welsh Development Agencies
suggest that much public sector intervention in industrial
development will emanate from these organisations. Local
authorities may well indeed increasingly prefer or be directed
towards partnerships with the private sector as will be
discussed shortly. In passing however it should be noted that
any weakening of local government activity in the industrial
development area will inevitably mean that certain objectives
often assumed by local government, such as attempting to
ensure that units are used for industrial purposes, or that
the building of new factories should assist in reducing
unemployment, may be lost. Market criteria will clearly come
increasingly to dominate the construction and leasing of new
units.

(c) Public-private sector partnerships in the industrial
     development process

Although this book deals largely with local authority economic
intervention, it becomes increasingly difficult to ignore the
private sector especially as much recent entrepreneurial
innovation has been of a partnership nature attempting to
combine the talents and attributes of the two sectors. Much
of this activity has been described elsewhere (Barrett and
Boddy 1981; Boddy and Barrett 1980; Williams 1980). But
reference needs to be made to it here. Initially some mention
ought to be made of the structure of the industrial market in
the United Kingdom.

By 1977 there were about 350 million sq metres of industrial
and commercial warehouse premises in England and Wales almost
three times the combined figure for commercial and retail
premises. The relative increase in industrial floorspace in
the 1960's and 1970's was however much less than for commercial. More than half of the total industrial floorspace was,
by 1977, in units of less than 500 sq metres. About two-
thirds of industrial units are owner-occupied. This proportion is however declining as an increasing number of industrial

establishments seek out leasing or renting arrangements. Such arrangements avoid the tying up of capital in buildings rather than capital equipment, allow for relatively rapid movements between factory units as firms expand or contract, and distance companies from the problems associated with owner-occupied buildings.

One cause and consequence of the tenurial shifts identified above has been a growing interest in the industrial development process on the part of both developers and the financial institutions. Traditionally in fact the development market has shown a marked reluctance to invest in industrial property or the rehabilitation of older infrastructure. This was due to a number of factors. These included the specialised nature of industrial buildings, complex managerial problems, a high rate of wear and tear, technological outdating, difficulties in securing adequate rent reviews, and so on. Industrial rehabilitation was in many respects even more unlikely to attract private investment because of the same sorts of problems as those associated with industrial development, combined with the peculiar problems specific to improvement such as the high cost of refurbishment, especially high management costs and the technical difficulties attendant upon converting older industrial buildings into new uses.

However by the mid to late 1970's the market, especially the major institutional investors revealed a markedly more enthusiastic attitude to industrial property. This was due to, amongst other factors, the increasingly standardised nature of industrial and warehouse activities, a more attractive yield, lack of alternative investments, heavy refurbishment costs of commercial property and improvements in industrial building techniques which have allowed for the more rapid construction of units and therefore a quicker return on investment.

This change in attitude on the part of the investment market has been seen by some authorities as an opportunity for the creation of public-private sector partnerships in the field of industrial development. Whatever the potential conflicts between the two sectors, and these will be mentioned later, industrial partnerships hold out distinct advantages from the point of view of local government. Industrial units can be provided using private capital, unemployment moderated and scarce public resources used for other aspects of economic development and employment creation.

In one sense partnerships might imply, say, the simple sale of industrial sites freehold with appropriate planning permission. Normally however in this context partnership implies a sharing of risk and reward. Typically, although there are many variations in practice, the partnership will involve some sort of lease-leaseback arrangement. Here an authority will guarantee rentals on a completed development. This commitment will often allow an industrial developer opportunities to raise development capital from major investors. Crewe for example in its Gates Industrial Estate granted a 125 year lease to a major insurance company in return for a premium and subsequent peppercorn rent. A 35 year leaseback was taken on by the authority on completion with an agreed rent payable by the council reviewed every five years.

Other forms of partnership exist such as the 'two-slice' method whereby the developer recovers cost and profit first with the local authority taking the whole of any residue. As with the leaseback arrangements there are distinct advantages in these co-operative developments. Authorities may be able to ensure the implementation of industrial development, sometimes on difficult sites or in problematic locations without having to raise development capital. They may too find that they are in a position to control the use and management of completed units.

On the other hand partnership arrangements can produce genuine problems for authorities concerned. Completed units may be difficult to let. Finished units may prove more expensive than had been thought thus inhibiting their letting to new, smaller units seeking out cheaper property. The complexities of partnership negotiation may be lost on less experienced authorities. This can lead to the selection of developers unable to ensure the completion of the development on time, the signing of agreements that prove of limited use in practice, and an underselling of the overall scheme, which the authority concerned is after all guaranteeing.

Nevertheless it appears that partnerships will continue to play a part in industrial development. It brings forth private and institutional capital, it stimulates development projects and it can ensure the implementation of schemes that would not otherwise occur. It may be however that in the future there will be growing conflicts between major urban authorities and the institutional funds. The latter increasingly are likely to support well-serviced green field developments of a better quality, particularly perhaps those located in areas in the South of England where economic growth appears more likely. These objectives will prove at variance with the aims of the older cities where inner urban developments of a relatively simple nature catering for the lower end of the market will be perceived as a priority.

THE IMPROVEMENT OF OLDER COMMERCIAL AND INDUSTRIAL PREMISES

Since the mid 1970's there has been a marked increase in the
improvement of older industrial and commercial premises by
local authorities. For much of the post-war period local
authorities had instigated redevelopment policies designed to
remove the worst excesses of 19th Century urbanisation.
Extensive areas of the major cities were thus designated
Comprehensive Development Areas after 1945 wherein existing
buildings were completely removed. However in the
reconstruction of such areas the mixed land use pattern
typical of Victorian urban development was replaced all too
frequently by a single land use: residential. By the early
1970's these policies were giving rise to considerable disquiet. Partly this was because of the social and economic
costs inherent in new high rise, high density, residential
development. But increasingly too some urban authorities (for
example London Borough of Wandsworth 1975) were becoming aware
of the employment consequences of redevelopment proposals.
Older industrial and commercial premises were being lost which
provided cheap and flexible units particularly suited to new,
small enterprises. In fact as later research was to indicate
(Chalkley 1979) many firms compulsorily acquired during
redevelopment frequently used the compensation they received
as a result of the expiration of business to re-equip and to
re-capitalise in other premises. Nevertheless the demolition
of older industrial and commercial premises clearly involved
a loss of cheap and flexible infrastructure.

In order to retain older industrial and commercial premises
many authorities have implemented improvement policies.
Sometimes this might involve the rehabilitation of a single
unit or a small group of buildings. Southwark for instance
has converted a nineteenth century riverside warehouse into
small workshops (London Borough of Southwark 1978). Green
and Foley (1983) have examined the scale of conversion of
older, redundant buildings in West Yorkshire. In similar
vein Darley (1978) and Falk (1978) have pointed out the degree
of industrial improvement throughout the country. These range
from the house shells schemes in Nottingham wherein blighted
and condemned residential units are converted to small
industrial units, to the substantial conversions of textile
mills in the North West.

(a) Area improvement

Much of the industrial and commercial improvement which has
been undertaken in recent years has not however concentrated
on the individual building but rather has been concerned with
the implementation of area based proposals. The area based

approach has been a consistent theme in urban policy for many years. Housing improvement and many aspects of inner city intervention, such as enterprise zones, have adopted the areal approach. This allows for the concentration of resources and may prove an effective way of engendering individual and corporate interest. On the other hand of course the areal approaches raise issues of equity, in that some individuals or companies receive assistance but others do not, and may suggest that problems, such as poor housing, are contained in small areas when this can prove far from the truth.

Nevertheless there has been considerable local authority interest in the regeneration of older industrial and commercial areas. Sometimes in areas of architectural or historic interest substantial improvements and the engendering of economic activity can take place using legislation governing conservation. The Nottingham Lace Market is one such example (Nottingham 1976). Here an area of attractive nineteenth century industrial buildings had by the 1960's fallen into some state of disrepair because of changing market fashions, foreign competition, and planning proposals for road widening and extensive redevelopment. The area was however declared a Conservation Area in 1969 and more intrusive planning proposals were abandoned in 1973. Since then the area has been declared a Conservation Area of Outstanding National Importance and an agreement between relevant local authorities and the Department of the Environment in 1976 ensured that the Lace Market became a Town Scheme. This latter declaration recognising the national importance of the area ensured in turn that grants would be made available for the repair and improvement of buildings within the area. This approach combined with environmental policies designed to improve street furniture and to control through traffic have undoubtedly stimulated market interest in the Lace Market. Industrial and commercial buildings have been retained and refurbished. The overall improvements to the Market combined with the existence of a number of listed buildings of historic and architectural interest will undoubtedly too help stimulate tourism.

(b)   Industrial and commercial improvement areas

It has to be recognised however that most areas of older industrial and commercial development are unlikely to be declared Conservation Areas and still fewer to receive national acclaim and hence any substantial financial support for rehabilitation. For most authorities the concept of the Industrial Improvement Area (IIA) will prove of greater relevance.

Although similar policies were being developed in the mid 1970's in the North East, the concept of the IIA is usually seen to have originated in Rochdale where the Crawford Street IIA was declared in 1974. Here an area largely dominated by long-established firms in the textile and engineering sectors with a deteriorating environment and with little new industrial development was selected for improvement. The overall objective of the scheme was to secure the future of the area for modern industrial activity whilst at the same time making it environmentally acceptable to residents remaining in the area (McDonald 1979).

The ultimate success of the Rochdale scheme, about which more later, stimulated national interest in the concept of the IIA. This culminated in the 1978 Inner Urban Areas Act. This Act allowed, amongst other powers, certain specified authorities powers to declare industrial or commercial improvement areas. The accompanying circular (Department of the Environment 68/78) indicated those authorities which would be granted such powers. They fell into three categories. There were to be seven Partnership areas where inner city problems were apparently most acute; 15 Programme authorities with slightly less acute problems and a third tier of 19 other districts. All these authorities were to be eligible for 75% per cent grant from central government under an enhanced urban programme for expenditure within IIAs approved by the Department of the Environment. This expenditure could be directed towards grants and loans for the conversion or improvement of industrial and commercial buildings or for environmental improvements designed to assist the IIA as a whole. In some cases grants were limited either to a certain proportion of total expenditure or to a fixed figure relating to the numbers of jobs created or preserved as a result of improvements to buildings.

In the first two years after the passing of the 1978 Act, some 60 IIAs were declared by over 30 authorities. As Young et al (1980) have pointed out, the Act did not stop other authorities unable to declare IIA's under the 1978 Act from implementing area-based policies. Trafford Metropolitan District Council for instance in association with local industrialists and the Civic Trust has initiated an environmental improvement scheme for the Trafford Park industrial estate. Nevertheless the emphasis in terms of improvements to older areas of industrial and commercial development has moved firmly to the concept of the IIA. It is obvious too that the approach has raised a number of pertinent issues which will now be explored.

(i)   As others have pointed out (Cameron et al 1982) a number
        of objectives may be assumed within the declaration of
        an IIA. These include the removal of obsolescent
        buildings, improvements to the environment and physical
        infrastructure, stabilising or increasing employment,
        boosting commercial as well as industrial development,
        industrial redevelopment, bettering the environment for
        remaining residents and so on. It is apparent that
        these objectives may conflict. For example as Williams
        et al (1980) establish, the single greatest constraint
        facing many inner urban companies is the difficulty of
        expanding in situ. Factories tend to be cramped and
        inefficient affording few opportunities to expand or
        to improve accessibility. But providing additional
        land for expansion, for plant rationalisation, car
        parking or improved internal communications may well
        reduce existing industrial stock and quite probably
        local employment too. It is by no means obvious either
        that industrial rents will remain stable in an IIA
        subject to extensive improvements. This will influence
        the type of establishment moving into or remaining
        within an IIA and may inhibit the smaller, newer
        company seeking out cheaper accommodation.

(ii)   The scale of local authority action within an IIA can
        be considerable. It may well embrace land reclamation,
        demolition, site preparation, factory construction,
        improvements to communications, landscaping, and the
        provision of grants and loans to firms. This formidable
        list of powers raises two questions: internal local
        authority structures and the particular problems
        associated with certain local authority programmes.
        The latter theme will be developed later. It is worth
        pointing out here however that the successful imple-
        mentation of any IIA will require the creation of
        effective management organisations. The evaluation of
        the initial Rochdale IIA (Tym and Partners 1979)
        concluded that the relative success of the project was
        due, amongst other factors, to the creation of a
        knowledgeable core team, recruited largely from one
        department, headed by an enthusiastic, entrepreneurial
        leader given wide local political support. This team
        provided a permanent point of contact for local
        industrialists and through its determined efforts to
        concentrate on action rather than on planning or data
        collection, mutually supportive links were created
        between the officers concerned and local industrialists.
        It seems too that the concentration of resources on a
        particular area can help engender confidence on the part

of local industrialists and may provide a useful framework within which environmental improvements and other
policies can be organised.

The area approach inevitably however raises the issue
of selection. Areas where there is some evidence of
economic vitality, where vacant land exists, and where
land ownership is relatively simple may provide better
opportunities for the successful implementation of IIAs.
This last point may prove especially important. There
is evidence of considerable delay in the implementation
of local authority proposals within IIAs (Dabinett and
Whisker 1981; Tayler 1982). Such long-lead in times
may be due in part to the bureaucratic problems
associated with the concentration and possible
re-organisation of local authority resources but often
reflect too the complexities of implementing environmental and traffic improvements in areas with diffuse
patterns of land ownership.

(iii) In the implementation of IIAs certain policy issues
have cropped up in the areas of traffic management,
environmental improvements, and refurbishment of older
physical infrastructure.

1   Traffic management   One of the major objectives within
many IIAs will be improving the circulation of traffic and
access to buildings. These policies might however result in
conflict with other goals such as preventing industrial traffic
from using residential streets. Equally so bettering the
circulation of traffic through an IIA might require the strict
control of on-street parking, closing some accesses on to major
roads and the introduction of a plethora of signs and yellow
lines. Such policies are likely to prove unpopular and
difficult to sustain. Not surprisingly as Tym and Partners
(1979) point out, traffic proposals can prove extremely
contentious and may highlight the markedly different objectives
being sought by local residents, local industrialists and the
authority. Such detailed proposals may tend to deflect attention too away from car-sharing, the re-organisation of bus
services or the staggering of working hours which could have
a considerable impact on the problems of accessibility and
traffic intrusion.

2   Environmental improvements   One objective assumed within
the IIA concept is that of local environmental improvements.
These can include landscaping, demolition of intrusive
buildings, wall cleaning and painting and the creation of
either temporary or permanent public open space. Funding for
such activities can come from urban aid, the Manpower Services

Commission, derelict land grants and so on. And indeed as the detailed evaluation of the Crawford Street IIA in Rochdale (Tym and Partners 1979) makes clear, total costs to any local authority for environmental improvements may well prove relatively limited and yet can bring forth substantial private sector investment in the way of additional environmental improvements and other benefits. On the other hand authorities ought not to introduce unrealistically high environmental standards. IIAs essentially consist of older industrial and commercial property in which relatively small environmental improvements can help instil confidence in the long term future of the area. In some cases too there will anyway be the problem of polutant and intrusive uses (Tayler 1982) that might inhibit the introduction of more intensive forms of environmental improvements.

3   The rehabilitation of older industrial stock   The improvement of older industrial buildings or the conversion of non-industrial buildings into industrial use can prove a problem. As Topham (1978) has pointed out probably the greatest difficulty is in raising finance for such projects. This issue will be taken up later. In addition however there may well be substantial technical difficulties. The installation of services can be expensive. Ceilings heights and illumination levels may be too low. The problems too of improving internal access and of creating servicing and reception areas in high density industrial development can prove formidable obstacles in the implementation of industrial rehabilitation projects. Fire and building regulations can add substantially to the costs. The former in particular can prove expensive to satisfy. Escape routes may have to be provided, combustible elements in the structure may have to be protected and large spaces compartmentalised.

4   IIAs and the market   Successful implementation of any IIA will require the effective combination of public sector infrastructural investment with private sector spending. The public sector can undoubtedly stimulate and direct private sector investment. It can do this through spending on environmental improvements and traffic management, by providing business and advice, and by promoting the concept of the IIA through surveys, consultations and personal visits (Local Economic Information Service 1982). Ultimately, however, it is essential that the private sector responds through enhanced investment in production, physical infrastructure, environmental improvements and so on.

It is clear that some areas are more likely to bring forth private sector investment than are other potential IIAs. The

apparent early success of the Rochdale IIA for instance was
seen by the consultants (Tym and Partners 1979) as being due
in part to the relatively good performance of the town's
economy compared with the North West as a whole, local control
of the economy stimulating greater loyalty to the area than
would have been the case with externally owned firms, and a
compact travel to work area which allowed for the easy
recruitment of labour. These sorts of factors were recognised
by central government in the guiding circular governing the
implementation of IIAs (Department of the Environment 68/78).
Here it was recommended that authorities selected their IIAs
with care. In particular IIAs might best be declared in areas
with some spare land for new development or bettering
accessibility, where there was a concentration of firms in
expanding sectors, where production dovetailed into local
skills, and where local firms showed on preliminary survey
that they would be likely to co-operate with the IIA
programme.

Nevertheless even bearing in mind these criteria it is
apparent that in some IIAs the take up of grants and loans has
been poor (Cameron et al 1982; Tayler 1982). This may be due
to a number of factors. The performance of the economy as a
whole inhibiting economic investment; poor regional performance in areas such as the North East; the bureaucratic and
uncertain nature of grant and loan application; the small
size of grant.

It is by no means inevitable of course that expanding firms
will require or bother with grants and loans under the 1978
Act or that these powers will prove particularly useful in the
retention or creation of jobs. Returning again to the
detailed evaluation of the Rochdale IIA it becomes apparent
here however that local authority action in the area has had a
considerable impact on employment prospects in the area. In
particular policies designed to bring forth land for either
additional floorspace or improved servicing have been
instrumental in securing or creating several hundred jobs. An
equivalent number is likely to be forthcoming too from new
industrial development on sites made available by the
authority. Moreoever local authority expenditure in terms of
the acquisition and servicing of land brought forward private
sector assistance on an altogether great scale.

5   The legislative and financial framework   It seems
apparent that there are problems in the implementation if IIAs
because of the relevant legal and financial framework.
Authorities may for example have to decide in their grant
allocations for industrial or commercial improvement or
conversion whether a developer or firm is to obtain an

excessive rate of return as a result of the receipt of grant.
This may be difficult to determine. Some authorities moreover
will not be faced with such technicalities since under the 1978
Inner Urban Areas Act they are unable to declare IIAs.
Informal improvement can of course proceed but grants and
loans available under the 1978 legislation will not be
available. Other legal and financial modifications proposed
in the early evaluation of the Crawford Street IIA in Rochdale
include the granting of wider land acquisition powers to
authorities, some relaxation of building regulations and a
speeding up of statutory approvals for compulsory purchase
and traffic management (Tym and Partners 1979). In addition
it is clear that because of the somewhat diffuse nature of
the legislation it is vital that local authorities ensure a
concentrated attack on the problems of the declared improvement
area. This should involve the creation of an action team
promoting the concept of the IIA possibly with a decentralised
presence within the area. Individual firms will need to be
approached, surveyed and consulted. Equally so the authority
should be prepared to bend main programmes to benefit the area
under consideration. Highway expenditure in particular may
need to be directed into the action area in an effort to
improve circulation, access and parking which are often major
problems in inner urban areas. The bending of highways and
other expenditure will need moreover to occur relatively
quickly since IIAs are expected to last no more than 5 or 7
years. In practice too since the take-up of grants can be slow
in the first few years, much of the implementation of the IIA
will occur in a relatively short period of time.

INDUSTRIAL DEVELOPMENT AND REFURBISHMENT: A CONCLUDING
COMMENT

Industrial development and refurbishment have become, and are
clearly very much likely to remain, central policy objectives
within local government's overall determination to consolidate
intervention in the economic development and employment
creation areas. There are certain distinct advantages in
pursuing these objectives of development and refurbishment.
They are politically uncontentious. Central government has
shown a willingness to increase, if only on a limited scale,
the legal framework and financial resources dedicated to these
areas. They are likely moreoever increasingly to attract
private sector support. They encourage public-private sector
partnership. They represent obvious areas for enhanced
intervention, especially perhaps within the larger cities.

It should be pointed out however that expansion into these
policy areas has not been without comment or criticism. In

terms of industrial development for example, as Chalkley and Perry (1984) point out, the enormous expansion in the construction of small units by local authorities begs a number of questions. For instance, how many jobs has the programme created and for whom? Would resources used for industrial development have been better employed elsewhere? Is there substantial evidence for a shortage of small units? And if partnerships are likely to prove the norm will local authorities retain adequate control of tenants? Evidence from radical commentators in London Docklands suggests that private industrial estates have encouraged the proliferation of low employment creating and low wage paying firms (Joint Docklands Action Group 1977). Whilst not all authorities will agree with the political approach adopted by the Joint Docklands Action Group it seems reasonable that local government should retain considerable control over lettings. This will help ensure good employment standards and, for more interventionist authorities, affords the opportunity of guiding even if marginally, the direction of local economic development.

Industrial rehabilitation has similarly been the subject of more reflective evaluation. What for instance are the opportunity costs of investing in older urban infrastructure as opposed to newer green field locations? Some might anyway argue that boosting national wealth may require the pursuit of policies whose impact is to run generally counter to those of the local improvement of the industrial sections of the inner urban areas (Town Planning Review 1978). Clearly many authorities in the depressed regions would argue that older industrial infrastructure can provide the basis for an enhanced local economy. Older buildings can be retained for new and established firms. Local environmental standards and traffic circulation can be much improved. New units can be constructed and older ones retained. Jobs can be secured. But whatever the merits of the inner city versus green field debate, those implementing IIAs will no doubt reflect on some of the evident discrepancies in the approach. Much private sector investment might occur anyway irrespective of any IIA declaration. The approach might prove purely cosmetic, an irrelevance compared with other structural forces affecting an authority. Grants, loans and environmental improvements moreover will not guarantee the retention of local firms. They may do little either to encourage the creation of newer enterprises. Area action in the form of IIA treatment may well involve a gradual rise in industrial rents to the detriment of potential entrepreneurs. But for many authorities faced with acute industrial decline older industrial and commercial areas offer opportunities to intervene. These will undoubtedly be grasped.

7 Local authorities and enterprise: co-operatives, community business and high tech

Local authorities have become increasingly aware of the need to help establish new enterprise. Traditionally the creation of new businesses has been undertaken by the market. In recent decades however the retreat of capital from the older cities and depressed regions has stimulated a much more interventionist attitude on the part of local government towards enterprise and innovation. Frequently this involves local authorities acting as co-ordinators and catalysts rather than as independent entrepreneurs. This appears a reasonable approach since local government may operate most effectively in the creation of new enterprise when its powers and expertise are combined with those emanating from individuals and organisations more familiar with the workings of the market. In time however as local government becomes more aware of the dictates of the market so it can be anticipated that local administrations will become more willing and able to intervene effectively in the creation of new companies.

One classification within which to explore local government and new enterprise is that which distinguishes between high technology developments, co-operative enterprise, community businesses, and small firms. Inevitably there is some overlap here. Inevitably too at times reference will be made to policies towards existing rather than new companies. These constraints seem unavoidable. The approach nevertheless provides a framework within which to identify and to evaluate local government activities in this field.

LOCAL AUTHORITIES AND HIGH TECHNOLOGY INDUSTRY

There has been immense recent interest in the likely impact of new, high-technology industries. New products, processes and ways of distribution information will be introduced that will have the most profound of influences for some industrial sectors and few areas of employment will be untouched. Much of the innovation will be in the microelectronics field although substantial changes are likely also to occur in

biotechnology. The macro-economic impact of the new technologies has been the subject of some debate. Some observers have
suggested that dramatic unemployment will accompany any widespread introduction of the new technologies (Pahl 1978). The
Treasury too (1979) has accepted that new techniques will lead
to job losses in both manufacturing and service sectors which
at times will be both substantial and rapid. On the other hand
the introduction of new products, new services and new
processes will at the same time create additional jobs. The
exact equation between jobs gained and lost will thus prove a
complex one to unravel even at the national scale. Clearly
for many local authorities this problem is likely to prove more
acute. Some will find themselves in the fortunate position of
presiding over increases in employment in high-technology
industries. Others may find that they are adversely affected
both because of the introduction of new processes making
traditional skills irrelevant and because little in the way of
new production occurs within their administration. Not
surprisingly local authorities are steadily moving towards
policies designed both to understand the impact of what has
been called the third industrial revolution (Stonier 1980) and
to intervene within it.

(a) The new technologies: Local Authority research bases

National forecasts as to likely job impacts attendant upon the
introduction of new technologies may be of only limited use to
local authorities. It will be important for many of the
larger ones to establish likely employment changes. Taylor
(1984) has described this process in one London borough. By
disaggregating the local economy and considering the existing
and potential impact of new products and processes some assessment of job loss and employment change can be established.
Such an analysis will need to explore the impact of innovation
across the entire spectrum of employment opportunities in both
public and private sectors. As a similar study in Tameside
points out, analysis will be needed of both job change within
an authority and the probable impact of technological innovation for those resident in the administration but working in
another (Green and Coombs 1981). Moreover as Green and Coombs
(1981) establish, there will be a marked discrepancy between
jobs potentially at risk and those actually lost. Trade union
resistance or natural wastage for instance may reduce actual
redundancies. Equally so the overall equation must determine
net and not gross change. Although many jobs will be lost,
some will be created in the new industries and services and
there will be some retraining of those made redundant from
declining sectors. In passing it may be pointed out that
accurate forecasts of both job loss and job creation is

fraught with problems. If new products and services are
brought on to the market at steadily declining prices, output,
productivity and employment may rise. On the other hand, the
scale of retraining, the ability of British industry to respond
to market demand and the overall level of aggregate demand in
the economy may well operate to depress output and potential
employment in the new sectors. Interestingly enough too, and
this will be developed later, Taylor's (1984) evaluation of
job change and employment restructuring in Hammersmith adopts
a markedly more optimistic tone than does the Tameside analysis.
Quite simply some authorities will undoubtedly benefit more
than will others.

(b) Local Authorities and new technologies: lobbying for
     intervention and accommodating change

The widespread dissemination of new products and new processes
will stimulate a range of responses from local government.
For many, the most appealing policies will be those designed
to create production centres based on high-technology industry
and these developments will be explored later. The apparent
proliferation of science-parks and the like ought not however
to lead local authorities into ignoring other policy modifications that might be implemented. It will be important for
instance for authorities to consider their attitudes towards
the introduction of informational technologies within local
government itself. Retraining programmes may need to be
created, possibly with the assistance of local educational
centres. Policies towards redeployment will require consideration. Ultimately however, as Green and Coombs (1981) suggest,
communication technologies hold out the possibilities for a
much wider and more comprehensive dissemination of information
through for example the decentralisation of terminals to
schools, libraries and the like. Such policies ought too to
be combined with a general programme designed to familiarise
the public with the potential and constraints of the new
informational technologies.

  Other policy innovations may be required. Cities historically dependent on older manufacturing bases may have to
re-align their attitudes towards future employment creation as
a result of technological innovation. Tourism and the leisure
industry for example may be new areas of economic expansion.
For those in work there will be much greater opportunities for
travel, sport and recreation. Jobs in these sectors are
traditionally seasonal and often poorly paid but may represent
nevertheless sectors in which more of the semi-skilled and
unskilled can find work.

Planning policies may need to be reconsidered too. For example the assumption that office employment ought to be located within central business districts may need to be re-examined. New informational techniques will free many routine service sector jobs from city centres. Person-to-person contacts will no longer be required. Instead office employment may become increasingly decentralised from the older urban cores. It is likely instead to locate in smaller communities with attractive local environments, good shopping and housing facilities and so on. The same sorts of considerations will apply too to manufacturing employment, as will be explored later. These factors will clearly necessitate changes in orthodox land use planning. New suburban or green field sites may have to be allocated for service and manufacturing employment. The relationships between new employment sites and transport, residential and retail services will need to be fully explored too. And certainly older attitudes towards the location of offices and industry, the one to be located in city centres, the other in extensive, environmentally unattractive, zones will effectively disappear.

Of course local government can only make certain responses to the problems emerging and opportunities created through any widespread introduction of high-tech industry. Much more will need to be done by central government. Here local authorities will need to lobby long and hard to ensure that some of the institutional changes that the new industries may require will at the very least be the subject of intense national debate. Three issues at least will necessitate considerable discussion. First there will have to be a much expanded and intensified programme of retraining to guarantee that the opportunities provided in both service and manufacturing industry are not neglected. Post 1945 expansion has frequently been muted because of bottle-necks created by labour shortages. Bearing in mind the low level of national resources dedicated to training and higher education this is all too likely to occur again. Secondly exactly because some parts of the national economy will benefit far less from structural changes that will occur, so national government must be prepared to consider implementing public works programmes. Many of those made redundant from declining industrial sectors will not find employment in new industries. Programmes such as house improvement and construction, energy conservation, environmental improvements, and updating public utilities can prove labour intensive, utilise British rather than imported goods and services, and can prove relatively inexpensive because of concomitant reductions in the social security budget. And thirdly it will be important for local authorities to lobby for an extensive review of welfare

provision. It does appear probable that, at least in some
parts of the country, there will be a considerable net loss
of jobs. This situation should help stimulate debates on
early retirement, job creation, job sharing and so on.
Local authorities of themselves can help ensure that these
issues remain central to political debate.

(c) Local Authorities and job generation in High-Tech

One of the problems inherent to discussions about local
authority involvement in high-technology industry is the lack
of terminological precision. A number of myths cloud the
issue (Debenham, Tewson and Chinnocks 1983). The phrase
'high-tech' conjures up certain types of innovative companies,
producing technologically advanced products within architecturally and environmentally attractive locations. This is
however frequently not the case. Many existing companies
and organisations are now using new informational systems but
in standardised functions in older buildings. Equally so the
production of some high-tech hardware is undertaken using
largely labour intensive methods. And the assumption that
advances in new technology will emerge primarily through the
electronics industry may prove far from the truth. Much of
the change associated with the widespread introduction of
newer technology will involve the application of new processes
to the production of the same sorts of goods and services.

There appears too to be some misunderstanding of the sorts
of physical developments within which technologically advanced
production and process innovation can proceed. In particular
there has been considerable interest in the concept of science
parks on the part of many authorities without perhaps an
adequate appreciation of what is implied by the term or what
requirements such developments demand. Synthesising
classifications made elsewhere (Debenham, Tewson and Chinnocks
1983; Taylor 1983) it can be argued that innovatory production can be located within a variety of related facilities.
Five types of provision can perhaps be identified: innovation
centres, science parks, technology parks, commercial/business
parks and upgraded industrial estates. Clear distinctions may
not always be possible between these developments, and some
schemes may well embrace characteristics typical of more than
one category. Nevertheless classification is important
because appropriate local authority responses need to be
rooted in a thorough appreciation of the requirements of, and
products emanating from, different types of provision.

(i)   Innovation Centres are usually located in converted
        industrial buildings close to an institute of higher

education. The objectives of an innovation centre
will typically include exploring the commercial
applicability of a product or process, the provision
of technical, financial and marketing advice to
potential entrepreneurs and the forging of links with
educational establishments. The Merseyside Innovation
Centre for example provides almost 10,000 sq ft of
usable space and is managed by an independent company
sponsored by the local institutes of higher education
and Merseyside County Council. It is intended to
foster closer relationships between the economic
development objectives of the County Council and the
research activities of the Polytechnic and the
University. Other centres of innovation will not
embrace such a close relationship with higher
education. The enterprise workshops for instance,
about which more later, instigated by Strathclyde,
Birmingham and many other administrations may be more
concerned simply with providing opportunities for
those intent upon bringing a product or process on to
the market which may not represent the application of
any aspect of innovatory production. In this case
quite simple, often very small, units will be
provided. Sometimes rent and rates will be waived and
technical and financial assistance provided. Ideally
too, local authorities may move towards providing a
hierarchy of industrial units. Successful development
of a product may lead to the re-location of the
emerging company into a standard, often proximate,
unit.

(ii)   Science parks have received considerable interest in
the United Kingdom in recent years. This undoubtedly
partly reflects the development of, and evaluation
into, the science park concept in North America which
has been discussed elsewhere (Markusen 1983;
Saxenian 1983).

Science parks are developments designed for growing
or established firms in research and development
which retain or establish close links with university
or polytechnic departments. A distinction is sometimes made where between a research park and a science
park. The former, epitomised by Heriot-Watt
University's Riccarton development is not for manufacturing but is intended for research and development
emanating from government sponsored research
organisations, or major companies. Science parks will

110

contain firms involved in mass manufacturing of specialised goods within a complex intermixture of offices, laboratories, workshops and production units. Typically the parks in the United Kingdom will be under 100 acres, and will be developed at low density according to high architectural and landscaping standards. Facilities within the overall development might include libraries, computing services, sporting and recreational facilities, and extensive parking space.

The involvement of local authorities can vary considerably from one science park to another. Perhaps the best known science park, that at Cambridge, was largely implemented as a result of Trinity College's determination to forge close links between pure research and production. In other cases, as for example in the Birchwood scheme at Warrington, the local Development Corporation has been much more active in devising and implementing the overall project. It has been involved in land allocation, design, construction, and the creation of the Genesis small unit scheme whereby innovative spin-off companies can lease very small units in their early stages of development.

In general, local authorities might be involved in a number of ways in the creation of science parks. They may help to establish the essential academic/ administrative/financial nexus essential for the creation of parks. They may be involved too in land allocation, estate management, landscaping, design, financial support for new firms, and flexibility in terms of planning permissions. To expand on some of these issues, a pleasant location within easy Commuting distance of good suburban housing and national and international communication links appears an important consideration in the establishment of science parks. Room for estate and company expansion is crucial too. So too is a flexible attitude towards design and ownership. In terms of the former, many companies appear not to need purpose built accommodation but do require space to expand, to meet uncertain future demands and to accommodate a wide variety of functions: research, office activities, production, storage, demonstration, assembly and so on. On the question of ownership, newer companies in particular appear to prefer to lease rather than to own their accommodation. Successful science parks need therefore to provide a range of units some for short and long lease.

On the crucial question of finance most of the parks developed in the United Kingdom have involved the incorporation of public capital in some form or other (Debenham, Tewson and Chinnocks 1983). A few developments in the high-tech area have been funded exclusively by new town development corporations or local authorities. Far more however have involved the establishment of partnerships between public and private sectors. Over 70% of the Birchwood Science Park was funded by the private sector with the rest emanating from the Development Corporation.

(iii)   Technology parks although similar to science parks differ from them in that tenants will be limited to purely high-technology production which may not be the case on all 'science parks'. Again the authority may be involved in a variety of ways: land allocation, overall design and landscaping, funding, estate management and so on. Lynch Wood at Peterborough has been seen as one example.

(iv)   Commercial/business parks are high-quality, low density environments with accommodation for commercial companies requiring a prestigious site. Proximity to good suburban housing, shops, banks, leisure facilities and the motorway system and important locational requirements. Links with academic institutions may however be limited or non-existent. One example is the Aztec West development near Bristol.

(v)   Upgraded industrial estates in many respects may offer a more realistic objective for many local authorities than will any proliferation of science or technology parks. Higher standards of design and landscaping, an increase in the proportion of office space, more sensitive letting policies, and a more adventurous approach to industrial location can all help to create industrial estates of far greater appeal than a standardised development. Such new schemes need not involve the creation of any links with educational or research bodies, nor culminate in the production of new goods or services. They nevertheless represent one step in the re-structuring of industrial development and as such lie firmly within the grasp of many administrations.

Local Authorities and High-Tech Employment: some concluding
comments

Although many authorities will no doubt eagerly seek out the
opportunities afforded by high-tech schemes there are a
number of considerations that should be borne in mind before
any intensive intervention in this area is attempted.

(a)   As Williams (1982) establishes there are distinct
      locational criteria demanded of genuinely high-tech
      developments. Many authorities will simply be unable
      to meet them. Typically these include access to high
      quality environmental and residential development;
      access to motorways, airports and research establishments;
      proximity to a highly trained workforce; good cultural
      and recreational facilities in the vicinity; links with
      other high-tech companies and so on. No matter how much
      an authority may wish to intervene in this area it may
      simply be unable to provide essential locational require-
      ments. It is not, in the context of the United Kingdom,
      surprising to find that certain parts of the country
      notably the South-East and especially the South-West
      along the M4 corridor proving so much more attractive
      to the market than other regions (Thwaites 1982). Nor
      surprising either to find the market extolling the
      virtues of this area (Herring Son and Daw 1983).

(b)   It is important to remember that high-technology
      industry is dominated by market criteria. Growing
      companies may simply seek out the best subsidies
      available amongst bidding local authorities and indeed
      between various countries all eager to attract their
      share of sunrise employment (Dumsday 1984). Whether this
      publicly funded auction will actually involve the creation
      of new jobs that would not otherwise have occurred or
      whether any jobs so created will actually assist the
      locally unemployed is another matter. Independent
      observers might reasonably suggest the introduction of
      some form of regional dimension through which certain
      sectors of high-tech industry might be guided to certain
      parts of the economy (Taylor 1983). This appears
      extremely improbable however when state intervention
      might discourage investment anywhere in the United
      Kingdom. It may well be however that in the long run
      some form of spatial intervention may moderate some of
      the overheating problems likely to occur in the South
      East and South West as suitable land becomes more

expensive, skilled staff more difficult to recruit, and congestion of all kinds more evident.

(c)   There is of course no guarantee that high-tech developments will actually succeed and that new companies and new jobs will emerge out of science park and the like. By the mid 1970's there were apparently over 80 'science parks' in the USA employing about 150,000 people (Goddard and Thwaites 1983). But not all of these by any means had proved total successes and very few had 100% occupancy rates. Any suggestion that the United Kingdom was over-supplied with high-tech developments would appear somewhat premature. But there may be institutional constraints that operate against the widespread dissemination of successful science parks. The concept of the academic entrepreneur hardly exists in the United Kingdom compared with the USA. The major institutional investors have proved reluctant to invest into uncertain and complex projects based on high-technology schemes especially those located outside the South of England. Perhaps the generation of enterprise generally has not been great anywhere in the country compared with international competitors. There has been little in the way of sympathetic intervention and guidance from central government a situation by no means common to all countries eager to expand innovative technology. Quite simply the ability of many authorities to attract and create jobs in high-tech will be severely circumscribed by factors beyond their control.

LOCAL AUTHORITIES AND THE CO-OPERATIVE SECTOR

Although the development of producer co-operatives in the United Kingdom has lagged behind the considerable advances made in some European countries notably Italy and Basque Spain (Oakeshott 1978) there has been substantial progress in recent years. Whereas there has since at least the 19th century been interest in retail and wholesale co-operative ventures it has only been within the last decade that producer co-operatives have come to the fore in the British context.

Proponents of producer co-operatives would argue that there are inherent advantages in this approach to industrial organisation. It can enhance industrial democracy (Watkins 1978). Co-operatives reduce the dependence of communities on economic and employment decisions made by controlling boards divorced from the social consequences of their actions (Cockerton et al 1980). From the Left have come indications

that co-operatives retain economic surplus for re-investment
and the material benefits of workers (The Labour Party 1980)
and from the Right it can be argued that co-operatives weaken
the power of trade unions and ensure that workers are
directly responsible for their actions. An finally from the
point of view of local authorities it is apparent that
co-operatives can fulfil a number of vital functions.
(Rigge and Young 1982). They can assist local economies in
decline, provide goods and services not previously available,
produce socially useful goods, employ the socially disadvantaged and retain local skills.

However before any local authority elects to pursue the
development of producer co-operatives it is important that
consideration is given to two issues: the variety and
complexity of co-operative organisation and the national
.structure within which the producer co-operative movement
has developed. Although the 1976 Industrial and Common
Ownership Act sets down a proper legal definition of common
ownership and industrial co-operative enterprise, there are
still considerable variations in the structure of co-operatives. As Cockerton et al (1980) point out there are
variations even in terms of the legal structures that can be
adopted by co-operatives. Partnerships, companies limited
by shares, registered co-operatives and companies limited by
guarantee without share capital can all be acceptable.
Equally so variations can exist in terms of membership, the
provision of management, the introduction of outside
finance, and the allocation of surplus profit. Some
co-operatives moreover will emerge as new ventures, others
as worker takeovers of existing organisations, others from
the relocation of output to other parts of the country or
abroad. It is clearly important for any authority wishing
to provide support for the development of co-operatives to
realise the variety of co-operative organisation.

Local government must be similarly aware of the national
administrative infrastructure within which local intervention
must proceed. Amongst the institutions that local government
should consider are the Industrial Common Ownership Movement
and the Co-operative Development Agency. ICOM was established
in 1958 and its financial arm Industrial Common Ownership
Finance in 1973. ICOM has promoted a pure form of co-operative
based on rules that insist on all members being workers and
only workers being members. As such it has operated as an
advisory and lobbying body for many years. ICOF has had the
more distinct role of creating a revolving loan fund for
worker co-operatives. Like ICOM it was recognised as a
relevant body which could make grant assisted loans to

co-operatives under the 1976 Industrial Common Ownership Act. In the ten years between 1973 and 1982 ICOF made around 45 loans totalling about £450,000 (Rigge and Young 1982).

The Co-operative Development Agency was given legal status in 1978. Amongst its many functions are to promote the concept of co-operatives, to provide a forum for discussion, and to identify ways in which more co-operatives might be established. The CDA has not however been given powers to provide financial assistance to co-operatives. Its funds indeed make this improbable. From 1982 total grant amounted to only £200,000 per annum which represented a substantial cut on annual expenditure allowed in its first three years of existence. Not surprisingly bearing in mind the jejune nature of the national framework governing the advancement of co-operatives there have been calls for a concentration of effort at the local level (Whyatt 1983). There may be a deal of sense in this suggestion bearing in mind the inevitably decentralised nature of co-operative formation. Certainly the apparently meagre nature of national intervention has done little to stem the considerable growth in the co-operative movement. One co-operative was registered under ICOM rules in 1976, but 337 in 1982. Interestingly enough too there appears to have been a change in the sort of factors that have been responsible for the creation of co-operatives. Until relatively recently many jobs in co-operatives were in larger manufacturing plants which had been handed on to workforces by benevolent owners. In recent years however many new co-operatives in printing, retailing construction and manufacturing represent the emergence of alternative movements concerned with the purpose and control of employment (Taylor 1983). These considerations will need to be embraced by any authority eager to promote the co-operative ideal in a sensitive manner.

Local Authority Intervention in the Co-operative Sector

Local authorities can assist in the creation of co-operatives either directly or indirectly by using financial support available in a number of acts. Under Section 3 of the 1978 Inner Urban Areas Act local authorites can make loans and grants to cover the costs of establishing a co-operative. Specific powers may exist too under local acts of parliament and powers exist under sections 111 and 137 of the 1972 Local Government Act which allow authorities to incur rate expenditure on developments such as co-operatives.

In practice some limited functions have been undertaken directly by authorities wishing to see an expansion of the

co-operative sector within their administration. This might
involve providing industrial premises, establishing advice
centres, increasing local awareness of the co-operative ideal
and some direct financial support (Jolley 1980). On the
whole however much of the local emphasis has been directed
towards establishing local co-operative development agencies.

Local authorities have been involved in a variety of
organisational arrangements designed to establish local CDA's
of which, by the early 1980's, there were over 60. Sometimes
they will be bodies registered as companies limited by
guarantee, sometimes there will be an executive board with
local government representation, sometimes CDA's will be
incorporated bodies with powers to invest in co-operatives.
The City of Sheffield for example has, with the County
Council and the Co-operative Bank, provided grants for the
creation of a Co-operative Development Group in association
with the local trades council and the traditional co-operative
sector (Mawson and Miller 1982).

The initiation of local CDA's is likely to prove particularly important in the fostering of the co-operative ideal.
There is evidence that where CDA's have been established
the creation of co-operatives is much greater than where
other or no, arrangements have been devised (Taylor 1983).
They can provide a whole range of commercial financial and
managerial advice. They may be able to provide small grants
and indicate alternative sources of finance. They can
provide mutual support and generate local awareness of the
co-operative ideal. And they can help create links between
local producer and consumer co-operatives. By ensuring too
that local CDA's are controlled or at least influenced by
those drawn from local co-operatives the situation should be
avoided whereby paternalistic attitudes towards existing and
incipient co-operatives can be avoided (Taylor undated).

Local Authorities and Co-operatives: An evaluation

Despite the eagerness with which many administrations have
embraced the co-operative ideal it is important to realise
that there are constraints governing the creation and
expansion of this form of enterprise.

(a)   Not all local CDA's will be able to provide a package
      suitable for a comprehensive expansion of co-operatives.
      Some such as those in the West Midlands can provide
      support in product identification and development,
      training and financial support for viable producer
      co-operatives (Titley 1983). Not all CDA's will under-

take these functions. There may be the problem too that local CDA's providing only limited assistance will delay the development of co-operatives by establishing support criteria not suitable for, say, other organisations providing funding. Similarly CDA's must take a realistic attitude to product definition and marketing. Co-operatives must exist within the market. In this context, although there are problems with the approach. the idea of the market gap appears useful. Local authorities or local CDA's if thoroughly familiar with the local economy, can begin to identify goods and services not produced locally which might prove suitable for some form of co-operative or community enterprise (Taylor 1982).

(b)   Local authorities must remain aware of the needs and aspirations of the co-operative movement in any proposals for expansion of this sector. Authorities may wish to use co-operatives to expand employment, provide jobs for the socially and economically disadvantaged, and help develop socially useful goods and services. These goals may lead to the creation of too interventionist an approach governed by too complex a bureaucracy for many interested in the co-operative ideal. For the latter, goals such as job creation may be secondary to other objectives such as the organisation and purpose of work. Certainly it appears the case that authorities are more likely to see an expansion in co-operatives if they utilise agencies such as local CDA's and resist the temptation to become too heavily involved themselves.

(c)   In any case local authorities must remain realistic about expansion in the co-operative sector. It still represents a tiny proportion of productive output. Partly this may be due to lack of interest in the United Kingdom. although this may change in time. Partly too there has been the political question. The Labour Party (1980) has strongly pursued the ideal of the co-operative suggesting that workers in any private company should have the legislative right to convert that firm into a co-operative. Whatever the virtues of this proposal it is unlikely to recommend itself to any Conservative government. Indeed despite the fact that the co-operative movement can be perceived by any right-wing administration as a mechanism through which, say, workers can become more aware of their actions and more responsible for production, the approach has been largely ignored by Tory governments. By European standards

118

indeed the co-operative movement in the United Kingdom
has received short-shrift (Titley 1983). Tax advantages
and the establishment of substantial funding organisations which have been implemented in Italy and France
have not really been seen as central to the British
political agenda. Perhaps in the longer run it will
require EEC directive to ensure the creation of a
satisfactory financial and legal base within which the
co-operative ideal might flourish.

LOCAL AUTHORITIES AND COMMUNITY ENTERPRISE

The burgeoning interest in co-operatives has been paralleled
by a similar concern on the part of many administrations to
encourage community enterprise. This is usually seen as
economic activity controlled by local people to generate
employment and economic activity to benefit their local area
(Newnham 1980). As such, community enterprises are usually
evaluated as advantageous in that they create and secure
worthwhile jobs, provide goods and services needed locally,
retain surpluses for community benefit and increase the local
circulation of income   (Newnham 1980). It appears too that
community enterprise may be particularly suitable for older
infrastructure (Steward 1978), may help to conserve
historically or architecturally worthwhile buildings, can
help to boost local entrepreneurship, and can help ensure
that economic decisions are taken locally. In many respects
co-operatives fulfil the same objectives and are perceived
to engender the same sorts of advantages. A distinction can
however be made here in that co-operatives tend very largely
to be organised along specific lines guiding the creation and
operation of the establishment.Community enterprise however
can in practice mean many things. Sometimes indeed such
organisations may differ little if at all from orthodox
companies.

Three issues appear to merit consideration here: local
authorities and community enterprise in general; the specific
question of local enterprise trusts and agencies; and some
more reflective considerations that have emerged in recent
years.

Community Enterprise and Local Government: A framework for
action

Community enterprise is very much bound up with concepts such
as self-help and community action. As such a wide range of
community based groups have taken initiatives intended to

119

create or retain jobs (Pearce and Hopwood 1981). Inevitably
therefore local authorities will wish to move cautiously.
Their actions must be seen as supportive rather than imperial-
istic. Supportive too to a wide variety of community based
organisations. Not necessarily that many will have employment
creation as a primary aim. Nevertheless recreational,
cultural, welfare, legal and housing organisations may create
or retain jobs as a result of their activities.

The range of community based organisations is formidable.
A substantial number of voluntary and community organisations
have been supported in the past through urban aid, the
Manpower Services Commission, and other national and local
bodies. Traditional urban aid alone has helped fund
hundreds of voluntary organisations since the late 1960's
(Lawless 1979). It is only relatively recently however that
an emphasis on economic development and employment generation
has come to characterise the community and voluntary sectors.
The Community Projects Foundation for instance a nationally
supported body devoted to innovatory work in community
development was by 1981-1982 supporting 14 current projects
of which 3 had a specifically economic function, normally the
provision of economic advice or dealing with the social
consequences of redundancy (Community Projects Foundation
1982). This proportion is likely to grow.

Any expansion of economic and employment dimensions
on the part of national bodies such as the Community Projects
Foundation will depend on a strategy designed to utilise
appropriate local authority support mechanisms. Hayton (1983)
has suggested that there are three main local authority bases
that can prove of value to community business: financial,
physical and staff resources.

Financial resources will normally come through local
government's main programmes or via the 25% contribution made
by local authorities towards urban aid funding. Only some
community projects will be approved not all. In West Scotland
for example, where there has been a strong community business
dimension, proposed urban aid funding will only be forthcoming
normally if it is supported by the local Regional Council
member and is located within one of the region's designated
areas of deprivation (Hayton 1983). Even then the time-lapse
between grant application and approval can be too long for
many incipient community businesses a problem which
Strathclyde has attempted to overcome by establishing an
urban aid supported Minor Projects Fund which can make small
interim payments. An additional difficulty with urban aid
is that 3 to 5 year funding may not prove adequate to ensure

the continued viability of a community business. It can be argued that any business should show longer term security within 5 years. On the other hand the extremely successful promotional and informational functions undertaken by, say, LEAP (Local Enterprise Advisory Project) in Paisley will not probably survive a reduction in urban aid funding. Equally so urban aid can prove of considerable value in establishing community business which can then seek out MSC and private funding, and in turn obtain charitable status. This reduces rate demands and makes funding from trusts and other organisations more probable.

What sort of community businesses have been supported by local government? The range is considerable (Calouste Gulbenkian Foundation 1981). Goodwill Incorporated (Glasgow) for example collects and renovates older furniture and bric-a-brac. It obtains support from a variety of local and central government agencies and intends to provide training and rehabilitation places for disadvantaged employees. Somewhat different objectives have governed the development of Lambeth Industrial Enterprises. Here the local voluntary organisation, Lady Margaret Hall Settlement, identified the extremely high failure rate of small firms. In order to retain some of these concerns and to help establish others, 32 separate workshops units were created at relatively low costs with in-house financial, technical and managerial support. The local authority has helped in a variety of ways including allocating Inner City Partnership finance to the project for the purchase of a lease and necessary conversion costs.

Local authorities can assist in two other obvious ways towards the expansion of community enterprise: allocating property and staff resources. Old, especially inner city, physical infrastructure can be leased at or given to community projects. This can ensure the occupancy of derelict buildings, some of architectural interest, which might otherwise fall into disrepair. Once a lease is granted moreover this can allow some leverage on the part of the community enterprise towards other public or private sources of finance which can assist renovating or converting unsuitable premises. In essence because both the authority and the enterprise are prepared to enter into a legal agreement cementing the organisation for a period of time so other charitable and private sector organisations may be willing to provide support.

The importance of adequate premises should not underestimated. Flagstone Enterprises Limited operating in Ferguslie Park in Paisley have been given the use of a disused school by the Strathclyde Regional Council. This has been used as a storeroom, office and workshop space and has proved invaluable to an organisation committed to employment creation through labouring, cleaning, sandblasting, environmental improvement services and so on (Local Government Research Unit 1982).

Finally local authorities can assist the creation of community enterprise through appropriate use of staff resources (Hayton 1983). Such staff will act as co-ordinators, planners and administrators. Once a business is established managerial and entrepreneurial roles will be filled from the market or through secondment from the private sector. Prior to this however local government staff can be involved in activities such as urban aid grant application, secretarial support, establishing which local goods and services are not provided locally and which might thus provide product outlets for community businesses, identifying needs of minority groups, fostering the concept of community enterprise, considering the provision of legal, financial, creche and catering facilities at locations appropriate for community enterprise, exploring purchasing policies adopted by the authority and so on.

Local Enterprise Trusts and Agencies

Mawson and Miller (1982) have indicated that by the early 1980's there were over 60 enterprise trusts or agencies throughout the country. Although they differ in detail they are essentially business development organisations. They will assist both existing and new companies. Usually their functions will include providing advice on financial issues, management, marketing, legal questions, accommodation, and the availability of grants, encouraging the secondment of managers and technical experts from larger to smaller firms, holding start-up conferences and surgeries, stimulating bigger companies to assist smaller ones through purchasing policies and assistance with exports, and acting as marriage brokers bringing investors into contact with producers.

In some cases, as for example with the London Enterprise Agency the private sector will prove influential in the creation and running of a trust. On other occasions, the St Helens Trust for example, the private sector will enter into a formal agreement with the local authority to guide the development of the resultant organisation. Sometimes too, local educational establishments will be incorporated into the overall project to provide technical and advisory support.

Community Enterprise and Local Government: some issues for consideration

There has been a remarkable proliferation of interest in community enterprise on the part of local and central government, the voluntary sector and private industry. It seems probable that national politicians, encouraged by big business, will increasingly promote the idea. The Department of the Environment has for example created regional Enterprise Units one of whose functions is to stimulate the formation of enterprise agencies. Local authorities will in many cases inevitably respond positively to these moves. It needs to be remembered however that there may be genuine shortcomings or constraints in the expansion of community ventures.

(a) The concept is wide open to different interpretations. Not all community enterprises will be locally based organisations committed to social and economic objectives. Some will vary hardly at all from orthodox companies. Some authorities may prove reluctant to enter into agreements with private firms, say in enterprise trusts, on the basis that it has been the operation of the market that has so radically worsened the economic position of many older towns and cities.

(b) However much local authorities may wish to see job creation as a central objectives of community enterprise this may be difficult to achieve. Many community development projects may adopt somewhat different objectives such as increasing self-reliance, widening community awareness or enhancing welfare and legal services. Community organisations based on these goals may in practice boost employment creation but may not regard the enhancement of local jobs as a central objective. Community business may anyway employ few overall, few locally unskilled and unemployed, and may, as even long established organisations have done, fail. There may be conflicts between goals of community development and economic viability. Wages may have to be relatively low for example in order to maximise profits; skilled personnel may have to be recruited from beyond the immediate area and from the ranks of the employed. Few women may be employed despite general commitments towards equal opportunities on the part of many authorities and community enterprise generally. Finally there may too be conflicts between management and workers particularly where community business

ventures adopt company structures limited by guarantee
where decision making may ultimately be centralised in
the hands of a manager.

(c)   As with co-operatives, local authorities will need to
      tread carefully in their dealings with community
      enterprises. There may be activities in the early
      development of community ventures that authorities can
      undertake in a sympathetic manner. Many of these have
      been identified above. But in general there will need
      to be a co-ordinated and catalytic response to the
      demands from community business Ventures. Probably too
      in the longer run many authorities will perceive
      community business as but one part of an overall move
      to decentralised administration, a move which has been
      advocated by a number of commentators. Area teams
      dealing with a wide variety of issues, notably housing,
      detailed planning issues, and personal social services,
      may well provide that administration structure most
      likely to stimulate local economic ventures (Donnison
      1983).

(d)   The ultimate scope of community enterprise may be
      formidable. The possibilities of job creation in
      environmental improvements alone, an ideal focus for
      community activity in being locally based and labour
      intensive, would be considerable. Areas such as thermal
      insulation, cycle routes, paper re-cycling, and an
      enhanced allotments programme could provide over
      40,000 jobs in the longer term (Barbier 1981). The
      problem with programmes such as this is the perennial
      question of funding. Local authorities through, say,
      the urban programme and funds raised through the 2p
      rate in the pound provision contained in the 1972 Local
      Government Act can provide some support. But these
      funds may be limited in size, and uncertain in the
      longer run. MSC funds may similarly be of a temporary
      nature and subject to tight governing criteria. Not
      surprisingly wider investigations into the area have
      argued for the creation of a national development fund
      for community business (Calouste Gulbenkian 1981). Such
      an organisation could have a considerable role to play
      in stimulating the creation of community ventures, in
      providing a legal, advisory and financial base, in
      undertaking necessary research and monitoring of
      community organisations, and in liaising with other
      interested bodies. In 1984 the creation of such an
      organisation appears remote.

LOCAL AUTHORITIES AND THE SMALL FIRM SECTOR

There has been unprecedented interest in recent years in the
small firm sector. Partly this has arisen because of the
allegedly high proportion of new jobs created in small
companies in America (Birch 1979). Partly too it has been
argued that small firms still represent a high proportion of
companies within certain sectors; and that small firms can be
innovative, prove suitable for older infrastructure, take on
employees more readily than larger companies, and act as seed
beds through which larger concerns will emerge   (Advisory
Council for Applied Research and Development 1978; Bolton
Committee 1971). In addition it has been suggested that small
companies can help both to promote a healthy national economy
and boost local economies (Bannock 1976, Confederation of
British Industry 1977). Although these assumptions are
questionable (Green and Walker 1980) it is not surprising,
bearing in mind the assumed advantages of small firms that
such a concerted emphasis has been placed upon them. Two
points ought to be made here however before more detailed
discussion of the small sector is undertaken. First, and
this needs to be stressed, in many respects a multitude of
initiatives developed throughout the book will prove of
relevance to small companies. The questions of premises,
financing, community and co-operative enterprise and so on
in many cases relate directly to smaller companies. Local
authority initiatives towards smaller concerns explored in
this section of the book will therefore inevitably prove no
more than a sample of the totality of relevant innovation.
And secondly, and this to be developed briefly below, local
authorities are but one of three sectors exploring small
firm policy. Central government and the private sector, and
combinations therein, are proving important here too.

By 1984 over 100 incentives were being provided by central
government to boost the small firm sector. Many of these
were of a fiscal nature. Thresholds at which various taxes
are to be levied have been increased to benefit smaller
companies for example. Smaller firms similarly may be exempt
from certain legal and financial regulations governing larger
establishments. At times too central government has instigated development organisations concerned primarily with the
creation and fostering of the smaller firm. The Council for
Small Industries in Rural Areas (CoSIRA) formed in 1968
supports employment in small firms in rural areas. The
Scottish and Welsh Development Agencies provide advice and
assistance to smaller companies. So too do the Highlands
and Islands Development Board and the Local Enterprise

Development Unit in Northern Ireland. In the 1970's too central government instigated a number of conferences designed to identify the problems faced by small firms in inner city area (Department of the Environment 1978). Amongst the multitude of other services provided by central government mention ought to be made of the Small Firms Information and Counselling Services run by the Department of Industry and the Loan Guarantee Scheme which has increased the supply of low security credit (Collinge 1983).

Interest in the small firm sector has not been limited to the public sector. Organisations such as the Confederation of British Industry (1977) and the London Enterprise Agency (1980) have argued for the small firm sector. In particular big business has in recent years promoted the interests of the small company on the grounds that the latter can help reduce unemployment, maintain the local economy, provide inputs for larger concerns, create innovative products and processes and so on. As such some of the major multi-nationals have helped create, fund and service enterprise agencies one of whose major objectives is the fostering of small establishments. Other activities undertaken by the market directed towards smaller companies are the provision of venture capital by institutions such as the Industrial and Commercial Finance Corporation, the creation of a number of investment organisations based on the Business Start-Up Scheme introduced in the 1981 Finance Act, and the increasing provision of small units as a result of the industrial building allowances scheme. A number of public-private sector agencies, some of a non-profit making nature have emerged in recent years too which have attempted to devise physical, and economic packages designed to boost older run-down areas. Such strategies usually involve both private and public sector support directed towards the retention of existing, and the creation of new, small firms (for example IBM/URBED 1977). Nevertheless however important such developments may prove in the future the focus of interest here remains local government innovation and the small sector.

It would appear that local authorities can assist small firms via research, advice and consultancy, physical measures, subsidy, procurement policies and changes in planning and other internal procedures. With some of these areas, notably the provision of promises and financial support extensive information is provided elsewhere. For the sake of completion however brief mention of all initiatives will be made here.

(a)   Local authority research into the structure and organisation of small firms and the constraints

operating upon them can be useful in a variety of ways.
Work undertaken in Leeds (1977) for example indicates
the problems faced by local companies, their relationship with larger concerns, disincentives to capital
investment, the impact of local authority activity and
so on. Strathclyde Regional Council has similarly been
active in compiling registers of local companies which
can prove of value in indicating local market gaps that
might prove suitable for small establishments.

(b) Advice and counselling services have been provided by a
number of authorities, these can prove of value for both
existing and potential companies. Information typically
will be made available on the scope of central government financial support including the availability of
regional assistance, employment subsidy, fiscal incentive
and so on. More interventionist authorities such as
Mid-Glamorgan have developed comprehensive approaches
whereby firms are interviewed in the area and resultant
problems directed to an advisory service. The latter
in turn might expect to deal with issues relating to
premises, marketing, the legislative framework, input
requirements and so on. As authorities move towards
creating the one-door approach towards problems
emanating from smaller companies so more in turn will
develop contacts with local educational, financial and
professional services to which specific issues can be
directed. Such an approach may well require the local
authority to use its own and the business community's
local expertise if it is not to duplicate counselling
and informational services run by the Department of
Industry. Many authorities might anyway argue that at
limited costs a comprehensive counselling service can be
provided to deal with the problems of all companies,
large and small, within their administration. In many
respects this might prove of relevance in securing
existing, as much as creating new, jobs. Certainly this
would appear to be the case with the more interventionist
strategies being devised by Wandsworth, Mid-Glamorgan
and East Sussex. Activities here indicate that
eventually business advisory services might undertake a
wide variety of functions. These might include the
creation of a resource group from local political and
business circles, a refined informational service
dealing with premises, the operation and structure of
particular industrial sectors, marketing, input-output
linkages, market gaps in the local economy, and the
creation of closer links between new companies, educational establishments, libraries, local banks and

established local firms with the authority acting as an initiator and co-ordinator.

(c) The development of small premises has been dealt with elsewhere and need not detain us too much here. Suffice to say that many authorities, and indeed central government and the market, have been attracted towards the provision of smaller units. Such developments result from both the conversion of existing premises and the construction of new factories. Councils such as Nottingham and Liverpool have converted larger residential, commercial and industrial infrastructure into small units. Sometimes an authority may be eager to use cheaper improved premises for the creation of co-operative or community ventures. This may involve the waiving or lowering of rents and rates for a period of time. Similarly authorities such as Tyne and Wear have built mini-units of less than 1,000 sq.ft especially for new small enterprises.

One approach to small companies not developed extensively elsewhere in the book is the enterprise workshop approach. Although varying in detail, typically they involve initially the creation of small units from the rehabilitation of older premises. North Tyneside (1981) for example has implemented a Development Workshop Scheme where the units will be between 200 and 700 square feet. The idea of a development workshop is to encourage the creation of new products and new companies by providing a sheltered environment within which innovation can proceed for a limited period of time. Normally a manager and a business panel will select appropriate projects. These would then be allocated a development workshop. Here managerial, technical and financial support will be forthcoming. Some charge may be made for services but common secretarial, security and clerical services may be provided, advice will usually be free and rent and rates may be too. Typically too, successful companies emerging out of enterprise workshops will be encouraged to take on local authority units after their initial exploratory periods.

The early evidence from development or enterprise workshops is that some at least of these projects have proved successful. The Tollcross Industrial Village implemented by BSC (Industry) Ltd is usually seen as a particularly good example of small industrial units being supported by common service arrangements and managerial staff. Elsewhere it appears that not many starters will be involved with innovative products or processes; that the choice of a manager can be crucial; that a wide range of support and advisory services may be required, and that by no means all concerns achieve a permanent status.

(d) The question of financial support to local companies will be developed later in the book. Suffice here to say that a variety of loans, grants and equity investments have been made by authorities to small local companies. For instance Merseyside County Council has promoted a CHASE (County Help for Active Small Enterprises) scheme and a venture fund (Struthers and Williamson 1979). The former provides a variety of interest and rent relief grants, environmental and capital grants, and loans for construction, plant and machinery with firms in certain areas eligible for all forms of assistance and others in non-selected areas able to claim a more limited number of grants and loans. The venture fund is designed to assist firms unable to qualify under the CHASE criteria say because they have an insufficient track record.

(e) Local authorities can adopt procurement policies whereby a certain proportion of goods and services required by a council is provided by small firms. Leicestershire's Library Department for instance has used a small local firm to import books from the Indian sub-continent. Not all authorities would however necessarily be prepared to distinguish between small and larger companies in any policy designed to increase the proportion of locally produced goods and services used by the administration concerned.

(f) Planning procedures have been seen as responsible for the decline of small companies (Righter 1977). Whatever the merits of these and similar allegations against the planning system of which there is infact considerable doubt (Chalkley 1979), many authorities have elected to clarify, and in some cases change, their planning procedures with respect to small firms. Following Department of the Environment (1977) advice many authorities have been prepared to deal rapidly with industrial development applications, look more favourably on mixed land-use proposals, and accept industrial developments that may not confirm exactly with zoning schemes but which do not prove environmentally intrusive. Some authorities such as Leeds have declared minimal change areas which can prove important in reducing uncertainty about planning proposals thus encouraging private investment. Similarly most authorities will ensure that future redevelopment proposals do not involve unacceptable or avoidable loss of industrial floorspace and that any firms displaced as a result of necessary development schemes are offered suitable alternative accommodation.

Local Authorities and Small Firms: some constraints and shortcomings

Whereas the international and national interest in small firms and their role in economic development and employment creation has inevitably stimulated many local authorities into action in this area it is essential that administrations remain aware of the undoubted shortcomings of too heavy a reliance on the small sector. These debates must in their entirety be beyond this book but some indication ought to be provided of more pertinent issues. Three in particular appear relevant: the constraints operating generally on smaller firms; their job creating potential; and radical political evaluations of small establishments.

(a) Local authorities should be fully aware of the sorts of problems that constrain the small firm. The overall state of the economy will prove crucial for instance for many companies. Pursuing supply side economics, as epitomised by the fostering of small companies, will prove of relevance only when combined with satisfactory demand-management policies. Other problems and constraints typically characterise the small firm sector. Marketing and the establishment of business structures acceptable to lenders seem particular difficulties faced by smaller concerns. There appears too to be a consistent shortage of venture and development capital (Collinge 1983, Wilson 1979). And it may be far from easy for many smaller companies to pay market rates for skilled labour.

(b) Small firms do not create many jobs in the United Kingdom even in the long term (Fothergill and Gudgin 1979). Many new enterprises die quickly and very few grow to medium sized companies with a decade (Firn and Swales 1978). Even when smaller companies become viable it is by no means certain that the jobs so created are genuinely new jobs or whether they represent activities previously carried out by larger concerns. Certainly few small companies appear to be innovative thriving concerns dealing with the creation and

dissemination of new goods and processes (Lloyd 1980).
Many indeed are out-dated, under-capitalised, non-
diversified establishments dependent upon contracts from
larger companies, the activities of which will have a
far greater impact on most local authorities than will
the small sector. Interestingly enough too where more
innovative companies are created, and this tends to be
increasingly in the South and South-West, there seems
to be strong correlation between the rate of new firm
formation and the existence of both a pool of well
educated managers and a substantial number of pre-
existing small companies (Storey 1981), factors over
which local government intervention will have only the
most limited of impacts.

(c) By no means all authorities are convinced of the small
firm emphasis. The Greater London Council for instance
has initiated a marked attack on any policy designed to
boost smaller concerns to the detriment of, or without
taking account of, larger units (Greater London Council
1983b). Amongst the arguments presented by the GLC are
that small firms are not expecially innovative; that
where small firms are important in an industrial sector
this tends to represent a weakening of labour or a
displacement of risky activities from larger to smaller
companies; that small firms are less productive and
contribute less re-investable surplus than do larger
companies; and that much of the increase in small firm
employment in London is specific to a small number of
service sectors. Moreover the widespread application
of Birch's (1979) American findings to the United
Kingdom is irrelevant in terms of the job generation
question. Birch, for example, argued that there were
minimal variations in birth and death figures between
states. In the United Kingdom however there are marked
variations between the older cities and depressed
regions on the one hand and innovative areas
especially in the South of England on the other. Birch
anyway indicated that much of the employment growth
was concentrated in the service sector when local
authorities are generally more eager to promote manufacturing jobs. In essence the GLC concludes that its
strategy should on the whole not be supportive of small
firms except in some cases such as with co-operatives
or where, as with clothing and printing, industrial
sectors contain a high number of small firms. In
general however the Council was not prepared to support
enterprises which were frequently under-unionised,
offered low wages and in general remained economically

backward. Instead attention should be focused on larger
companies whose contractions, expansions and rationalisa-
tions would have a far greater impact on the economy of
London.

LOCAL GOVERNMENT AND THE CREATION OF ENTERPRISE: A CONCLUDING
STATEMENT

This chapter has attempted to indicate something of the
variety of initiatives implemented by local government
intended to boost enterprise and hence employment.
Inevitably this has created problems: the difficulties of
classification for instance, and the need to embrace the
constraints as well as the opportunities presented by this
evolving area of local government activity. At this juncture
a few final comments might profitably be made. First it
should be stressed that the area is complex and expanding and
will attract a wide range of authorities. Secondly many
initiatives will depend on the co-ordinated activities of a
local government, central government and the private sector.
A substantial number of innovations in, for instance, the
high-tech area will require the support of individuals and
organisations emerging from both public and private sector
backgrounds. Thirdly for there to be any considerable boost
to employment prospects in areas such as community and
co-operative development central government will need to
establish financial and administrative frameworks of an
altogether more interventionist nature than now exist. And
finally local government must remain realistic about the
numbers and kinds of jobs that will emerge from the policy
areas discussed here. Some jobs would have occurred anyway,
many will only prove suitable for skilled and professional
employees, and many initiatives will create few jobs overall.

It is important of course to realise here that local government economic intervention will anyway prove minimal
compared with the potential impact of the market. For some
authorities, particularly those located in the more prosperous
regions of the South, East Anglia and the South West there
are some encouraging trends. Industrial investment is
occurring in selected locations. Commercial development has
taken place and a substantial number of new jobs has been
created in high-tech sectors. For other administrations,
especially the larger cities in the older industrial
regions, the outlook is of course bleaker. Market
contraction and relocation have severely undermined
industrial and commercial confidence; industrial investment

by the major institutional investors has proved limited,
even nonexistent in some cities; the creation of a substantial number of new jobs through the revitalisation of
the market appears improbable. For these urban administrations in the mid 1980's as so much new public and private
sector investment is directed to more prosperous regions,
and even to other countries, local government intervention
in the formation of new enterprises will surely prove a
necessary, but sadly marginal, activity.

8 Pressure, research and advice

Local Authorities will create few jobs without co-operation from employers and workers. Almost all of their actions in this field involve an interdependency between organisations requiring the active participation of industry and commerce in initiatives made by the local authority. The local economy is also, in part, dependent on the actions of central government, as is the extent to which a local authority can take interventionist initiatives. Most actions taken by Local Government either to create or to save jobs are therefore in a broad sense interest group actions since they seek to persuade employers, workers or government agencies to adopt particular courses of action.

Persuasion and advice are intimately connected. In as much as a local authority acts as an interest group in creating or saving jobs it also acts as an advisor to businesses, employees or the government. In many cases advice is given unsolicited but most officers and councillors involved in employment work are also engaged in answering queries, complaints and cries for help which may in turn motivate the council to put pressure on some other organisations. The ability to persuade and to advise is also closely connected with the capacity of the local authority to understand the economy of its community. To be effective in the arts of advice and persuasion it is essential that councillors and officers are able to conduct research into local economic problems and build the results of this work into a store of information that they and other groups may use to advance their aims.

The content of this chapter has been selected in a rather arbitrary fashion since so much of the work of local government already discussed in this book is in a sense an interest group function. The effors of local authorities to persuade industries to locate in their territory or to promote tourism are for example as much pressure group activities as are efforts to persuade central government to provide an area with an enterprise zone. The strategies of attraction of industry and tourist promotion have however assumed such widespread importance in employment creation that they have been considered in separate chapters leaving in this section an analysis of less widely developed or smaller scale interest group activities and also a more detailed discussion of the underlying research work conducted by local authority employment creators.

RANGE AND EXTENT OF INTEREST GROUP ACTIVITY

Local pressure on central government to gain economic advantages for a particular area is not a new phenomena and is arguably less important today as an element of the British political process than it was in the 19th Century. Manufacturers were then often represented as councillors within local authorities and were therefore able to use local government to lend further weight to their campaigns for industrial protection. Cotton manufacturers in Lancashire had, for example, a significant impact on the Liberal Party at the turn of the century and consequently on tariff and colonial policies. Although many industries in Britain are today still confined to a particular region they are now owned by interlocking financial interests that may have little collective allegiance to any particular nation let alone a specific locality. The dispersal of manufacturing ownership along with the rise of working class influence in local authorities has brought the relationship between local capitalists and local government to an end but has also left the local authority as the remaining element of a coalition that once fought for local employment.

Alongside support for individual industries local councils have from time to time attempted to use their influence, or have been used on account of their influence, to demand more general reforms in central government economic policies in order to solve the difficulties faced by more depressed areas of the country. The Jarrow hunger march, sponsored by the controlling Labour Group and Trade Unions within its local council, was a well publicised attempt to change the attitude of central government on regional economic policy. The efforts of these campaigners alongside several other similar demonstrations in the 1930s helped to pave the way for the pre-war special area commissioners and later regional development policies.

During the immediate post war years full employment and relative prosperity along with an established scheme of regional economic assistance put an end to the hunger marches.

They were replaced by a regular march of councillors and their officials to the offices of junior ministers and civil servants in Whitehall to press for more limited goals of improving their status in the scale of development area assistance. The greater the involvement of central government in promoting economic development the greater became the concern of local authorities to press for help from London as the solution to their local economic problems.

A survey of local authorities in England and Wales conducted by Chandler and Yates in 1980, which received a 78% response rate from a sample of 183 indicates that in the preceeding three years 83% of responding authorities had made an approach to government concerning economic development within their community, whilst 26% had petitioned the EEC and 31% a nationalised industry. County councils and metropolitan districts were more likely to put pressure on government than non-metropolitan districts but as many as 75% of respondents from these smaller authorities had made some form of economic submission to central government.

The survey shows in Table 8.1 that the most frequent subject of local authority pressure on central government are issues that facilitate the attraction of industry.

Table 8.1
% Local Authorities in England and Wales approaching central government on the following subjects:

Assisted Area or Inner City Status	38
Industrial or Office Development Premission or Certificates	13
Factory construction	8
Release of land	5
Infra-structive improvements	17
Aid to a specific industry	15
Other	18
None	22

The data clearly underlines the importance given by most local authorities in the late 1970's to schemes for attracting employers rather than saving jobs or aiding established firms. Among the much smaller proportion of local authorities that sought aid for established industries the majority were county councils and metropolitan districts and within these areas a number of major schemes, such as the efforts to gain protection for the textile industries that are described later in the chapter, account for the responses of a number of authorities. Submissions to the EEC were similarly largely concerned with acquiring aid from the social or regional funds whilst a majority of the approaches to nationalised industries concerned the release of land for industrial development particularly from British Rail

Although Table 8.1 gives some indication of the number of local authorities engaged in particular types of pressure group activity aimed at promoting employment the survey does not provide any information on the intensity or sophistication of interest group campaigns. Attempts to persuade the government or a naticnalised industry to aid the local economy can vary from sending a letter expressing the concern of a council at some Ministerial decree to a sustained campaign involving a number of council officers on a full time basis and recruiting the support and involvement of many local interests in addition to the local authority.

RESEARCH AND PRESENTATION

Demands for economic aid by local authorities are more likely to be recognised if they are well argued and effectively presented. Pressure group activity therefore requires local authorities to have resources enabling them to conduct research into local economic and social problems and to present their findings in a form that will gain the attention of civil servants or executives of major industries. A request for inner city funds or assisted area status requires information on the recent history of business firms within the area, the numbers of jobs lost in recent years, the numbers likely to come on to the job market, the availability of land for industrial use and other relevant data on the social and economic structure of the area. The information must however be packaged in a reasonably brief document that does not tax the patience of civil servants.

The ability of smaller district authorities to conduct such research and present it in a manageable form is, as

will be shown in the case of Chesterfield, often limited.
Most local government personnel are trained for specific
specialised professions and if they are not social science
graduates will be unlikely to have had any experience of
social and economic research and analysis. Some authorities
may nevertheless try to use the resources they have at hand
and call on the abilities of officers within planning
departments or chief executives offices. Where an industrial
development officer is employed the task of formulating a
case for the authority may be placed in his hands.

Smaller authorities may be able to overcome some of the
problems of developing and presenting their demands by
enlisting the help of better resourced organisations.
District councils can often gain help from the county council
which is more likely to employ professional economists.
They can also hire private sector organisations such as
accountancy firms, or planning consultants to conduct
research and produce a supporting document. On all too few
occasions they may seek the help and expertise available
within local centres of higher or further education.

The larger authorities that have some concern for employment
creation are much more capable of conducting their own
research into local economic problems. Among county councils
the need to develop structure plans has obliged them to
appoint individuals who can collect and order data on
industry and employment within their territory. As a
consequence of this demand the research capability of many
of the larger authorities is located within planning
departments. Many of the metropolitan county councils
recognised at the time of their creation the need to collect
and process information on the local economy and developed
units usually based within their planning departments that
employed economists and were specifically concerned with
economic research and monitoring industrial production and
employment. Within some of these authorities and a number
of the larger metropolitcan and non-metropolitan districts
that have a major interest in employment creation these
initially small units have developed into much larger
organisations capable of conducting sophisticated economic
research and analysis and of presenting their findings in
a manner that can be absorbed by the civil servant or the
citizen in the street. The West Midland County Council for
example employs around 60 personnel in its Economic
Development Unit of whom a majority will be concerned with
research in pursuit of the many objectives of the Employment
Development Committee. Senior officers within these units
have rarely been employed exclusively by local authorities

and many have had experience of research for higher degrees, or work within industry or larger pressure groups. Many employment units will also employ or be able to call on the assistance of graphic artists and designers to illustrate promotional and campaign material.

The research output of the larger employment departments such as those of the Greater London Council or Sheffield is considerable. These departments issue each month a facts sheet providing basic statistical data on the local economy such as the changes in the levels of local unemployment and those firms which have announced redundancies. These papers are distributed not only to local councillors but members of parliament for the area, trade union officials and employers' organisations. In addition to monitoring the progress of the local economy as a whole the West Midlands Economic Development Unit charts the progress of larger companies within the County which may be facing economic difficulties. The larger employment departments also conduct studies of sectors of local industry in order to aid policy making on employment creation and to develop a thorough understanding of their local economy. The Greater London Council has for example published over thirty studies of aspects of the metropolitan economy during the last three years. These papers, headed 'Economic Policy Group-Strategy Document' can be up to 100 pages in length and have covered industries as varied as flour milling, engineering and publishing. Alongside studies of specific industries further research has been published on alternative policies for London's docks area or on subjects such as an analysis of energy saving schemes that could cut industrial costs and save jobs.

The research findings on studies of the local economy alongside the data on local industry collected by research workers in employment departments build up into a valuable information resource for groups within the community campaigning to save or create jobs. The Greater London Council has funded a number of resource units for Trade Unions including one in co-operation with Hackney Borough Council that monitors local industries within the borough and helped through the information obtained to build up trade unionism within the local clothing industries. (GLC 1983 d)

PRESSURE FOR DEVELOPMENT AIDS

It has been indicated in Table 8.1 that the majority of attempts to influence central goverment concerning the local

economy have attempted to gain resources such as improved
grant status, advanced factories or better infra-structure
which will promote the attraction of new industry to the area.
Pressure to achieve these aims usually proceeds along well
accepted lines. The local authorities demanding better
facilities will either write to, or obtain an interview
with, the appropriate Ministers or senior civil servants
presenting to them written evidence in support of their
demands. Contact with government ministers is frequently
obtained through the intermediary of local members of
parliament.

Approaches to the government may often be occasioned by
protests at an executive decision that affects the development status of the local authority. West Glamorgan County
Council for example reacted critically to an announcement
by the newly elected Conservative Government in 1979 that
there would be a reduction in the number of areas eligible
for regional assistance. The County argued that:-

'the economy of the Swansea/Port Talbot coastal belt
will have to compete from August 1980 as an
intermediate area with South Glamorgan/Cardiff area
as a Development area'(West Glamorgan County Council,
1979 p8.)

To reverse what was seen as a decision favouring an economically more secure County to the detriment of West Glamorgan
the County Clerk stated that:-

'I have conducted a correspondence with the local
member (of parliament) most involved in countering
the effects of cuts in Wales. Copies of my correspondence has been sent to the Welsh Office.

I recommend that representations are made in writing,
and personally on the proposed visit of the Secretary
of State for Industry and in writing to the Secretary
of State for Wales in order to attempt to prevent
local areas from being downgraded to Intermediate
Areas; and at the very least improving the range of
assistance available to this status' (West Glamorgan
County Council, 1979, p8.)

Local authorities not only react to changes in government
policy but may campaign to acquire development aid which
they have not received previously. Chesterfield District
Council successfully sought intermediate assisted area
status in 1974 on the grounds that the community was failing
to attract industry in competition with the neighbouring

assisted regions of South Yorkshire. The District Council
lacked sufficient resources to make an effective submission
to the Government and enlisted the help of a private firm of
economic consultants to bring together the necessary data
to make an effective case. The District was fortunate in
respect to the help given by its Member of Parliament,
Eric Varley, who became a cabinet minister in the year that
the proposal was tabled.

Similar pressure group campaigns are waged by local
authorities interested in gaining improvements to infra-
structure. Sheffield Metropolitan District Council calling
on much greater resources than a non-metropolitan district
such as Chesterfield was able to wage a protracted and
elaborate siege of a public body for better communications
even before the establishment of its Employment Committee.
The city in the latter half of the 1970's became concerned
about the lack of any modernisation to rail connections with
London which was seen both by the local authority and the
Chamber of Trade as deleterious to the local economy. The
City Council organised a campaign to persuade British Rail
to use High Speed Trains on the Sheffield to London line
initially sending delegations of councillors and local
industrial interests, brought together through the authority's
industrial advisory committee, to demand a better service from
British Rail. Their efforts were supplemented by lobbying
and parliamentary interventions from local MPs and later
through joint action on the rail connections with other East
Midland authorities. A regular High speed London to Sheffield
service was instituted in 1982 although the extent to which
this was due to sustained pressure or planned modernisation
on the part of British Rail is difficult to determine. By
this point the Sheffield campaign had moved on to encompass
the much more ambitious aim of securing jobs for local
industry and nationally through the electrification of the
Sheffield to London line as part of a nationwide railways
modernisation policy.

CAMPAIGNS TO AID EMPLOYERS

Pressure for incentives such as assisted area status,
advanced factories and, in many cases, infra-structure, will,
if successful, have an impact largely on the ability of an
area to attract new industry. Concessions from government
on these matters will be of much less value in giving ailing
companies a new lease of life and therefore saving jobs.
Efforts to aid established firms are less frequent and
usually require more complex campaigns integrating the

interests of employers, Trade Unions and the local
authority.

In a number of conurbations economic decline is associated
with the demise of particular industries. Cotton manufacturing for example lost 20,000 jobs in 1980 (Local Authorities
Textile Action Committee, nd) whilst the Sheffield cutlery
industry employed 30,000 in the 1950's and only 5,500
workers by 1977 (Chandler and Templeton, 1981). Local
authorities active in employment creation are aware that the
continued failure of these industries has a major impact on
the local economy and, if possible, defence of jobs in these
sectors may be the best means of strengthening the local
economy. Much research has therefore been conducted into the
declining traditional industries by those local authorities
with the capacity to carry out such work as this activity is
backed by strategies to arrest decline. It is however
accepted by most local employment organisations that they
cannot on their own solve problems of technological change,
foreign competition and undercapitalisation. They must act
as a catalyst through pressure group action working on both
government and the employers to restructure the economic
regulations confronting the industries and the management
practices within the firms themselves.

Some of the most ambitious attempts by local authorities
to develop a co-ordinated approach to reduce an ailing
industry have concerned textile manufacturers. In March 1980
Oldham Metropolitan District Council called a meeting of all
local authorities in Lancashire and Greater Manchester to
discuss, with representatives of the Textile Employers
Federation, possible ways in which local government could
help the industry. Although the employers were initially
sceptical about the value of such support the meeting laid
the foundation of a body, the Local Authority Textile Action
Committee (LATAC) to campaign on behalf of the industry. The
organisation included 15 local authorities although in practice much of the work was carried forward by a smaller group
representing Lancashire and Greater Manchester County
Councils and the Districts of Pendle and Oldham. The
secretarial and research work of the committee was largely
entrusted to Oldham Metropolitan District whose Chief
Executive had been most responsible for its creation.

LATAC since its formation has largely been concerned with
monitoring the progress of closures in the industry and
preparing delegations of local authority and employers
representatives to petition the EEC and the government on
the need for:-

'measures which will establish the right climate in which the textile industry - traditionally a self-help industry - can re-establish itself in an internationally competitive role.' (LATAC nd p8)

These measures include changes in import quotas, protection from 'dumping' by United States manufacturers and cheaper fuel prices. The committee is exclusively concerned with putting pressure on governments for better trading conditions within the industry and has not for example attempted to instruct the manufacturers about how to run their businesses. Efforts to expand the committee's function to consider more widely the problems created by the decline of the cotton industries and how the jobs lost could be replaced were resisted by some of the participating local authorities.

A somewhat more interventionist minded attempt to deal with the similar problems facing the woollen textile industry across the Pennines has been developed through the organisation of the Woollen Textiles Action Committee (WOOLTAC), under the leadership of West Yorkshire Metropolitan County Council. This interest group has a much closer working relationship with the industry and is guided by a committee chaired by a textile manufacturer consisting of two local authority representatives, two from the employers' associations, two Trade Unionists, an MP and an MEP. The research and secretarial work of the group is handled by the Economic Development Unit of West Yorshire County Council which also provides most of the funds required by the organisation. The organisation has, like LATAC, fostered delegations of employers, Trade Unions and local authorities to petition government on trading conditions for the industry and has also induced local MP's to raise issues concerning woollen textiles in parliament. Considerable research and campaign work has been put into influencing the British government's attitude towards the Common Market Multi Fibre Agreement, and more recently work has concentrated on ensuring that product labelling of imported goods means what is says. The local authorities on the committee have also made some attempts to change attitudes within the industry but have been quickly rebuffed by employers who will only accept local authority help as a fellow appellant to government. Suggestions that the industry's attitude to marketing was at fault received only objections from the industry that such comment amounted to interference with their private interests.

The cotton and wool textile campaigns have been almost

exclusively pressure group actions designed to convince governments of the need to protect these industries. Co-operation between local authorities and particular industries can however lead to more concrete schemes for joint action. Sheffield Metropolitan District Council for some years struggled to generate sufficient unity in the declining cutlery industry to press government for protection from much cheaper imports of stainless steel cutlery. Although it made little impression on this issue it was able to push more successfully for tighter regulations governing the use of the 'made in Sheffield' trademark and also provided a certificate signed by the mayor of the city in each canteen of high quality cutlery attesting to its manufacture in Sheffield. (Chandler and Templeton, 1981).

An example of the possible value to be obtained from co-operative meetings between industries and local authorities can be illustrated by the ideas flowing from a seminar organised by the Northamptonshire Enterprise Agency, an organisation established by the County Council, and representatives of footwear manufacturers established in the County. The Enterprise Agency is actively investigating setting up a visitor's centre for the industry which would depict the history and present development of shoe manufacture within the area and serve both as a showcase for sales and an attraction for visitors. It was also decided to provide burseries to young designers which would allow them to travel abroad to study shoe design and then return to work within local firms. A further idea under investigation is that the County Council should convert out of date shoe factories into workshops for smaller businesses and thus allow the footwear firms to move to more modern premises with the assurance that they would not be left with an unwanted and unsaleable factory.

Local authorities can attempt to aid industry not only by supporting their efforts to gain better trading conditions from government but by directing their attention to new business opportunities and influencing investment decisions. Such pressure is rarely applied although the basis of an initiative in this area is being developed by West Yorkshire and Greater Manchester County Councils who have jointly launched a scheme to persuade financial houses and property developers to find alternative use for derelict factories in their areas. The Councils commissioned research, principally through a private planning consultancy, to identify the extent and pattern of vacant factory floorspace within the two Counties. The resultant report also suggests ways in which new investment could transform particular buildings by making them tourist attractions illustrating Britian's industrial heritage, or by converting them to other industrial purposes. It is also argued that less desirable buildings should be demolished to raise the value of remaining units. The conclusions of the survey are to be sent to property developers and agencies such as pension funds and insurance companies that have funds to invest in the hope of persuading these organisations profitably to aid the regeneration of older industrial properties.

Approaches to pension funds have also been made by the West Midlands County Council which has reached an agreement with a number of London based public sector pension funds to invest in projects being supported by the County's Enterprise Board. West Yorkshire has also, sought, with limited success, to persuade the Midland Bank to provide investment for larger industries in partnership with the County Council pension fund. Loans from this source are however only available at rates offered widely by financial institutions and the scheme has consequently received few takers. Several other authorities, as will be indicated in the latter chapter on finance, try to interest banks in jointly investing in local firms. There is nevertheless much that can still be achieved by local authorities by putting pressure on major financial institutions to persuade them to invest in companies within their communities.

Co-operation between employers, trade unions and local authorities to aid a particular industry can have few disadvantages apart from its relatively modest use of the resources of the participating organisations. On occasion, as the Northhampton example suggests, a single meeting may lead to the development of a number of practical ideas. Councillors and employers may learn through such work something of each others concerns and problems and joint meetings of employers and local authorities may also, as in the case of the tortuous negotiations between Sheffield City Council and the divided cutlery firms, generate some self criticism and a necessary understanding of the overall problems of an industry. Success in achieving the principal aims of campaigns to protect an industry has however been limited and general run up against established government policies that are bound by international trading agreements and EEC directives.

The problems of many declining industries are not however solely due to international agreements on trade. Firms may fail to take advantage of conditions created by, for example, the EEC due to their own failure to modernise. Efforts by

145

local authorities to suggest to employers that they need to rationalise their industries have however usually met with a stern rebuff from larger firms and employers' associations. In 1980 both of the cutlery manufacturers' associations then representing the industry argued that Sheffield District Council had no understanding of the industry and therefore no grounds for suggesting how the employers could put their houses in order. Only when firms are small and in difficulty is it probably feasible for local authorities to make a direct impact on industrial reorganisation through direct financial intervention rather than persuasion as is the case with the attempt by the West Midland County Council to reorganise the foundry industry in the County which is discussed in Chapter 13. In the absence of direct influence on employers, socialist minded authorities may turn increasingly to trade unions in an effort to gain some improvement within the local economy, or to developing public campaigns to change government policies.

AID TO EMPLOYEES

In a number of local administrations research facilities and the authority of the council are linked not so much to industry-wide campaigns in which employers predominate but to the efforts of workers, usually in association with their trade union branches, to secure their right to work. These authorities are, not surprisingly, larger Labour Party controlled councils. Most trade unions employ few if any research staff even at a national level so that factory branches of trade unions have almost no access to resources that would enable them to present a well researched case in opposition to closures or redundancies. The local authority can therefore serve as a valuable source of information and advice to groups of shop floor workers or even regional and national trade union organisations. The resource centres established by employment departments are of particular value to shop floor workers who may in turn be able to supply information of value to the employment departments.

In addition to the provision of basic information local authorities can also conduct research on behalf of workers faced with the closure of their factories and provide them with support in any negotiations or confrontations with their employers. The following extract from a report of activity in this area conducted by the Sheffield Employment Department illustrates the nature of this work.

'WOODHEAD COMPONENTS

At the end of 1982 the closure of Woodhead Components'
Globe works was announced with the loss of 244 jobs.
We provided financial information on the company and
held discussions about possible alternatives to the
closure with the shop stewards. Research revealed
that the company's plans would have important implications for a number of other plants in Sheffield -
information which was passed on to the relevant full-time
officials.

GKN

The threat of 280 redundancies at GKN Shardlows in
December 1982 led to a number of informal discussions
between the Employment Department and the Conveners
about plans for the plant in the context of GKN's
overall operations, both nationally and overseas.
Although the future of the forge remains uncertain
there have been no compulsory redundancies at the
plant. More recently assistance has been given to the
trade unions on interpreting the Company accounts.'
(Sheffield Metropolitan District, 1984a, p5.)

The Report from which this extract has been taken lists
several similar cases of help given to local shop stewards
who had approached the Employment Department with concerns
over their future.

Sheffield is not the only city where such help may be
given to groups of workers. Both the GLC and the West
Midland Employment Departments can provide advice and
conduct research on behalf of workers facing factory closures.
In a few cases these local authorities have consulted one
another on the plans and progress of companies that have
factories in a number of cities. Possible redundancies at
GEC Traction plants following the failure of the government
to enact a major electrification scheme for British Rail
led to joint discussions between the Manchester Employment
Research Group and the Greater London Council. The Greater
London Council and Sheffield have also pooled information to
help headquarters staff in the Midland Bank who have been
faced with redundancy. An even more ambitious co-operative
venture has been fostered by the GLC which has attempted to
ensure co-operation between workers for Kodak in London and
Paris concerning the company's future rationalisation plans.
(Greater London County Council, 1983d)

147

The West Midland County Council's Economic Development Unit
is not only prepared to advise workers concerned about
closures but has developed a system of monitoring larger
companies within the County which may be facing economic
difficulties in order to give workers early warnings of the
possibility that they may lose their jobs. The system not
only allows workers to be able to prepare a case against
possible redundancy but they can also, through advice given
by the Economic Development Unit prepare plans to salvage
something from a possible wreck. Groups of skilled workers
may therefore be able to remain together and through
negotiations with the ailing company and aid from the County
Council form co-operatives to continue profitably using their
skills.

POLITICAL CAMPAIGNS

The level of unemployment and the general prosperity of most
cities and towns is dependent upon the policies of large
employers and they in turn may be highly dependent on the
policies of governments. Central government has direct
influence over the plans for major investment or retrenchment
within the nationalised sector and can determine the fortunes
of private industries through its fiscal policies, provision
of subsidies and procurement decisions. Local authorities
can therefore do much to influence the fortunes of their
local economies in as much as they can determine the industrial and financial policies of central government.

Few authorities openly attempt to persuade central
government to modify or to change its policies even though,
as observed earlier in this chapter, most local authorities
lobby Whitehall concerning their communities' economic
interests. A distinction must however be made between
campaigns, such as an attempt to gain assisted area status
for Chesterfield, which seek to gain an interpretation of
current government policy in favour of a particular locality,
and a campaign that attempts to change the whole tenor of
that policy.

Whilst a Conservative Government is in power the local
authorities most active in openly opposing its policies are
Labour controlled but only a small number of these councils
have either the resources or the temerity to take on the
entrenched opinions of the cabinet. Among the most
adventurous in this respect is Sheffield Metropolitan District
which has a particular concern for the development of the
special steels industry. Between 1971 and 1983 employment in

the steel industry within the city declined from 45,000 jobs
to 18,000 and resulted in the area for the first time this
century having a rate of unemployment greater than average
for the country as a whole (Sheffield Metropolitan District
Council, nd). The City Council had begun monitoring the
fortunes of the steel industry during the late 1970's and
became increasingly involved in attempts to present its
decline as Conservative Government policies started to cut
the steel industry at the same time as the city, through the
creation of its Employment Department, gained greater
resources for campaigning on industrial issues.

Sheffield City Council realises that it cannot resurrect
many of the jobs that have been lost in the industry but
wishes to prevent a continued loss of employment which it
sees as, to a considerable extent, the consequence of
government policies.

'The alternatives may be limited: they cannot recreate
the 110,000 jobs lost to British steelworkers, nor the
35,000 lost in Sheffield and Rotherham. In themselves
they cannot repair the damage done by the unsatisfactory
nationalisation, the collapse of the market for steel
(rather than the need for steel) and the crippling
effects of government policies directly and indirectly
on steel. But they do indicate that practical campaigns
around concrete issues and projects provide the basis
for arguing that steelworkers' jobs and capacity in
South Yorkshire special steel industry, are essential for
future social and industrial development.' (Sheffield
Metropolitan District Council nd, p40)

The 'concrete issues and projects' designed to save jobs
in the industry have most recently centred around government
proposals known as the Pheonix plans to rationalise the
public and private steel sectors through the merger of plant
in both sectors to produce smaller units owned privately or
jointly by British Steel and private investors. The Pheonix
III which most seriously affects Sheffield has so far
resulted in the merger of the private Firth Browns steel
company with the BSC River Don plant with the loss of an
estimated 1,600 jobs, As soon as rumours of the proposed
merger were received by Trade Unions and the local authority
a committee was formed which included local authority
representation to link all the Unions in the plants
concerned. The committee produced, with the aid of the
Sheffield Employment Committee, leaflets and newsletters
alerting the workforce to the consequences of the proposed
merger. A public information exercise was staged by the
City Council which arranged a week long public investigation

of the proposal. A more widespread campaign is also underway
to challenge the Pheonix II proposal to rationalise the
production of engineering steels which would involve mergers
between BSC plants in South Yorkshire and the Midlands with
the private sector GKN plants in Wales to form a jointly
owned British Engineering Steels Company. It is feared that
the proposal is in effect being implemented with the closure
of a number of private steel making companies in Sheffield
and would result in the closure of at least one major steel
making plant either in Wales or Sheffield. A campaign
committee with a similar composition to that used in the
Pheonix III action has been formed and the City Council held
a conference in Sheffield that included steel workers,
workers from industries using steel, Members of Parliament
and local authorities in order to further a co-ordinated
campaign. In preparation for this event the Employment
Department published a 40 page booklet 'Steel in Crisis' with
the sub-heading 'Alternatives to Government Policy and the
Decline in South Yorkshire's Steel Industry', a 20 minute
video tape and several smaller summary documents and
information sheets. These materials are made available to any
local organisations wishing to gain information on the issue.

Apart from the steel campaigns Sheffield City Council has
also organised a National Conference and brought together a
package of detailed information on the suggested electrification of British Rail. The 1984 coal miners strike has
received considerable sympathy and help from the Council
since it aims to save jobs in an industry active in South
Yorkshire and whose Union headquarters has recently been
established in the city. The Employment Department has also
produced literature at the request of British Telecommunica-
tion workers to aid their campaign against the probable loss
of jobs through privatisation of the industry.

Sheffield Metropolitan District Council was in 1984 the most
active in the country in staging campaigns against the
industrial policies of the government. It is possible that
their concern in this sphere has not been matched by other
radical Labour authorities such as the Greater London Council
since Sheffield is much more dependent on nationalised
industry than other parts of the country governed by radical
Labour controlled councils. The Greater London Council has
however shown a willingness to campaign against the Thatcher
government not only to ensure its continued existence but in
devising an alternative planning strategy for London's
Docklands which is very different to the business orientated
strategy developed by the London Docklands Development
Corporation. A considerable number of Labour controlled

councils are also active in combating government policies
that directly affect the powers of local authorities. These
campaigns, discussed in more detail in Chapter 9 are
directed against the proposals to abolish the GLC and the
Metropolitan Counties, cap the rates and privatise a number
of local government services.

WORKING CONDITIONS AND EQUAL OPPORTUNITIES

Radical employment departments are not only interested in
creating or saving jobs but also wish to ensure that employment is open to all groups within their community at fair
rates of pay and working conditions. This concern is best
articulated if it permeates the thinking of politicians
and officers concerned with employment creation so that
regulations promoting equal opportunities or better
conditions of work are attached to a whole range of activities
sponsored by an employment department. Many of the strategies
used to achieve these aims are dealt with in other chapters
and in many cases are secured not solely through persuasion
but through compliance with conditions laid down by the
local authority for the use of its facilities. The emphasis
on the need for acceptable employment practices imposed
through these means nevertheless has an important socialising
effect on both employers and employees and it is therefore of
value to consider in this chapter the range of strategies
used to secure better working conditions and equality of
opportunity.

Although employment departments are usually alert to the
need for equality of employment opportunities they are
clearly not the only or the most important defenders of this
interest within their communities or often even with their
authorities. Particularly in the case of racial discrimination, organisations such as local community relations councils
or as in some multi-racial authorities such as Hackney, council
operated units take on much of the work needed to secure
equitable employment for all races in the community. There
are fewer well established local agencies to secure sexual
equality and it is therefore more open to employment
departments to establish an interest in the rights of women
to work. Sheffield's employment department has consequently
appointed two, as yet, temporary officers to investigate the
female employment pattern in the city. There appears to
have been far less activity in local authorities to secure
employment opportunities for disabled workers although this
may reflect a practitional view that these individuals should
be the responsibility of social services departments and be

considered as cases for compassion and charity rather than as ordinary members of their community.

Local authorities realise that pressure for equal opportunities must begin at home. The employment practices of local authorities controlled by the most anti-racist and feminist minded councillors are usually far from perfect. Sheffield City Council Employment Department conducted a study of female employment within its workforce and found that 56% of salaried women employees were on the lowest salary range as opposed to only 10% of male employees. (Sheffield Metropolitan District Council 1984b). Having completed the easier task of establishing the size of the problem the Council is now faced with the more difficult task of implementing changes in their employment pattern. Suggestions concerning better promotion prospects for women, and improved services for aiding women who have to care for dependant children or elderly relatives are under consideration. A related concern of the Council is to improve pay and conditions for their part time workers since 90% of these employees are women. Sheffield is also proposing to conduct similar studies of its employment practice in relation to ethnic minorities although work in this area has been developed much more extensively by cities with a larger proportion of non-white citizens. The 1981 Labour Party manifesto for the Greater London Council for example advocated positive discrimination in favour of ethnic minorities in its recruitment of council workers.

Outside the local authority the principal means of ensuring that private companies establish better employment practices is through the development of clauses in contract compliance agreements. These schemes, which are considered further in Chapter 9, commit firms trading with a local authority to accept working practices demanded by the council. In all such contracts there are clauses requiring firms to comply with legislation on equal pay for women and equality of employment for all racial groups. Similar conditions can be attached by enterprise boards as a condition for obtaining financial aid.

A further area in which local authorities can help ensure equal opportunities is through its sponsored training schemes. In Sheffield an electronics training workshop and a unit to train plasterers have been opened specifically for women. The latter scheme in particular generated considerable publicity which has helped alert employers and women to the possibility of wider opportunities within the labour market.

ADVICE

It has been observed earlier in this chapter that so many
employment creation activities of local authorities involve
advisory work, a separate section on how and when such help
is provided by Council officers to businesses, would repeat
much that has already been discussed in this book.
Information is for example readily given to firms wishing to
relocate on the availability of sites and premises within a
local authority. Advice is often available to tourists and
conference organisers on accommodation and attractions of an
area. In this chapter it has been shown that a number of
local authorities are concerned with building up a library
of information on local industries and economic development
to aid groups of workers to challenge the policies of their
employers.

Despite the wide and extensively used range of advisory
activities carried out by local authorities wishing to create
employment a number of Councils consider that their main
role in this area is to act as advisors to small businesses.
The principal role of an industrial development officer in
many authorities is to act as an advisor to small firms.
Much of their work involves providing information and support
to small companies trying to understand how to raise capital
or extend their premises or master the intricacies of
corporation tax. A few local authorities have abstracted
this element of the industrial development officer's work
and established small business advisory centres. Northampton
County Council in partnership with Chamber of Commerce for
example formed in 1980 under the acronym of INPUT an office
employing a permanent officer which could provide advice to
local businesses. The organisation has now been incorporated
into the Northamptonshire Enterprise Agency but still retains
its specific advisory functions. Dudley Metropolitan District
Council set up a small firms centre to give advice and hold
courses for intending businessmen (Boddy 1982). Calderdale
Metropolitan District Council had by 1977 appointed an
information officer to answer enquiries from firms concerned
with the area and this work was supported by the establishment
of a library of relevant information based with a local further
education college. This organisation along with the Chamber
of Commerce also ran several business and accountancy courses
for small businessmen (Mawson, 1983). Seminars and short
courses to aid individuals running or wishing to establish
small enterprises have been operated by a number of local
authorities.

The schemes to advise small firms set up in the late 1970's have tended to become submerged in some of the larger and more active authorities with the growth of large and diverse employment creation interests. In cities which have some form of employment or economic development unit employing several staff, small businessmen will have several possible channels for gaining advice depending upon the problem at hand. Different officials may have to be consulted on the availability of premises or the possibility of obtaining capital and there may be a danger that these organisations will become too complex for many small businessmen to use as a means of overcoming several interrelated business problems. It must however be observed that apart from local authorities several other organisations exist to advise small or prospective businessmen on how to make a success of their enterprise.

EVALUATION

The value of research, advice and pressure group activity on behalf of local employment cannot be assessed as simply as a Which survey that abstracts the best buy from a number of competing products. It is difficult and sometimes impossible to estimate the extent to which an institution such as the government decides to follow a particular policy as a result of pressure from one particular source. Pressure group campaigns may also involve questions of value. It is not possible to assess objectively whether a campaign to prevent closures of marginally profitable coal mines is of greater importance to a local economy than efforts using the same resources to designate an area as an enterprise zone since the worth of both strategies may be dependent on differing views of the morality of the capitalist system.

It may nevertheless be argued that some measure of the success of pressure group campaigns can be gained by estimating the extent to which their objectives are realised. Many of the examples of interest campaigns cited earlier in this chapter have clearly failed to achieve many of their aims. In the case of the defence of the textile and cutlery industries the government has refused to grant substantial protection from cheap imports and it is doubtful if the Thatcher government will reverse their policies on the steel industry as a result of local government objections.

These criticisms must however be tempered in the light of some of the smaller but nevertheless valuable achievements of these campaigns. Better trademarking standards may not be all

that the woollen textile industry would like to gain from
central government but a measure of success in this
direction can save some jobs in the industry at little cost.
In some cases pressure from local government on behalf of an
industry can have long term effects that are not immediately
realised. Demands by Sheffield Metropolitan District Council
that the government should abandon its policy of severely
curtailing the steel industry may not immediately influence
the Cabinet but can have a considerable effect on Labour
or even Liberal Party policy on this issue and could even
help to motivate Conservative opponents of the Thatcher
government to push for changes in prevailing policies.
Even though the success of such a campaign to evaluate and
if at all influential may have no immediate effect it must
be emphasised that the possible impact of changes in policy
on an issue such as the steel industry can be of major
importance to a locality. It is highly unlikely that any
local authority can finance local industry to the extent that
they could create jobs to match those that may be lost
through government policy on steel closures.

Apart from the importance of the possible successes
achieved through local government pressure the strategy has
the further advantage of requiring relatively few resources.
Apart from large scale advertising aimed at mobilising
public opinion the major and at times the only cost involved
in an interest group campaign is its use of professional
officer's time. The principal cost involved in arranging a
delegation to petition a government Minister is in the
preparation of a case to present to the government. This
task may be carried out somewhat expensively through hiring
a professional agency to conduct the necessary research but
it is frequently possible for larger authorities to second one
of their officers employed in a relevant area to work on the
campaign or, in the case of larger authorities, employ full
time research and campaign staff. Although such work
commands considerable resources it remains a much less
expensive exercise than a strategy directly to fund local
firms or to attract industry into the area. The provision
of grants and loans to local firms requires staff to evaluate
the economic viability of applicants in addition to the
funds given to the more acceptable projects, whilst efforts
to induce industry to move into the local authority also
involves staff time in devising information on the area
along with highly expensive advertising costs.

The research and advisory work involved in developing a
pressure group campaign may moreover have a value that
transcends its original purpose. Information on the local

economy gathered for a particular issue may add to the wider understanding within the local authority of its economy and be of use in later campaigns or other policy initiatives. Co-operation between industry, trade unions and local councillors occasioned by an interest group campaign can have a similarly lasting value in other policy areas whilst the amassing of a store of information and spirit of co-operation between local politicians, industry and employees can form the basis of a valuable advisory service.

A further advantage of pressure group as opposed to other more directly interventionist economic activities reflects the particular ideological positions of certain local authorities. Councillors on both the left and the right of the political spectrum may be wary of providing direct financial aid to local enterprise. Politicians on the right will consider that the local authority should not be involved as a public body in the process of economic enterprise but nevertheless has a duty to represent the general economic interest of its area. Left wing councillors may on the other hand be reluctant directly to aid local capitalists even though they wish to demand that the government enacts policies that will promote more extensive local employment. In both these cases pressure group and advisory work enables the political actors to retain some influence in local economic matters whilst at the same time retaining their ideological purity by avoiding direct monetary involvement with industry and commerce.

9 The local authority as employer and consumer

However insensitive local authorities may be to the needs of their local economy they will nevertheless have a significant impact on employment, industry and commerce through the pursuit of their powers. Local government is one of the largest employers within the country and spends considerable sums on goods and services. It is also a major source of taxation both directly through the rates and indirectly through revenue raised by central government to fund grants to local authorities. It is however only in recent years that serious attention has been paid by local authorities to the economic consequences of their purchasing powers. Some interest was shown by a few larger city councils in the 1930s on the impact of their personnel policies on prevailing levels of unemployment. A number of construction projects were initiated by local governments during this period with the aim of giving work to the unemployed. The scope for such action was however limited by the difficulties of raising capital to fund major building schemes. The consequences of paying for local authority expenditure has however always exercised the minds of local businessmen.

RATES

In the 19th Century many city governments refused to develop their services so as not to increase rates. This attitude is still prevalent today. Traditionally promises to restrain local authority expenditure, and as a result the rates, were used to influence voters by appealing directly to their wallets and purses but in recent years a number of organisations have also suggested to the public that high rates harm their interests by undermining the profitability and competitiveness of local firms. The CBI in April 1980 began a campaign to highlight the effect of rate increases on businesses and demanded that a ceiling was placed on the upward movement of their payments. (The Times 30th June 1981). The London Chambers of Commerce and Industry maintained

before the 1981 Greater London Council elections that rate
increases consequent on the introduction of the block grant
would lead to the loss of 25,000 jobs in the South East
(The Times 7th March 1981).

These arguments are incorporated in a more general ideological objection to high rates of taxation that forms a
central element of Thatcherite neo-liberal ideology.
Taxation, it is argued, undermines the ability and desire of
individuals to create wealth through their spirit of
competitive initiative and thereby develop the economy for
the benefit of all. Local authorities such as Birmingham
City Council, when under Conservative control during the early
1980s, accepted these ideas and consequently cut their
expenditure and the rates. Their tax reductions were in part
justified on the grounds that they were a positive contribution to local economic development and the alleviation
of unemployment.

Industrialists can rightly argue that they have not been
exempt from bearing the burden of the higher cost of local
government rates. It has been calculated by the Greater
London Council that rates have increased by 125% on average
between 1978/79 and 1983/84 (Greater London Council, 1983e).
There is however considerable doubt as to whether this
increase has created as great a problem for industry as the
employers' organisation surveys suggest. It has for example
already been observed in Chapter 3 that the rate burden on
firms appears to have little or no effect on their decisions
to relocate. Attempts to calculate the extent to which rates
are a major element of industrial costs also suggest that they
are not as onerous as many employers would like the public
to believe. The Layfield Report calculated on the basis of
the 1968 Census of production that local authority rates
as a percentage of industrial output varied from 1% for light
industries to 5% for heavy industry. (HMSO, 1976a). Greater
London Council research shows that:-

> 'At the aggregate level, rates made up only 0.6 per
> cent of turnover in manufacturing industry, under 2
> per cent of gross value added, and only 3 per cent of
> the total wages and salary bill (data for 1974-9).
> Between 1975 and 1981, non-domestic rates fell in
> real terms by 20 per cent. Since then they have
> risen because of the reduction in central government
> finance of local government. Even so, the size of
> the increase is dwarfed by other factors .... The
> increase of value added tax from 8 per cent to 15
> per cent in 1979 is one example.' (Greater London
> Council 1983e, p 7).

158

Not only are local authority rates a relatively small item of business expenditure their real cost to a firm can be lower than is suggested by the preceeding estimates since rates are regarded as an expense which can be used to gain relief from co-operation tax. High rates may also significantly decrease the rent for commerical and industrial premises. A property company complained that due to rate increases the rent that can be obtained from shops in the West End of London has been reduced by a third in the early 1980s (The Times 22nd February 1982). It is argued by the Greater London Council that this factor ensures that rates

'are inversely related to property prices, not industrial profits' and that

'It is the landlords who should be opposed to rates, not productive industry.' (Greater London Council, 1983 e, p 8).

Although it can be argued that in general local authority taxation is not a serious burden on industrial profitability it must be observed that this is a sweeping conclusion that pays no attention to variations in the type of industry and its profitability at any particular moment. The rateable value of commercial and industrial premises is calculated on the basis of the estimated rent that could be obtained from the property. This calculation hits hardest commercial ventures such as department stores occupying large premises in city centres. Factories housed in similarly sized sites in rural or suburban areas will have a much lower rateable value. The system of valuation makes no allowance for the profitability of a firm, the assets it may hold in terms of plant or machinary, or the number of its employees. Retailing ventures are therefore obliged to pay a higher proportion of their turnover in rates than most industrial firms. The size of the rate demand in comparison with the total costs for a firm will also vary with the economic well being of the business. If a firm is in economic difficulties it can decrease its costs by ordering less stock or by cutting its workforce. The rate demand will however remain constant when other expenses are reduced and thus form a larger proportion of overall costs.

Although the burden of rates will vary from one industry to another it can be generally concluded that their reduction will do little to solve the economic problems of a particular community. Lower rates will lead to lower expenditure and fewer orders from the local authority to industry which may seriously damage firms reliant on contracts with the public sector. Financial losses may also result from poorer services and infra-structure. A rate reduction will also lead to fewer jobs within the largest employer for many communities and this will also have an effect on depressing the local economy and profitability of its local commerce and industry. These economic arguments must moreover be weighed in the final analysis alongside the social benefits that flow from full employment and good services.

EMPLOYMENT

Local Authorities are major employers with a full time equivalent workforce in December 1983 of 2,265,000 in England, Scotland and Wales. This represents 10% of total employment within Britain. In many small County towns local authority work will be the largest sector of employment and even in major cities the local authority is usually the largest single employer. Cuts in local government manpower will therefore contribute significantly to the prevailing level of un-employment. Between June 1979 and December 1983 there was a loss of 96,000 jobs in local authorities (Employment Gazette, 1980, 1984).

The reduction in the number of local government employees has not in general been the result of large scale redundancies for employees in post. Councils such as Wandsworth that felt obliged in 1981 to reduce its workforce by 9% occasioning 700 redundancies are exceptional (The Times 8th January, 1981). Rather, faced with a need to meet the financial squeeze on local authorities most councils have frozen or abolished posts when they became vacant. Such schemes have often been tied to agreements reached with Trade Unions to provide incentives for early retirement. This policy has been used most extensively to reduce the number of school teachers and lecturers in teacher training. Although freezing posts has the advantage of not creating the painful and, at times expensive, problems associated with compulsory redundancies the policy has had serious consequences for unemployment among school leavers and newly qualified graduates. Few vacancies have been open to young people within local govern-ment since 1980 and the continuation of this trend could have a serious effect on the structure of the local govern-ment service in terms of age balance and career opportunities.

The diversity and location of local authority work does not lead to the creation of severe rates of unemployment in any particular locality. Local Government workers are generally employed in the field rather than being concentrated in any one location. The largest single occupational group are teachers and lecturers scattered in small units throughout the area of the local authority. Other field workers include police, firemen and social workers. Town Hall administrators who form the most concentrated group of local authority employees will account for at most 25% of the total workforce. The effects of cuts in local government employment is therefore not as dramatic in its impact on any particular area as is the closure of a large industrial plant, so that the overall effect of the reduction in the numbers of local government workers has not appeared to be as great as it is.

Despite appearances the scale of local authority employment is sufficient to make a considerable impact. Liverpool City Council under the control of a radical Labour group of councillors has concentrated its efforts to alleviate unemployment through the expansion of its workforce employed in the traditional areas of local government activity. In particular the Council has attempted to increase the number of its employees and improve its housing stock through an ambitious house building and modernisation programme. The strategy led to the long running threat by the Council to approve a deficited budget if the government did not allow them the means to carry out the programme on which they were elected. Other local authorities have so far not followed the Liverpool example to the exclusion of other means of alleviating unemployment but many have shown a determination to at least retain their workforce at its present levels.

Many local authorities which have sought to retain their existing labour force despite government cut backs have established a no redundancy policy. A NALGO survey of councils that have adopted this stand shows that they include Conservative councils such as Devon as well as Labour controlled authorities. The precise nature and purpose of a no redundancy policy can however vary considerably. In Sheffield the policy is viewed as an extension of their interest in maintaining full employment in the city. The Council has in theory agreed not only to retain in employment the present workforce but to fill vacancies as they arise. Other Councils may however adopt a no redundancy policy in order to assure their employees that they have secure employment although they have kept to government targets for spending cuts by freezing new appointments.

Despite the adoption of a no redundancy policy local authorities are in practice often obliged to abandon their resolution. In a few cases the policy may have been adopted solely as a means of keeping employees' minds at rest although councillors remain prepared to abandon the policy

161

for particular departments or in general at any time that circumstances dictate a reduction in the workforce. In authorities where there is a strong ideological commitment to prevent redundancies and avoid freezing posts it is in practice often impossible to maintain such a policy. In Sheffield for example despite agreement not to reduce the number of posts an exception is made in respect of the teaching profession where the Council's policy is to reduce staffing levels to the extent that present staff pupil ratios remain at the same level. It is also unlikely that authorities that face major reductions in the workload in areas such as direct labour organisation or architects departments could sustain a workforce in employment when they have no work. Such action would be regarded by the district auditors as unreasonable expenditure.

A few local authorities have attempted to ensure an adequately trained young workforce by employing junior staff on a temporary basis through the use of funds obtained under section 137 of the 1972 Local Government Act since the Government's manpower watch figures which help guide their grant allocations do not include individuals employed on this basis. Through such a scheme Wakefield Metropolitan District Council for example employ a further 100 young people who are kept in permanent work through this fund until jobs can be found for them on the established pay-roll. The people employed on this basis are normally given training within the authority to prepare them for a full time career in local government. The scheme has the advantage of bringing younger people into the local authority at a time when few vacancies are available. It can however be questioned whether this is the best use that can be made of section 137 funds in order to create jobs since the scheme provides work for a set number of employees and cannot be used to stimulate the generation of jobs by supplementing funds from the private sector.

Many local authorities have made considerable use of training schemes sponsored by the Manpower Services Commission in order to employ more workers. These schemes are con- sidered in more detail in Chapter 12. Efforts have also been made to mitigate the effects of unemployment through the use of more novel conditions of service. Job sharing is for example encouraged by a number of local authorities in order to ensure at least some work for a greater number of individuals and also to enable more women with children to gain work. Neither job sharing schemes nor the MSC training projects should however be considered as more than palliatives to unemployment since they do not represent the creation of permanent full time jobs.

PURCHASING AND 'BUY LOCAL' POLICIES

Although the greatest proportion of local authority revenue
pays wages, large sums of money are also spent by local
authorities on goods and services. A large authority such
as Sheffield Metropolitan District in 1983 awarded contracts
to businesses totalling £80 million of which £24 million went
to local firms. It does not require much imagination on the
part of local authorities to realise that the local economy
will benefit if expenditure on goods and services is placed
with local firms. An increasing number of Councils are
developing schemes to ensure that wherever possible they will
buy local goods and services. Mid Glamorgan County Council
has been one of the leaders in this movement and the idea
is also well established in Nottingham, Sheffield, Leeds and
South Yorkshire. Many other authorities such as Oldham
District Council are also aware of the value of buying local
products even though they have yet to develop a systematic
method of achieving this aim.

Despite the obvious value for a local authority of a 'buy
local' policy these schemes are faced with a number of
financial and legal problems. It is not possible for a
Council to affirm a minuted policy to buy solely local goods
since this strategy would be contrary to EEC regulations
which require any organisation to allow firms within the
Common Market to tender for contracts. It is also imprudent
for an authority to purchase local goods if they are more
costly or inferior in quality to similar products that can
be obtained elsewhere. A rigid local purchasing policy may
not only be impractical for many goods it could also run
foul of district auditors if a local authority does not
purchase goods at a reasonable price. Although these factors
require local authorities to be prudent in developing schemes
to buy locally, or even in a wider context to buy British,
they do not rule out the possibility of obtaining many goods
on advantageous terms from local businesses. Local authorities which have developed strategies to buy local products
do not usually give this policy formal status but ensure
that the Council's purchasing officers are aware of the value
of obtaining goods from local firms. This form of understanding is best facilitated if the council has a strong
continutity of political control and officers who are
sympathetic with the aims of the councillors. The strategy
also requires a well organised and preferably centralised
system of purchasing within the authority. If each

163

individual council department is permitted to buy goods and services it requires it will be much more difficult for councillors or senior officers to impose a think local attitude on a dispersed group of purchasing officers. It will also be less likely in such circumstances that the purchasing officers can pool information on the availability of local products and therefore gain a high level of knowledge about local firms and their potential. Many of the local authorities that attempt, whenever possible, to buy local goods, such as Leeds Metropolitan District, have established a strong central purchasing department through which all local authority buying must be channelled.

A further difficulty facing local purchasing schemes is the problem of finding out what firms within a particular area can or will make. In highly industrialised areas few councillors or officers will have an extensive knowledge of the range and scope of local firms let alone the nature and worth of their products. Councils have discovered that goods which were imported from abroad are made only a few miles away. A by-product of a local trade exhibition organised by Oldham District Council was that a local firm could supply goods to the authority that were previously obtained in Europe. Most councils with a well established strategy for local purchasing rely on the experience and knowledge of their purchasing officers and may expect them to acquire as much information as possible about local businesses. Mid Glamorgan County Council has developed a more systematic method of identifying local firms and their interests by constructing a products register which provides details of local businesses and the goods or services they can sell. The list is open to other small Councils, firms or individuals within the County and it is therefore hoped that it will enable other organisations to buy locally. Although of considerable value an effective products register requires considerable research and is a relatively expensive undertaking. Several other local authorities such as South Yorkshire County Council nevertheless regard the exercise as a success and have taken up the idea.

A strategy to buy local products will have several obvious advantages for any authority wishing to aid its economy. Money obtained from local taxation will be returned to the community and as a result local industry will gain con-siderable benefits. Firms operating close to the local authority may also be able to supply goods at advantageous terms to the council since delivery costs will be lower. It is also possible for local firms more rapidly to ensure maintenance of equipment and a number of authorities frequently devise tendering specifications to advantage these firms. The proximity of a firm to its local authority can also promote an understanding of each other's needs and capabilities. Such a relationship can lead to the local authority negotiating prior to tendering with a local business an arrangement to supply goods that is advantageous to both organisations and better than can be obtained from other firms in open tendering.

Local purchasing clearly has advantages from a parochial point of view but it may also be critised from this standpoint. If all local authorities insisted only on purchasing goods made within their area many industries would start loosing contracts to supply more distant authorities. Taken to its logical conclusion buying local could lead to the development of many small firms in each local authority area bound closely to the needs of the authority. These firms would be relatively small and vulnerable to changes in Council policy. Local purchasing clearly has its advantages but also must be managed with due regard to the needs of larger firms within a community to supply goods to a much wider market than a particular area of the country and the security and potential for growth of smaller companies.

CONTRACT COMPLIANCE

An important development flowing from a realisation by local authorities of their purchasing powers is to demand that suppliers of goods and services comply with acceptable working practices. Under section 135 of the 1972 Local Government Act all local authorities are obliged to maintain lists of approved firms which are allowed to tender for local authority contracts and must draw up standing orders to regulate admission to the list. It has been realised by a number of radical authorities and in particular Sheffield City Council and the Greater London Council that they can make stringent demands on contractors to provide acceptable working conditions for their employees. The process of establishing these conditions and ensuring that firms accept and practice them is referred to by these authorities as 'contract compliance', a term which was originally used in the United States when efforts were made to ensure that companies working for the Federal Government adopted policies of positive discrimination in favour of black people.

Contract compliance has been most extensively developed by Sheffield District and Greater London Councils in relation to the building and construction industry. They require

that firms wishing to tender for building contracts complete
a detailed questionnaire concerning their working practices
and capacity to undertake particular contacts. In Sheffield
they must be able to assure the Council that they will adhere
to the Health and Safety at Works Act and for contracts of
over £10,000 provide a detailed statement on how the project
will be executed safely. In order to ensure that promises
are fulfilled the Council's safety officers must be given
free access to the building site. The Authority also demands
that contractors employ apprentices who should number at
least 10% of the workforce and steps must also be taken
to encourage the employment of ethnic minority workers and
women. It is strongly recommended that all employees are
able to join a trade union and that the firm will itself be
a member of any appropriate trades association. It is
demanded that the builder pays a fair wage which is not less
than those generally applied throughout the industry. Firms
accepting a contract are also unable to employ sub-contractors
without the approval of the local authority and these will be
unacceptable if they do not conform to the standards expected
of the main contractors. In particular the Authority is able
to reject sub-contractors who supply only their labour and
are used by firms as a means of evading the responsibilities
they must accept to workers directly in their employment.
(Sheffield City Council 1984d)

The Greater London Council has adopted a similar set of
regulations to those imposed by Sheffield and lays particular
emphasis on the need for equal opportunities for women and
minority groups. Both Authorities have established small
departments to implement the strategy, which they initiated
in 1983. The process of monitoring contracts compliance is
a major undertaking. The Construction Industry Contracts
Compliance Unit which has been established by the GLC must
monitor the working practices of some 4000 firms and requires
officers who have considerable knowledge of the building
industry.

It is too early to assess the impact of contracts compliance
policies on the construction industry although it is probable
given the value of local authority building, modernisation
and repairs contracts that if effectively applied the
strategy can have a considerable effect on the industry. Both
the GLC and Sheffield have demonstrated that they are prepared
to use their powers to exclude firms that do not conform
to their conditions from their lists of approved contractors.
Businesses have been removed from the list in Sheffield for

reasons such as the failure to employ apprentices or provide
safe working conditions. The removal of a firm is not
however the object of the exercise and only takes place after
the company has failed to take heed of warnings from the
local authority. The purpose of the policy is to improve
the standards of working conditions within the industry
rather than exclude firms from taking on public works
contracts.

Although well developed in relation to the construction
industry the GLC and Sheffield City Council have not yet
turned their policy towards contractors and suppliers in
other areas of the Councils' work. A number of Enterprise
Boards however effectively pursue the principles of contract
compliance by demanding that firms which receive aid from
these organisations conform to working practices acceptable
to the local authority. It is also probable that the policy
will be extended to other local authority contracts if the
Government force local authorities to accept tenders from
private firms for many of their services. This course of
action will be adopted not only as a means of ensuring that
local authority departments can tender for their own contracts
on equal terms with the private sector. In services such
as cleansing or catering as well as the building industry
it is possible for private firms to undercut local authority
tenders by employing labour at lower than normal rates,
avoiding the responsibility of training apprentices or cutting
corners on safety. Local authorities argue that their departments should be allowed by central government to compete on
equal terms with the private sector and therefore have the
right to demand that private contractors submit to the
conditions that they expect from their own departments. The
imposition of such standards may well ensure that local
authorities can continue to provide services under their
direct control even when they are obliged to submit contracts
for services to competitive tender.

The possibility of legislation similar to that regulating
Direct Labour Organisations demanding open tendering for
local authority contracts has created considerable interest
within other local authorities. A conference organised by
Sheffield City Council in September 1984 on the strategy
as applied to the construction industry attracted over
200 delegates from local authorities throughout the country
and far exceeded the hopes of its organisers in respect to
its attendance. It is probable that in the next few years
the policy of contract compliance will become a much more
widely practiced strategy and also be adopted to a wider range
of local authority contracts and purchasing.

Few local authorities have been enthusiastic about the policies of central government during the last few decades and many are now in open revolt against demands for cuts or privatisation of services that are emanating from the Conservative Government elected in 1979, and again in 1983. More cautious minded councils find themselves caught between a desire to maintain their service and levels of employment and a fear of the electoral consequences of large rate rises. These authorities tend to steer a judicious compromise between cuts and higher rates but even when Conservative controlled are given to behind the scenes pressuring of government either directly or through the local authority associations, to improve their financial position. The more radical Labour controlled authorities are more publicly active in their opposition to any cuts in services or loss of powers that may be imposed by central government.

Many local authorities and at some time all the local authority associations have campaigned against the reforms of local government finance put forward by the Thatcher Governments. The Labour Group controlling Liverpool District Council in 1983/84 threatened to pass a budget based on a deficit if it were unable, because of Government policy, to carry out the policies for which it was elected. Their campaign made much of the loss of jobs in the city and their role in counteracting unemployment and was aimed at generating popular support for the Council. A campaign to prevent the 1984 Rates Act has also emphasised that council spending is closely interconnected with employment. Sheffield Metropolitan District Council for example has emphasised throughout its publicity opposing the bill that it is the largest single employer of labour within the city and spends over £24 million on goods and services purchased from local firms.

The campaigns to prevent the abolition of the Metropolitan Counties and the Greater London Council have also emphasised the implications of this policy for employment within the affected areas. (Greater London Council 1984c) Although the report commissioned by the threatened Councils from accountants Coopers and Lybrand suggests that jobs may have to be created as a result of the Government proposals if District Councils do not co-operate with one another (Coopers and Lybrand 1984). Both the GLC (Greater London Council 1983e) and the West Midlands County Council (West Midlands County Council, 1984) have issued reports emphasising the effects of their abolition on employment

168

creation within their regions. The West Midlands County
Council Report observes that:-

> 'Despite the importance attached to the Economic
> Development function by all seven authorities in
> question (together they now commit resources
> totalling at least £85 m per annum in this field)
> it is not treated as a distinct service by the white
> paper. (West Midland County Council, 1984   p1)

and notes that the Government considers that since district
councils already have powers to aid industry no new arrangements are necessary in this respect. It can however be
seriously questioned whether in London or the Metropolitan
Counties there can be sufficient co-ordination among district
councils to continue some of the more ambitious employment
schemes such as the Enterprise Boards that have been
developed by these authorities.

A number of Labour controlled councils are also becoming
concerned at the possibility that the government will demand
local authorities privatise many of their existing services.
Although local authorities, even on the left, may not, have
much enthusiasm for expanding their economic influence
through municipalisation they are clearly prepared to defend
their existing service roles. Although not directly
connected with employment a vigorous campaign was waged by
a few authorities against compulsory sales of council
housing and Norwich District Council pursued the issue to
the margins of legality. The GLC objected to the transfer
of London Transport to a Government appointed body designed
to run the organisation on strictly commercial lines
considering that the change in management could lead to a
loss of 12,000 jobs. Sheffield City Council is sufficiently
concerned at the possibility of further pressures to privatise
services such as cleansing that it is preparing information
to aid the defence of the service.

The methods used by local authorities to pursue campaigns
against loss of revenue, abolition or privatisation follow
the patterns outlined in Chapter 8 concerning political
campaigns. Considerable effort is placed not only on
developing well researched arguments in favour of a
council's position on these issues but in presenting them
not only to the good and the great of Whitehall but to the
public in general. The GLC, with resources unmatched by
other councils, has in particular waged a campaign against
its abolition that few can escape. Underlying such action
are efforts closely to co-ordinate local government
strategies through a growing industry of ad-hoc local

authority conferences to debate and to discuss challenges to
their powers. Within the councils efforts are made to form
joint committees between the elected politicians, trade
unionists and local government officers to develop solidarity
and unity of purpose throughout the service. At the end of
the day if these campaigns fail then many local authorities will
be forced to become contributors to the pool of unemployed.

10 Municipal enterprise

It has been shown in Part I that during the late 19th Century local authority intervention in the economy progressed largely through the process of municipalisation. As a consequence of a few general powers and for the most part private acts, city councils were operating gas, electricity and water undertakings, buses and tramways, ports and harbours, and as building contractors. The growth of this form of intervention declined by 1920 when it became difficult to steer private bills that extended municipal ownership through parliament. After 1945 successive Labour and Conservative governments removed from local control several of the more profitable commercial undertakings whilst other activities such as the provision of public transport were increasingly operated as social services rather than profit making ventures. Despite these pressures local authorities still retain considerable powers to establish commercial and industrial undertakings under their direct control. It will be argued in this chapter that local authorities have not developed their potential in this area despite their renewed interest in economic intervention.

The term 'municipal enterprise' requires some clarification since many local authority activities can be argued to operate along commercial lines in the sense that they attempt to minimise their economic costs. Municipal enterprise is however taken here to denote a local government activity which may be termed municipal trading in which a business is operated with a view to making profit for the local authority, or an undertaking that provides a service for the internal use of the council at a generally cheaper cost than could be obtained on the open market. In some cases such as the provision of public transport considerable argument may occur as to whether such an activity should be profitable or receive subsidies from the local authorities general fund. Since most if not all local authorities subsidise their bus services these ventures are not considered within this section and are discussed as an element of local authority infra-structure in Chapter 5.

If we exempt transport there are few examples of municipal trading in terms of an activity designed largely to make a profit from the public. General powers to establish profitable ventures applicable to all local authorities are few in number. The 1947 Civic Restaurants Act permits local authorities to establish cafes and restaurants provided that these can make a profit. Under the 1949 Air Corporations Act it is possible for local authorities to maintain municipal airports and through the Food and Drug Act of 1955 local authorities may establish markets or maintain slaughterhouses.

Even though successive governments have not encouraged municipal trading there is little to suggest that many local authorities are particularly interested in developing the opportunities open to them under existing legislation. The establishment of a municipal airport will be necessarily limited to a few cities which are sufficiently large to require such a facility but there is a need for cafes and restaurants in all parts of the country. Few authorities have however made full use of their powers to cater at a profit to the public.

Municipal catering

Local authorities obtained powers to sell food and drink in their halls and leisure centres through the Public Health Amendment Act of 1907 and the Physical Training and Recreation Act of 1937. Many councils made use of this legislation to set up small catering outlets and bars in public halls and parks but few developed their powers under the 1947 Civic Restaurants Act to run municipal restaurants in town centres. The Act allowed local authorities to take over the British Restaurants which had been formed by the government in 1941 in order to ensure that, despite the privations of war, the people of Britain could obtain cheap and nutritious if not exotic meals that would fortify them in their efforts to save the Nation. The British restaurants were managed by local authorities although their capital equipment was supplied by the government and any profit or loss made by the undertaking went to the Treasury. In 1947 the restaurants were quietly passed to local government as largely profitable undertakings.

Although municipal catering was relatively successful in the late 1940s many council managed restaurants went into a

serious decline in the 1950s and there are now very few
municipal restaurants catering for the general public
(Civic Catering Association 1977). The Civic Catering
Association, which was formed in 1962, has around 75 member
authorities but most of them are concerned with operating
services that can be accommodated within the earlier
catering acts in the form of bars and cafeterias in civic
halls, community centres or places for sport and recreation.
A number of authorities in coastal resorts such as Brighton
may nevertheless develop these outlets into considerable
ventures with a large financial turnover and pay roll.
Rotherham District Council remains one of the few authorities
still operating civic restaurants under the terms of the
1947 Act and has established the only separate catering sub-
committee within any English local authority. In addition
to its public restaurants Rotherham also holds contracts for
catering in a number of local factories and has sufficient
food processing requirements to operate a bakery and meat
processing plant. Birmingham Metropolitan District
developed a profitable trade in industrial catering and until
recently had contracts to provide food in some 50 industrial
plants within the city. These councils which are active in
providing public catering services are however the exception.

The atrophy of municipal catering has been argued to be in
part a consequence of:-

> 'the inability of councillors and senior officers
> to understand the principles of successful municipal
> trading in the catering field......the problems of
> setting up a business and operating a viable unit
> are not fully understood at the outset and not
> easily changed at a later date' (Civic Catering
> Association, 1977, p4).

The ability of local authority personnel, whether elected or
appointed to manage a business reflects a wider problem
within local government that undermines their ability to
successfully influence their local economies. In the more
interventionist minded authorities the controlling
councillors are rarely businessmen whilst the local government service rarely recruits officers with any direct
experience of industry and does not train its personnel to
appreciate the problems of business management. The Civic
Catering Association identified two further causes of the
failure of municipal catering which illustrate the lack of
business sense within local government. They complained of:-

> 'The tendency to set up a large organisation to
> control small businesses thus loosing sight of all
> common sense, particularly in financial matters.'

173

and:-

> 'Complexity in the financial structure of most
> catering departments and the apportionment of
> central administration charges for the services
> received from the Treasurer's and other Departments
> of the Council' (Civic Catering Association, 1977,
> p4).

These problems have been a particular concern of the
Director of Catering for Rotherham Metropolitan District
Council who argues that his organisation was faced with
higher charges than would be faced by a private catering
firm of equivalent size and that these costs resulted in his
department showing in recent years an apparent trading
deficit. Expenses included not only payment of rent and
rates to the Treasurer's Department but fees for central
administrative services. These costs may be offset by
lower rates of taxation but notwithstanding this factor
were being made by his department to other sections of the
same authority which obscured the fact that the catering
enterprise was probably putting more money into the authority
than it was taking out. At least in the case of catering
local authorities have been the reverse of the image of
reckless spenders of public money on non-viable projects.
They have instead been so cautious and insecure in their
accounting methods that they have made it almost impossible
to record profits on what may in many cases be financially
successful businesses.

Ports and airports

Municipal airports appear to be a somewhat more widely
recognised example of local authority trading since there are
at present 23 airports owned by individual councils or
consortia of local authorities. The largest of these is
Manchester airport which is controlled jointly by the
District Council and Greater Manchester County Council. It
employs almost as many workers as all the remaining
municipal airports put together. (Local Government Chronicle
27 Nov 1981). Several other airports owned by local
authorities such as Birmingham handle international traffic
although at the other extreme are a number of very small
ventures for light aircraft.

Despite the frequent nationalisation of local authority
ventures that cater for more than specifically local needs
the government has so far resisted the temptation to place
municipal airports under the control of the Civil Airports
Authority. Local authorities have maintained, so far

successfully, that the noise and inconvenience caused by
airports to local residents is a sufficiently serious
matter to require regulation by local representatives.
Ownership of an airfield has one further advantage of
enhancing the attraction of the area to industrialists. A
large airport such as Manchester which handles tourist
charter flights may also foster the development of hotel
facilities and can bring visitors into the city.

The Air Corporations Act of 1949 which allows the establishment of municipal airports does not demand that they should
make a profit. The government however affirmed in the 1978
White Paper on Airports Policy that they would not provide
any subsidies to local authorities wishing to set up an
airport. Until the late 1970s municipal airports rarely
made a surplus, although Manchester has been an exception
generating a profit of between 8 to 10 million per year in
the early 1980s (Local Government Chronicle 27 Nov 1981).
Much of the failure to make profits from airports was due to
unrealistic pricing by local authorities for their services
and to a lesser extent the added costs of internal administrative charges. In recent years most airport authorities
have been able to increase their charges to users of airports
without any diminution in business and have subsequently
become much more successful financially. In 1979/80 at
least half the municipal airports made a profit and the sum
of losses and gains for all airports was a surplus of around
£5 million (Local Government Chronicle 27 Nov 1981).

The successes of municipal airports are not reflected in
the returns for municipally controlled docks and harbours.
A number of local authorities act as port authorities
through private acts although the extent of council ownership
and management of harbours is less extensive than in the 19th
Century. The Borough of Liverpool for example at one time
owned docks but pressures from ship owners and the ability
of interested parties to build new harbours outside the city
limits have placed the control of most major port complexes
in Britain in the hands of private companies or public
boards. Bristol is the only local authority that retains
control of a major port facility. The docks of Bristol and
Avonmouth are administered by Bristol District Council which
has made strenuous efforts to modernise the facility although
the ports, like many other older harbours, lose money. In
1979/80 Bristol District Council lost £7.7 million on its
docks and harbours account (The Times 21 April 1981). Apart
from Bristol a number of other local authorities such as
Preston own smaller ports and harbours. Cumbria County
Council obtained at a minimal payment the docks at Workington

as recently as 1975 when the previous owners British Steel began closing iron and steel production within the town. The docks were obtained not with a view to making a profit on the acquisition but because 'the loss of the port would be a serious blow to West Cumberland's industrial prospects' (Cumbria Co-ordinating Committee, 1973, p1661).

Other trading ventures

In addition to powers to operate restaurants local authorities have general powers to control a few other profitable commercial ventures which can generate a modest if rarely substantial profit as traditionally managed. The 1955 Food and Drug Act permits councils to establish and maintain commercial markets and these are usually operated so as to bring the authority a modest surplus. Sheffield City Council for example raised over £1 million in 1983/84 through its markets account. The same Act allows local authorities, primarily in the interests of public health, to operate abattoirs although in recent years the establishment of large meat processing facilities by major food companies has led to the demise of many municipal abattoirs. In the case of both markets and abattoirs local authorities have shown no enthusiasm for developing their powers in these areas to establish major commercial ventures even though such action may be technically possible.

A number of local authorities still retain unique local trading practices which were obtained during the palmy days of private bills. These include the municipalisation of the St Ledger which is run on Doncaster Race Course owned by the Metropolitan District Council. More commercially significant is the telephone system operated by Hull District Council. The City established its own service in 1903 when the council bought a telephone exchange and in the following year an agreement with the British Telphone Company, later to be incorporated into the Post Office, to retain control of the Hull telephone services on a renewable contract which provided the national system with a 10% royalty on receipts (Calvert, 1978).

In terms of the impact a commercial venture can make on local economic developments financial institutions clearly play a major role and consequently municipalisation of banks would have a very significant value to present day efforts by local government to create employment. The rise and fall of the Birmingham Municipal Savings Bank is therefore an important illustration of the failures of municipalisation.

In 1916 legislation permitted the establishment of savings banks by local authorities as a means of aiding the war economy. The banks were only able to accept funds deposited by employers on behalf of their workforce and were to be disbanded three months after the cessation of hostilities. Only one authority, Birmingham City Council, took up the scheme. The venture was, after a faltering start, sufficiently successful to prompt the City Council to seek the continuation of the bank after the war on more commercial terms. In 1919 Birmingham gained powers within a private bill to establish a savings bank that would 'act in accordance with such regulations as the Treasury or Treasury with Corporation approval may provide'. (Committee on Municipal Savings Banks 1928).

In practice the bill allowed Birmingham's savings bank to receive most of its deposits from small investors in the manner of the Trustees Savings Banks. The city then re-invested the money either as loans to local people wishing to buy homes or in the City Council. It was also possible to invest in Treasury Stock but the bank rarely took up this option and preferred to keep the money deposited by Birmingham savers within the city. (Committee on Municipal Savings Banks 1928). Birmingham used its bank as an alternative means of providing council mortgages and could borrow money from it at a slightly better rate than could be obtained from other financial institutions. There were however major restraints on the use that could be made of the Bank which was unable to invest in equities and therefore be used to fund local industry.

Following Birmingham's success in establishing a municipal bank that provided cheap funds for the City Council and also generated a trading profit a number of other councils tried to found similar institutions. Swansea petitioned parliament on three occasions for such powers but was never successful. The possibility of extending municipal banking powers was finally put to rest in 1928 when a committee established by the Treasury reported that there was little justification in extending the powers of local authorities to cover a field of activity that was already adequately catered for by trustees savings banks and building societies. Municipal savings banks could only be successful 'at the expense of other institutions' (Committee on Municipal Savings Banks 1928 p34). The decision which was readily accepted by parliament is an indication of the changed attitudes towards municipal enterprise that had taken place after the First World War.

Birmingham Municipal Savings Bank continued to flourish until 1976 when it became, as a result of Labour government legislation on savings banks, a Trustees Savings Bank. The City Council was able to retain a measure of control through their nomination of trustees to the new institution. The move was however a step towards a further re-organisation in 1979 when the Bank was fully integrated into the regional structures of the Trustees Savings Bank.

The demise of municipal banking and the ineffectiveness of municipal catering illustrate the lack of enthusiasm for municipal trading among local authorities. This disinterest is still apparent even among the most radical and interventionist minded authorities. The Greater London Council has for example considered a number of possible ventures connected with internal trading but considers that the promotion of investment and control over public trading ventures lies in the activities of its Enterprise Board rather than in directly controlled operations whose profits could be used to subsidise other areas of the Council's activities. Sheffield Metropolitan District although much less enthusiastic about operating an enterprise board has sought to expand its internal trading organisations but not trading to the public. They have opened a recording studio as a means of giving help to hopeful pop music groups and taken over a failing commercial cinema but these ventures are as much motivated by artistic interest as a desire to develop their trading powers. The Council has investigated the possibility of offering estate agency or legal services to the public but have not pursued these ideas even though in the opinion of one officer concerned with developing activities in this field it is usually possible legally to find ways of carrying out most activities. It is even considered by the Authority that it may be legally permissible for them directly to buy equity in an external company without any intermediary organisation such as an enterprise board being established. The major restraint on developing municipal trading has been, at least for Sheffield, fears over the financial viability of possible schemes.

INTERNAL TRADING

Under section 111 of the 1972 Local Government Act it is possible for local authorities 'to do anything...which is calculated to facilitate or is conducive or incidental to the discharge of any of their functions'. This clause was designed to accommodate the considerable variety of municipal enterprises designed to supply goods and services that are needed by the authority. A council can manufacture goods or provide services that it requires not only for its own use but also through a consortium agreement for a number of authorities through sections 101 and 136 of the 1972 Local Government Act. It is also possible to sell surplus goods manufactured under these arrangements to the public and it could even be suggested that a local authority would have a duty to sell goods and services at a profit from such a venture because of its duty to minimise the burden on the ratepayers.

Despite the considerable opportunities for local authorities to manufacture their own goods and operate their own services either acting alone or with other public bodies they have with a few exceptions made little use of these powers. The most important exception is the widespread, though by no means universal, creation of direct labour organisations to construct and maintain council property. Outside the building and construction trades local authorities manufacture very few goods for their own use and are only slightly more enthusiastic about providing their own services with the exception of professional tasks such as accounting or soliciting in the legal sense, that have been accepted as an integral profession with local government.

Direct Labour Organisations

Direct Labour Organisations have had a considerable impact on the building and construction trades of larger cities. The first of these undertakings was established, under Fabian influence, by the Metropolitan Board of Works in 1982 and later was incorporated into the London County Council. Several other London authorities followed its example in the 1980s (Langford 1892). By 1980 before the passing of the Local Government Planning and Land Act which restricted the operation of direct works departments most council house building and repairs were carried out by direct labour organisations and their work at times extended to other forms of construction such as road building or water supply and drainage works. A large local authority works department could be a major employer within the local building and construction industry. In the 1970s the direct labour organisation operated by Manchester District Council provided work for 3000 individuals.

Conservative opposition to direct Labour Organisation has occasioned considerable controversy as to the merits in terms of profitability and efficiency between publicly and privately owned building contractors. It is however pointed

out by Langford (1982) that the value of direct labour
organisation should not be judged solely on these criteria
although he established a case study format in which:-

'D.L.Os and contractors of similar size operating on
similar types and size of contract were compared by
direct observation. The results of these observations
show that the output of direct labour and private
contractors are similar. (Langford 1982 p102).

Given a similarity of performance on criteria of efficiency
it may be argued that direct labour organisations have a
distinct edge on private contractors as a result of other
advantages. In private hands the building and construction
industry often fosters unsatisfactory working conditions
from the standpoint of a local authority that is interested in
ensuring that a high level of permanent employment opportunities is available within its community. Many of the largest
construction companies will be based outside the area of the
local authority and the award of contracts to such companies
will take money and control of employment out of the locality.
Construction companies frequently employ transient casual
labour for the duration of a particular contract and will
dismiss workers on completion with little obligation to
provide redundancy or severance pay. The casual employment
practices of building firms also allow companies to avoid
payment of pension funds to deal with the collection of
taxes. Although private building contractors may take on
apprentices and are encouraged to do so by training board
subsidies they have no obligation to keep them in their
employment once they have qualified in a trade. In contrast
local authority direct labour organisations normally employ
their workforce on a permanent basis under the same
conditions as council workmen in other departments. Many
direct labour organisations also feel that they are obliged
to train a number of apprentices even though they receive
less favourable subsidies for doing so than private firms
and have to retain the apprentices in their employment if
they choose to remain on the council's payroll.

In comparison with most private construction companies
direct labour organisations provide a source of considerable
employment stability within the building industry. They
ensure that local construction projects employ workers
resident in the local authority area and that their workers
can receive pension and insurance rights along with a
permanent job. Apart from the benefits that better working
conditions give council employees in the long term such
employment practices will prevent many workers from becoming
recipients of state and local authority welfare provisions

once they are unable to work. Local authority direct labour organisations are also frequently the only permanent employer of apprentices in the local building trades and may therefore have a significant role in training construction workers for both their own and private contractors.

The employment practices of direct labour organisations may be in the long term far more beneficial to the local community but such conditions can only be obtained at a cost. It has been estimated by one chairman of a direct works committee that their labour costs will be at least 20% higher than for a private firm tendering for the same contract. In addition to this cost, direct labour organisations are subject to internal authority charges which, like those imposed on catering departments, ensure that the costs of operating such organisations appear to be greater on the council than is the case. The implementation of the Local Government, Planning and Land Act which was designed to ensure that direct labour organisations compete with private firms for most contracts valued at over £1000 and for at least 2/3 of maintenance programmes has created serious problems for many direct labour organisations. A number of authorities such as Manchester have severely reduced the number of their employees whilst one authority, Hammersmith, has effectively agreed to hand over its building interests to Bovis a major private building contractor.

Other forms of internal trading

Apart from direct works departments other forms of municipal trading to supply the local authority are on a much smaller scale. Most larger authorities operate their own printing services and this work often extends to book binding. The need to produce volumes of legally required documents such as committee minutes at short notice ensures that a municipally controlled printing service that can order priorities to suit council requirements is of importance to a local authority irrespective of any savings it may make on the activity. Parks and gardens departments will frequently supply most of their own plants and some larger authorities have turned their attention to the production of trees.

Few authorities extend their internal trading beyond the activities already outlined and perhaps more surprisingly few appear to have much enthusiasm for expanding into new ventures. The Greater London Labour Party proposed in its 1981 manifesto an ambitious project to restore a bus factory to London by manufacturing vehicles for London Transport. The project however has sunk with the transfer of control over

London Transport. Sheffield City Council has investigated,
as has the G.L.C, the possibility of cleaning its own
windows with its own workers and Sheffield is to operate its
own security guard service.

THE ATROPHY OF MUNICIPAL TRADING

It has been observed in this chapter that local authorities
make little use of their opportunities to develop municipal
trading. Only in the area of building and construction
has the idea of municipalisation continued to flourish and
it is significant that this activity was established at a
time when municipal trading was a more acceptable venture.
In effect it is the one major activity remaining from the
better days of municipal trading that has not, like gas
and electricity supply, been removed from local government
or become, as public transport, more of a subsidised service
than a profitable venture. In areas such as catering where
later legislation specifically allows a local authority to
trade in a highly profitable industry little effort has been
made by local authorities to use the proffered powers. The
lack of enthusiasm appears to extend to radical local
authorities of the 1980s that are deeply concerned with the
need to intervene within the economy of their communities.

  Municipal trading has a venerable place in the written
cannons of British socialism with both the Webbs and
George Bernard Shaw enthusiastically working in favour of the
idea. Few British socialists however absorb their ideas
from the printed page. For Bernard Shaw municipal enterprise
was simply common sense (Shaw 1906). Profits obtained from
municipal trading can be used either to offset higher rate
demands or improve services. By developing its own enterprises for either external or internal trading it is possible for
a council to ensure that locally raised resources are
ploughed back into the community and used to create further
local employment. The policy may in this respect be seen
as having a similar role to 'buy local' strategies. In
addition to these advantages an authority can use enterprises
under its control to set standards for working conditions, job
training or consumer services that may be matched by private
firms within the area. Politically a business controlled by
the elected local council is likely to be controlled by
individuals who have the interests of the local community at
heart. If councillors fail to reflect local interests they
may be subject to pressures that could force them from
office. A privately owned business in contrast need pay
little attention to local interests when determining its

commercial policies. A municipally owned venture in Liverpool would for example be unlikely to move to the South East.

There are however a number of well tried objections to the use of municipal enterprise which helped bring to an end the expansion of this activity in the 1920s. It can be claimed that publically controlled business is likely to be inefficient since it is not based on the desire for personal gain, the profit motive. Without such a spur a local authority may be able to use its ability to raise taxation in order to offset losses and inefficiency within their businesses that would have driven a private company into bankruptcy. Private entrepreneurs are also concerned about the possibility that public monies could be used to undersell their companies.

Many conservative authorities will be easily persuaded that there is substance in these objections although their views are generally more a reflection of political values than empirically verifiable economic theory. It has been shown earlier in the chapter that in the case of municipal catering in Rotherham Metropolitan District the local authority imposes a more stringent test of profitability than would be faced by a private company. Even the most radical local authority will moreover be concerned at any serious losses made by a municipal enterprise. Sheffield City Council closed its abattoir in 1982 on the grounds that it was unprofitable. Local authorities are publically accountable organisations open to official criticism concerning financial loss from the district auditor, opposition parties, the press and finally and on occasion decisively through the ballot box.

Although 'free enterprise' arguments against municipal trading may influence most Conservative, and not a few cautious Labour controlled councils, this line of argument is unlikely greatly to exercise the minds of all Labour authorities and especially those that are in the forefront on employment creation initiatives. To some extent their lack of enthusiasm may be a reflection of the disappearance of the ideal of socialism through local government as a result of success at a national level. When in 1945 an approximation to the ownership of the means of production and the welfare state could be imposed throughout the country by a Labour Party in power there was little enthusiasm among its leaders for allowing such goals to be implemented by a motley collection of local authorities.

Radical labour councils of the 1980s do not however have a high regard for the centralising policies of the Attlee government. A more practical objection from councils dedicated to cutting unemployment figures is that many schemes of municipalisation would, if commercially successful, lead to a loss of jobs rather than their creation. A municipal housing office that replicated many of the services provided by estate agents would for example cut costs to home buyers but might remove rather than create jobs if it forced private estate agencies out of business.

A further restraint on the development of municipalisation is the divergent attitudes and values held by left wing Labour councillors and local government officers. Professionals in local government with few exceptions have little or no experience of business management and are tutored in more cautious forms of accounting and investment than would be practised by most successful entrepreneurs. The attitudes that, according to the Civic Catering Association, undermined the success of municipal restaurants pervades many other areas of local government. There may also be a reluctance on the part of some left wing Labour councillors to pursue policies of municipalisation since this may compromise their ideological position by forcing them into the role of an entrepreneur rather than a critic of capitalism. Labour Party politicians may also be wary of conflict with Trade Unions or in the case of industries such as catering be aware that profits are often made as a result of poor working conditions and opposition to trade unionism.

A combination of these factors appear to have motivated many radical councillors to edge away from economic intervention by means of gaining direct controls over new business ventures even though they may vigorously campaign against the privatisation of those activites which they have traditionally controlled. The antipathy towards acting as a capitalist may also incline many Labour controlled authorities more readily to turn to Enterprise Boards as a means of financial intervention in the local economy than municipal trading. The day to day work of most Enterprise Boards is conducted by its officers who are frequently recruited from business management whilst the control exerted by politicians is more distantly exercised through a board of directors that will be composed largely but not exclusively of a small group of councillors.

11 Economic activity and local authority organisation

The sheer scale of economic contraction occurring within some
of the older cities and regions has necessitated the adoption
of new administrative structures by many local authorities.
As Bramley et al (1978) have pointed out the adoption of
economically orientated objectives by local government raises
a number of issues relating to the emergence and implementation
of policy. For instance authorities will need to clarify the
direction of economic policy, debate the problems economically
orientated goals can create, achieve successful co-ordination
of activities, establish effective organisational structures
and create a strategy that can guide action. It is by no means
certain that many authorities have achieved these organisational goals. Nevertheless there has been a change in administrative structures within many authorities intended to improve
both the definition of policy and the organisation of relevant
expertise. Each of these developments will be explored in
turn.

THE STRUCTURING OF ECONOMIC POLICY

For much of the post-war period many cities and counties
adopted a laissez-faire attitude to economic policy. Struthers
and Williamson (1979) for instance in discussing Merseyside
point out that regional strategies for the North-West published
as late as 1974 continued to assume economic stability within
the area. This attitude would have been paralleled in many
other regional plans and the structure plans emerging out of
the 1968 and 1971 Town and Country Planning Acts. The economic
parameters within which national and local planners were
operating were of course different. Planning needed only to
guide, and indeed in some cases resist, economic growth. The
problems were those of over-heating, not severe recession.

Attitudes were rapidly to change in the 1970's and 1980's.
In areas such as Liverpool (Struthers and Williamson 1979),

Manchester (Manchester Metropolitan District 1981) and the West
Midlands (West Midlands County Council 1978) either through
analyses undertaken as part of structure plan preparation or as
independent exercises, it became increasingly obvious that
severe decline was occurring in many cities and regions of the
United Kingdom. This was becoming apparent because, in part,
of the activities of planning authorities operating at both
county and city levels. By examining local closures and
contractions, the likely performance of locally important
economic sectors, trends in the labour market, the likelihood
of new employment sources and so on, authorities began to
highlight the probable scale of impending employment contraction. These monitoring and research activities proved
invaluable to many authorities in that future trends were
identified and the case for intervention amply justified. In
particular it was apparent to many authorities that continued
decline would be associated with, and in turn accentuate,
unemployment, poverty, declining rate bases, social strife and
demand for welfare provision (Wandsworth 1972).

In considering their response to economic decline however it
became apparent to some authorities that the traditional
planning structure would not prove especially suitable for more
interventionist approaches towards regeneration. The system
consists of two main tiers: a local planning system and structure plans. The former are map based plans and will normally
indicate in some detail proposals for a particular area.
Although there are variations in local plans, it might be
expected that most will show land use, access, some design
detail and, in some cases, development agencies, financial
support and the phasing of development.

As has been pointed out elsewhere (Harrison 1978) local plans
can clearly be of value in, say, the reordering of districts
with mixed residential, commercial and industrial land use or
in the intensive replanning of smaller, older, industrial infra
structure. In particular local plans can guide development
control, boost environmental improvements, stimulate new
development, help instil confidence in an area, improve
accessibility and so on. On the other hand, formal local
plans, that is those implemented under the 1971 Town and
Country Planning Act, appear to have lost favour to some
extent. In part this reflects the emergence of policy instruments such as industrial improvement areas discussed in
chapter 6, which may make the preparation of specific local
plans unnecessary, detailed provisions being contained in the
improvement area declaration report. In addition too, formal
local plans may be both too rigidly land use orientated and too
bureaucratic to deal with what may be rapidly changing economic

circumstances especially in the older cities and more depressed regions generally. More informal policy documents,
co-ordinating a variety of economic and physical policies, and
adopting flexible attitudes towards land use zoning, design,
economic function and so on are proving more appropriate to
the needs of many authorities.

If some doubt has been expressed about the economic
effectiveness of local plans in ordering economic change this
is marginal compared with criticisms levelled at structure
planning. The system was established to co-ordinate strategic
planning within, ultimately, the counties established in 1974
in England. Many of the early plans proved long-winded,
technocratic, and over-ambitious. Eventually indeed the
Department of the Environment indicated that the plans should
concentrate on the key aspects of housing, employment and
transport. Even then there have been severe criticisms of the
approach as a whole. This debate cannot be entered into here,
although it has been explored extensively elsewhere (Centre
for Environmental Studies 1975). It is important however here
to consider the applicability of the structure planning system
for the ordering of economic intervention and employment growth

It is clear that there are major drawbacks in using the
structure planning system as a mechanism through which
authorities might intervene in their local economies. For a
start the objectives assumed by structure plans may not coin-
cide with those intrinsic to economic intervention. Structure
plans, although undoubtedly becoming more flexible in approach
are designed to guide long-term, strategic land use issues.
Economic intervention however requires politically inspired,
rapidly implemented initiatives designed to co-ordinate
limited resources from a variety of different sources. In
addition economically orientated strategies may not wish to
distinguish between 'land-use' policies and other objectives.
There is moreover the issue from the point of view of more
interventionist authorities that some of their more
politically contentious proposals contained within structure
plans may not be allowed when the plan is forwarded for central
government approval. The South Yorkshire Structure Plan (1978)
for example proposed the concentration of local authority
economic assistance in more deprived parts of the County. In
the event however the Secretary of State for the Environment
in effect overturned this Job Priority Area concept developed
within the Plan. For those authorities eager to adopt more
interventionist approaches towards economic development
structure plans will generally prove too rigid and too tightly
controlled by the centre.

187

There may of course be exceptions. The approach adopted
by East Sussex (1980) for instance is relevant here. Unlike
many other structure planning authorities which tended to
stress the overall process of plan making this authority has
laid much greater emphasis on annual reviews monitoring the
performance of the approved plan. This seems more appropriate
for employment creation and economic development than do
orthodox structure plans designed to last for up to a decade
simply because of the varied and rapidly changing nature of
intervention in these areas. As financial resources, legal
constraints and local and national economic climates can alter
so quickly so policy documents guiding local intervention in
these areas need to be capable of rapid modification.

For some authorities, the bigger urban administrations in
particular, the emergence of the inner city initiative has
provided an opportunity for refining economic policy making.
As part of the overall innovation, the 1978 Inner Urban Areas
Act gave legal definition to the concept of the partnership.
In authorities so declared by central government, partnership
committees were to be established consisting of central and
local government interests which would order the allocation of
urban programme funding. In the event some seven partnerships
were declared in England. In each of these areas a partnership programme was drawn up by 1979 which outlined the major
problems facing the partnership and indicated policy areas
to which urban programme funding was to be directed. Employment
and economic issues tended to figure prominently in the
programmes (see for example Manchester and Salford City
Councils 1979). Typically the scale of urban economic decline
and rising unemployment would be indicated and available
urban programme funding allocated to advance factory construction, land acquisition, industrial improvement and development,
retraining, infrastructural improvements and grants to
indigenous firms.

The shortcomings in the partnerships have been outlined
elsewhere. There was little in the way of overall policy
co-ordination (Spooner 1980). Emphasis tended to be placed
on capital spending rather than the devising of a suitable
policy framework for the inner areas concerned (Hambleton 1981).
Resources allocated to the urban programme were minimal
(Nabarro and McDonald 1978). But in terms of economic intervention the partnership programmes ensured that some effort was
made to identify problems, guide the allocation of urban
programme expenditure and monitor the overall impact of
resultant intervention.

Although not the recipients of comensurate urban assistance
the second tier programme authorities also produce annual urban

programme similar to those produced by the partnerships. The programme authorities were designated in 1978 as administrations with admittedly severe economic problems but which did not apparently equate with those endured by the partnership. Their programmes through which justification for central urban funding is developed, outline the social, economic and physical problems encountered in the relevant inner urban locality, indicate ameliorative spending and undertake appropriate monitoring. Taken together the programmes emerging from the partnership and programme authorities clearly provide a more flexible and immediate analysis of economic decline and prescriptive policy than, say, do structure plans.

For some authorities however the necessity to produce an urban programme has not inhibited the development of other, complementary forms of policy documentation. Two examples of this occur in the North East. Tyne and Wear County Council (1983) for example produces a three year programme of economic development works which, where appropriate, is fed into urban programme bids made by authorities within the County. The programme of development works indicates the scale of land acquisition, spending in industrial improvement areas, the extent of factory refurbishment and so on. At the same time, the policy context for economic development is outlined which might, for instance, point out the low levels of investment in the County, the generally poor standards of industrial estates and deficiencies in the range of industrial and service units on offer.

A more comprehensive approach to economic policy making is practiced within Newcastle Metropolitan District (1983). Here a separate Economic Development Committee has been established to initiate and to co-ordinate measures which will contribute to the development of the local economy. As part of this effort an annual Economic Development Policy and Programme is produced which indicates Council policy and financial support for a variety of initiatives ranging from product development to attracting new employment, from assistance to unemployed women to improvement area activities. In essence therefore the Policy and Programme provides a comprehensive assessment of Council activities in the area for the use of authority personnel, unions and business interests.

THE ORGANISATION OF ECONOMIC EXPERTISE

Until the late seventies much of the expertise in economic and employment fields tended to be scattered in a number of local government departments. An analysis undertaken by the London Voluntary Service Council (1979) for example indicates the ad-hoc, pragmatic nature of the structuring of employment

creation work. In local authorities with an interest in creating more jobs the task would be assigned to either or both of
the planning and estates committees. The former was involved
through its concern for local and structure plans whilst the
latter took on responsibility for the management of industrial
sites and premises. Occasionally a large authority would
assign the task of attracting industry to public relations and
publicity departments. This chaotic pattern is still much in
evidence in many local authorities.

Where there is only a marginal interest in economic development the work of answering queries from prospecting businessmen
is allocated to an officer in a department such as planning who
will provide what information he can to satisfy unsolicited
enquiries. More active local authorities have traditionally
appointed an industrial development officer (IDO) variously
to co-ordinate and to implement elements of policies concerned
with industry. The appointment of an officer to deal specifically with local economic matters was an innovation of
the 1930s development movement and the position has generally
remained in the amorphous form in which it was created. The
post can be assigned nominally to either the planning, estates
or chief executives departments and may be concerned with tasks
as varied as the management of industrial estates, industrial
training schemes, the attraction of industry and liaison with
established local firms. Most of these officers operate either
alone or with only a very small staff. In many cases IDOs work
in some isolation from the rest of the local authority and as
a role it has rarely been closely integrated into the central
structures of local government. The IDO for Doncaster
Metropolitan District for example is formally attached to the
Chief Executive's office but is effectively a lone officer with
one secretary to deal with all clerical work. Despite this
status she is able to co-ordinate other departments to facilitate the development of industrial estates and premises in
the District, attract new industry to the area and act as an
advisor to small businesses. Within resort towns a similar
position and status is often occupied by the Tourist Officers
or their equivalent. The lack of integration of the traditional IDO with the mainstream of local government work is
symptomatic of the failure of this post to evolve into a more
central position within the service and reflects in part the
stagnation of interest in employment creation after 1950 and
also, as shall be shown later, the background and training of
these officers.

In addition to the isolated IDO and the confused range of
committees responsible for implementing aspects of economic
policy, many local authorities in the early 1970s began taking

an interest in aiding the local economy by setting up liaison
committees comprising councillors and members of the local
business community. A survey of these consultative arrangements conducted by Chandler and Yates (1980) found that 42% of
a sample of 143 local authorities in England and Wales had
established some form of consultative committee on local
economic issues. Not surprisingly larger metropolitan
authorities were more likely to form such an organisation than
non-metropolitan districts and counties. Most included in
addition to employers' representatives, Trade Unionists and in a
few cases the local MPs. Many committees met regularly with
60% convening on at least a quarterly basis. In all cases
these organisations are purely advisory although they can be
an important forum for the development of significant initiatives by local authorities such as, in Sheffield, the campaign
to protect the cutlery industry. It is however probable that
most are little more than discussion groups which helped to
provide a better understanding between local authority members
and officers and local businessmen but achieve few tangible
developments. It has been observed in Chapter 8 that most
industries are unwilling to allow local authorities to inter-
fere within their concerns unless loans or contracts are
involved. One or two local authority respondents to the survey
moreover provided the unsolicited comment that the committees
had achieved very little. A final and significant factor that
will dull the effectiveness of such systems of consultation is
the absence of any coherent structures within the local
authority to develop and implement any suggestions that may
arise from the consultative group. The authorities surveyed
were asked to state the committees to which they reported the
deliberations of their consultative groups and gave answers
summarised in Table 11.1.

Table 11.1
Committees receiving reports from consultative groups on
the local economy

Type of Committee	% of authorities with consultative committees
No specific committee; reports may be sent to a relevant committee when appropriate	38
Planning Committee	17
Industrial Development Committee	17
Policy Committee	14
Finance or/and General Purposes Committee	6
Other Committees	6

n = 63

The Table clearly indicates the lack of structural co-
ordination of economic policy initiatives present within many
local authorities that have shown some concern over this issue

The emergence of a more coherent organisationfor employment
creation in some authorities has been facilitated more by the
structural consequences of the 1972 Local Government Act and
the Bains Report than an expansion of the role of IDOs or
consultative committees. The reform of local government gave
particular impetus to economic interventionism through the
creation of the metropolitan counties which, as suggested in
chapter 2, had responsibility for large populations but
relatively few powers and therefore an enthusiasm among their
leaders to establish new roles for their organisation. Their
responsibility for structure plans gave further impetus towards
policies for local industry. In addition to their ready
acceptance of new roles these authorities were also in a
position to organise their structures so as to take into account the recommendations of the Bains Report concerning corporate management. This system of management is ideally suited
to dealing with a task that required the help of a number of
traditional local authority departments. As a result of these
factors West Yorkshire Metropolitan District Council was for
example able to set up an Economic Development Sub-Committee in
January 1977 which was served by a small team of officers recruited on a corporate basis (Mawson 1983) who were later to
form the Council's present Economic Development Unit. In more
established authorities corporate management did not however
simplify an already complex system for economic intervention.
Sheffield Metropolitan District in the late 1970s was assigning
responsibility for economic development to the planning, estates, city promotion departments and the corporate management
unit.

Local authorities wishing to alleviate growing unemployment
began from about 1980 to create organisations that could more
adequately co-ordinate employment policy. Not only councillors
but some professional bodies such as the Royal Town Planning
Institute (1979) realised the need for action in this field.
To the Institute it appeared that as authorities moved into
areas requiring expertise in such diffuse topics as land
management, the creationof co-operatives, labour market intervention and financial support for companies it became
increasingly necessary to integrate these activities into a
separate section or department. In particular it was essential
to amalgamate forward planning in economic and employment
issues, typically a preserve of the structure or policy planner
with the day to day routine industrial enquiries normally
dealt with by industrial development officers.

The concern among local politicians over the industrial decline of their communities along with the previously chaotic arrangements for managing economic intervention has led to the formation by a number of councils of economic development or employment sub-committees. One of the most integrated organisations for employment creation was formed in 1981 by Sheffield City Council which re-allocated the scattered responsibility for this activity into an Employment Committee which is a full sub-committee of the Council under the direction of a chief officer. The Department is funded largely through section 137 funds and has a staff of 55 divided into sections dealing with Industrial Development, Research, New Technology, Training and general services.

It can be seen from Table 11.1 that a number of local authorities which are principally within metropolitan areas and London, have formed employment or economic development committees to formulate policy and oversee implementation of economic initiatives. None as yet have however followed Sheffield in organising its officers concerned with employment creation into a specific department with a status similar to other major service departments within the authority, although there are several authorities with economic development units or some equivalent designation, which effectively operate as departments.

Many local authorities that have taken a serious interest in employment creation began dealing with the organisational problem with the premise that the implementation of policy should be the province of traditional service departments or ad-hoc agencies such as Enterprise Boards which may operate at some distance from the council. The councillors' committees which formulated policy would therefore be aided by a small unit of officers who would have research and advisory functions. This view was clearly held by the leaders of the Labour Group of the GLC on taking power in 1981 (Greater London Council, 1981). An Industry and Employment Committee was formed to establish policy and this was advised by a small Economic Development Group of, initially, five officers. Many aspects of funding industry and property development were however to be handled by the Greater London Enterprise Board which legally is an independent company whilst training and manpower problems were dealt with through a Greater London Training Board. After a year's experience it was however realised that many of the schemes to aid the local economy that were being devised had to be implemented by the individuals or organisations who devised the ideas and there has subsequently been a considerable expansion in the size of the Economic Development Group

(Greater London Council 1983). Radical initiatives such as giving Trade Unions early warning of company policies or financial stability cannot for example be easily handled by local government officers with a traditional professional training.

The structure of the GLC's is similar to that which has developed in several other active authorities. The West Midlands County Council co-ordinates its economic initiatives through an Economic Development Committee, which is supported by an Economic Development Unit that appears to have outgrown its designation since it employs a staff of 70 workers, and the West Midlands Enterprise Board. West Yorkshire County Council has an almost identical structure on a smaller scale with an Employment and Economic Development sub-committee and an Economic Development Unit, which employs 19 staff and is a division of the Planning Department, plus the West Yorkshire Enterprise Board. Other approaches to organising employment initiatives include Bradford District Council's Employment Development Unit which is directly responsible to the Chief Executive and has been given considerable powers to implement strategies without detailed reference to established service departments. The Unit can for example grant loans or progress planning approvals with industrialists. It is also possible to put the principal burden of implementation on to an Enterprise Board. The Northampton County Council's Enterprise Agency is the authority's principal organisation for economic development initiatives even though it is not in a strictly legal sense part of the Council. At present the Agency is able to give loans and advice to industry but serious consideration is being given to its assumption of a publicity function to attract new industry to the County.

The re-organisation of economic and employment intervention within local authorities has inevitably tended to concentrate on overall corporate structures. Mention ought however to be made of the efforts made by Newcastle in particular to re-orientate their activities to the benefit of particular areas of the city (Local Economic Development Information Service 1983). As part of its determination positively to discriminate in favour of more deprived areas of the city the Authority has created some 12 Priority Area Teams. Each PAT is made up of political, resident and officer representatives and collectively in 1983/84 they spent over half a million pounds from either rate revenue or from partnership funding. Although much of the expenditure has been allocated to community and social projects there is a growing concentration on employment orientated projects.

These include sponsoring MSC schemes, training for the
unemployed and the creation of Employment Outreach Worker
posts who will work with the PATs in developing employment
initiatives. There may obviously be only limited scope to
deal with economic problems at the local level but as
interest in co-operative and community based employment
initiatives increases so it can confidently be predicted that
other authorities will move towards some decentralisation of
economic intervention in an effort to foster local enterprise
and initiative.

For most authorities the main focus of attention will
clearly remain on devising appropriate administrative
structures which allow for the effective creation and
implementation of employment policy. In practice this is
likely to mean the continued emergence of employment
committees and units producing and implementing economic and
employment policy statements. The creation of these sorts
of structures will undoubtedly cause problems with many
authorities. New employment policy statements may undermine
or outdate other forms of policy making. Economic policy
statements may need to be devised rapidly in the light of
changing economic or political climates. New employment
departments will antagonise more established departments
jealous of traditional preserves. It may be difficult in the
event to devise operational objectives that allow for the
permanent retention of, say, seperate employment departments,
planning departments and estates departments. Amalgamations
can be expected which will be resented. But ultimately,
especially for those administrations encountering massive
economic recession, the corporate objective of employment
retention and creation will assume primary importance.
Administrative structures will therefore be sustained which
encourage this goal at times to the detriment of other aims.

PERSONNEL

One of the more intractable organisational problems faced by
authorities involved in employment creation is the appointment
of personnel with sufficient expertise and political commitment to implement employment policies and at the same time
ensure effective liaison with other officers of a local
authority. Since many aspects of economic development such
as the provision of factory premises or the operation of a
policy to purchase local goods, require the co-operation of
other departments even the most integrated employment
department will need to secure a good working relationship
with other local authority staff. The problem of integration

of personnel has been one of the factors that has retarded the development of the status of IDO's. The majority of these officers are recruited from middle management in industry and commerce and may frequently be experienced in areas such as estates management or public relations. As a consequence of their background many IDO's will have little experience or patience before their appointment with the pressures and delays created by public accountability and committee cycle procedures of local authorities. On the other hand local government officers within traditional departments will expect conformity to time honoured procedures, and regard professional qualifications as an important asset for senior status within the authority. Many IDO's can find that good ideas are not accepted with enthusiasm and they will not be considered for promotion to the most senior positions within the local government service.

The lack of rapport that can exist between an IDO and more traditional local government officers can be exacerbated when individuals without local authority experience are appointed to newly created and relatively well resourced economic development units. In entrepreneurial economic development units such as that within Bradford District Council several officers may have a background in private industry similar to the IDO. A greater difficulty may occur in left wing authorities such as Sheffield or the GLC where several of the economic development staff not only lack professional qualifications normally recognised within the local government service but may have been recruited in part on account of a good record of active political work on behalf of the Labour Party or radical pressure groups. It would however be misguided usually to assume that such appointees have no further qualifications to offer. Many innovatory schemes require highly qualified graduates often with research experience in areas such as economics or management in addition to an ability for political organisation and publicity. Officers within economic development units tend to have practical experience ranging from industrial management to the organisation of community action groups but are also generally academically highly qualified.

The problems of friction that may result from introducing staff from non-traditional backgrounds into a job requiring close liaison with established professionalised departments can be overcome if officers within economic development units are recruited from established departments. Birmingham Metropolitan District Council has adopted this approach in the creation in 1984 of an Economic Development Unit whose 23 staff will be largely seconded from other sections of the authority. The strategy may also have the

advantage of saving money. It may however also encounter the
problems faced by the GLC when it was discovered that many
initiatives that it proposed could not be implemented by
officers with a traditional local government training.
Although it may be possible to forward a conservative economic
development policy using the skills available in planning,
estates and treasurer's departments focusing on the development of industrial estates and the provision of infra-structure
it is unlikely that such a department could successfully
generate the ideas or ability to implement strategies such as
acquiring equity in potentially successful companies or
campaigning to prevent the privatisation of local authority
services. In as much as many aspects of employment creation
are highly innovatory they require local government officers
with different skills to those normally present within the
service.

12 Local authorities and the provision of labour

THE STRUCTURE AND ORGANISATION OF THE LABOUR MARKET

Much of this book is concerned with efforts made by
authorities to boost local economic demand. In this chapter
consideration will be given to those initiatives emanating
from local government designed to improve the quality or
mobility of labour. Such innovations have not received the
same support as have policies designed to create jobs. In
periods of economic recession this concentration on enhancing
economic performance and hence the stimulation of employment
is understandable. It might be argued for instance that in
times of stagnation improving the quality of labour can
prove of little relevance when aggregate demand is so low
that skilled labour is either already available or has
bumped down the labour market to take on semi-skilled or
unskilled jobs. Such attitudes ought to be seen as misguided.
The allocation of national and local resources to training
is notoriously low in the United Kingdom compared with
virtually all European and North American competitors.
National expansion indeed traditionally has been muted
because of bottlenecks in the labour market. And for
individual local authorities improving the quality of labour
can have relevance in terms of attracting jobs into the area
from within and beyond the United Kingdom, of retraining
traditional skills, of retraining those whose skills are no
longer required, and of enhancing the position of the
socially economically and physically disadvantaged by
improving their ability to operate within the labour market.

Clearly for any authority intending to intervene in their
local labour market certain issues relating to the structure
of the national labour market and the role of national
organisations within it will need to be borne in mind.
Explorations into national labour trends and the labour
characteristics of those in the older urban cores have been
made elsewhere (Ball 1983; Cameron and Debinett 1980;

Lawless 1981; Mason 1983). Brief mention might however be
made of certain trends. At the national level major
structural changes have included the decline in manufacturing
employment especially for men; a marked increase in the
total labour force due especially to the rise in women and
school leavers; a marked rise in the long-term unemployed;
and a marked decline in unskilled jobs. There have been too
considerable regional differences in the operations of the
labour market. Some regions and cities dependent upon basic
industries have endured very marked economic decline as the
output of traditional products declines sharply and older
skills become redundant. In addition the older cities in
particular tend to contain high proportions of groups
especially vulnerable to unemployment. These include
single males, blacks, the unskilled, and the physically
disadvantaged. In effect there may be a dual labour market
operating within more deprived parts of the spatial
economy. In essence a high-wage, professionally structured
sector may exist in tandem with a secondary sector typified
by poor educational and vocational qualifications, limited
skills and few opportunities for advancement.

In the last twenty years efforts have been made by
central government to intervene more effectively in the
labour market in order to moderate problems of inadequate
skills, youth employment and so on. Mention will be made
of these later. It can be pointed out here however that
compared with virtually all developed economies national
investment into labour planning in the United Kingdom is
minimal. This seems surprising bearing in mind the repeated
occasions in recent decades that expansion has had to be
curtailed because of inflationary pressures caused by bottle-
necks, notably lack of skilled labour. Central government
appears equally unwilling moreover to raise fundamental
questions about issues such as job sharing, employment
creation and early retirement when quite clearly these policy
developments will have to occur if high rates of unemployment
are ever to be substantially reversed. As with other aspects
of local government economic intervention, it does appear
that in many respects it is the non-existence of central
government policy or its inherent weakness that stimulates
activity at the local level. And at this latter level we
are really talking about three inter-related issues: labour
mobility, training and educational provision.

Earlier in Chapter 5 of the book reference was made to the role that allied policy areas such as housing and transport can make in boosting economic development and stimulating job creation. Brief mention ought to be made here however of the ways in which transport and housing policies clearly have a direct relevance in the easing of labour mobility. Cheap and adequate public transport services can obviously widen job opportunities for those seeking work and ease labour supply for employers. The degree of central government control over support available to subsidise public transport may make substantial improvement to many forms of transport provision highly improbable however.

The problems of residential immobility have been high-lighted by a number of commentators (for example Lambeth Inner Area Study 1977). For many living in the older urban cores, and within the depressed regions generally, it becomes increasingly unlikely that sufficient new jobs will replace those lost through the recession and through rationalisation of output. In effect many will seek out employment in the South of England particularly as efforts to deflect employ-ment from the more prosperous regions through regional policy has been substantially reduced.

For many however wishing to move it does appear that there are severe rigidities in housing markets that constrain mobility. Owner-occupiers may have problems in selling older property unlikely to attract mortgage support for potential purchasers. The costs of moving may prove prohibitive to owner-occupiers too. For those in rented accommodation there are even more acute constraints limiting mobility between different regions of the country. In the private rented sector there may simply be very little accommodation beyond the major cities, within which of course there has been a dramatic decline in employment opportunities. In the public sector too much of the available housing is in the larger older cities and there remain considerable institutional problems in transferring local authority tenants from one city to another.

Central government has attempted to ease the problems of immobility. Through the sale of council accommodation for example public sector tenants have been moved into the owner-occupied sector where mobility is ostensibly easier. The costs of house purchase are likely to be reduced through reduction in stamp duty and an easing of the costs of conveyancing. National mobility schemes have been established too to assist the movement of public sector tenants from one region of the country to another. New efforts have similarly been made to increase the supply of private rented accommodation through for instance shorthold tenancies.

It is not appropriate here to discuss the effectiveness of these centrally inspired initiatives. Suffice perhaps to say that many have proved of limited value and that as long as so much new economic activity tends to occur in certain regions of the country where a large proportion of accommodation is relatively expensive owner-occupied housing so there will remain a continued problem in moving the economically weaker into areas of greater economic opportunity and so too will such areas continue to endure shortages in unskilled and semi-skilled labour.

Some authorities have reacted to potential labour shortages by introducing key-housing programmes which are discussed in Chapter 5. For the sake of completeness however it may be worth mentioning here the well documented case of Poole, Dorset (Mason 1983). Here the local authority, the Chamber of Commerce and Industry, and a major engineering firm have jointly sponsored a housing development funded by the Housing Corporation. The Corporation acquired land from the local authority and of the 100 plus dwellings constructed half were for key workers recruited from other parts of the United Kingdom employed in the public sector and half in the private. For an employee to be recognised as a 'key worker' in the scheme certain criteria have to apply. These include a condition that the relevant skill cannot be recruited locally, that the 'key worker' concerned will help maintain a firm's production, that he/she will boost the employment of semi-skilled or unskilled workers, and that the relevant person has received appropriate training.

LOCAL AUTHORITIES AND THE TRAINING OF LABOUR

As is briefly mentioned above central government has become intimately involved in training services. This involvement has however proved far from consistent. As Fairley (1983) points out, the training system has been totally re-organised three times in twenty years. The 1964 Industrial Training Act set up a network of Industrial Training Boards with powers to raise levies on employers. However the lack of adequate co-ordination between educational and industrial interests was not forthcoming and in 1973 the Employment and Training Act of that year created the Manpower Services Commission. Established initially to improve skills and co-ordinate services, by the mid 1970's the Commission was increasingly being called upon to run special programmes for the unemployed, notably the Youth Opportunities Programme and the Community Enterprise Programme. There has been considerable criticism of the Commission. It did not ensure the introduction of co-ordinated, national manpower planning. Different divisions of the Commission, Employment Services, Training Services and Special Programmes, often operated independently with little overall integration of effort and objective. Some of these criticisms have been taken on board by the Commission to some extent and new co-ordinated training initiatives have been initiated in the Highlands for example. Here a Joint Training Group is co-ordinating Public and private sector training provision in close association with the Highlands and Islands Development Board which is responsible for economic development in the area.

However this attempt to integrate manpower planning and economic development cannot be seen as typical. In a third major change in manpower planning since 1964 the 1979 and 1983 Conservative administrations indeed have clearly attempted to reverse governmental intervention in the area. Most of the Industrial Training Boards have been abolished for example. At the same time however the acute problems of youth employment have forced the government into developing the new Youth Training Scheme, a year long programme for unemployed school leavers which is to cover almost half a million young people at a, 1983/84, cost of more than £1 bn. Some effort has too been made to rationalise MSC activities by merging its Training and Special Programmes Divisions and the creation of new Area Manpower Boards to replace the existing MSC committees. Whether the new approach to national manpower planning proves notably more effective than previous efforts seems unlikely. Nevertheless it is important to stress that local government has to operate within structures and organisations laid down by central governments of varying political persuasions. Nevertheless whilst still accepting the primacy of central government in training and retraining initiatives it is clear that authorities can intervene in this area and, faced with acute problems of lack of skills, deskilling and unemployment, they are increasingly doing so.

LOCAL AUTHORITIES AND LABOUR MARKET RESEARCH

Intervention into local labour markets requires an adequate data base. Some authorities such as Newcastle (City of

Newcastle, undated) have produced comprehensive assessments
of labour market characteristics. These include details of
the structure of the labour market, skills, educational
standards, earnings, travel to work patterns and so on.
Research activities of this kind can highlight, for instance,
the markedly unequal impact economic recession can have,
affecting the old, women, the young, the unskilled and ethnic
minorities more than other groups in society. Establishing
the scale of these imbalances will assist in the creation of
city-wide labour market programmes designed to improve
opportunities for disadvantaged groups. Research into the
local labour market can too begin to highlight the extent of
cut-backs in training and retraining facilities implemented
by Conservative central governments elected in 1979 and 1983.
The GLC Labour Party Election Manifesto (1981) for example
points out the extent of skill centre closures within London.
The West Midlands County Council (1983) similarly highlights
the likely local impact of a rundown in training implemented
by Industrial Training Boards. Finally for a more
comprehensive view of the effectiveness of training in
London in the late 1970's a London Voluntary Service Council
report (1979) makes interesting reading. Industrial training
boards had reduced their activities, training in general did
not meet the needs of employers, and there was little to
suggest that the MSC had managed to produce an integrated
training programme for London linking training to economic
trends. Across the board in fact the strong impression
emerges from local authority and voluntary organisation
evaluations of labour market planning that the system remains
inchoate, fragmented and generally unsatisfactory. Not
surprisingly local authorities have seen this evidence as
more than sufficient justification for their greater involvement in labour market planning.

LOCAL AUTHORITIES AND LABOUR MARKET INTERVENTION

The scale and scope of local authority intervention in
labour market planning has increased considerably in recent
years and hence this analysis will of necessity prove
selective. In general discussion will proceed from the least
to the most interventionist strategies.

Local authorities have undertaken a major role in the
sponsoring of placements on the Youth Training Scheme and
the Community Programme and their predecessors. The West
Midlands County Council (1983) for example established a task
force under the old Community Enterprise Programme to provide

work experience and sustain vital construction skills for a work force of more than 200 selected from the long term unemployed.

These sorts of initiatives, and especially placement under the Youth Training Scheme, are commonplace amongst authorities. That is not to say that all councils are satisfied with the schemes on offer. Wages are frequently seen as too low for example, real training minimal and employability hardly affected. For interventionist authorities efforts have been made to introduce and sustain more intensive training initiatives. Sheffield (1983b) has for example negotiated a block MSC grant but allocated additional funds to this to ensure that union rates are paid during training and that training received will actually increase the chances of employment for the trainee concerned. Similarly the Greater London Training Board established early in 1982 has created an exemplary training project partly funded by the MSC but where training will be more intensive than is normally the case and where every effort will be made to place trainees in permanent posts (Greater London Council 1983 c).

Although for most authorities the greater proportion of resources allocated for training will continue to emerge from the MSC there are many new initiatives emanating from local government in which the Commission is either not involved at all or only partially. For example Chesterfield has used European Social Fund and MSC assistance to establish a Training Centre because of inaccessibility to regional skill centres. The innovation proved successful in terms both of occupancy and placement figures and involved limited expenditure per trainee.

The major cities, where problems are probably more acute and diverse, have developed a wide range of training programmes. Manchester for example has used Urban Programme Funds to create an Information Technology Centre (Kitchen 1983). Sheffield (1983 b) has established a Community Apprenticeship Scheme to provide new employment, training and educational opportunities in local government for local unemployed, unqualified people with previous trade union, voluntary or community experience. A whole range of initiatives has emerged too from the Greater London Training Board (Greater London Council 1983 a). These include the creation of training and skill centres for women, training for ethnic minorities designed to improve both skills and language ability, the provision of public transport facilities for those distanced from skill centres, and major new training centres, such as that at Charlton, begun after its closure as an MSC Skill Centre. Authorities such as Birmingham suffering from the particular problems associated with decline in one industrial sector, in this case engineering, may attempt to boost training resources in that sector, especially, as with the abandonment of many Industrial Training Boards, private sector training has declined in recent years. In this Birmingham example for instance urban programme expenditure has been increased for training schemes with the Engineering Skill Award (Birmingham Metropolitan District Council 1981).

As Mason (1983) points out the voluntary sector has not been particularly forthcoming in terms of labour market innovation, partly because many authorities have been neutral at best in their support for community based ventures. This is not perhaps so true of the inner city Partnerships wherein frequent exhortations are made by central and local government politicians to local and voluntary groups to boost their activities in the labour market and indeed in the employment field generally. A number of schemes designed to assist say, the young or ethnic minorities in both training and production have indeed been implemented. One example of a community based project discussed at length by Mason (1983) is the Notting Dale Urban Studies Centre in Hammersmith. Here funds from a variety of sources including the MSC, Hammersmith's Urban Programme, charities, trusts, banks and the Department of Industry, have allowed for the creation of a centre designed to boost technical skills amongst the less able young whilst at the same time establishing a number of permanent jobs for those receiving training. The scheme proved complex to organise and to fund, raised administrative problems for the MSC whose financial criteria were not always met, and required formidable organisational skills. Such projects will not be commonplace but can be supported in a sensitive manner by local government through the provision of secretarial and administrative assistance, premises and limited funds.

Although the initiatives mentioned above inevitably appear somewhat ad-hoc, fire-fighting devices, it would be wrong to assume that more comprehensive approaches towards local labour market planning have not been developed. Indeed for many of the major cities it is crucial that broader strategies incorporating specific political and social objectives are developed as a matter of priority. It is only with the creation of such programmes that individual schemes can be evaluated, supported or rejected.

A number of motives lie behind the determination of more interventionist authorities to create comprehensive labour market strategies (Greater London Council 1983 a; Kitchen 1983; Sheffield Metropolitan District Council 1983 b). These include high and rising rates of unemployment, a marked contraction in employment opportunities especially amongst marginal groups, and fears as to the longer term impact of technological change. In addition proposals emerging from the MSC, for example the New Training Initiative launched by the Commission in 1981, have been seen by more radical authorities as quite inadequate to meet the needs of contemporary British society. In particular likely funding for initiatives emerging from the Commission is generally seen as untenable, the retreat by private industry from training merits insufficient attention, too little is being done for the unemployed, and there is nothing like enough co-ordination between labour management and economic planning.

To overcome these defects through local labour planning will be a formidable, if not impossible, task. Nevertheless a number of local administrations have produced overall strategies in consultation with appropriate employer, trade union and community organisations. Typically such programmes will embrace a number of objectives and policies (Greater London Council 1983 a; Sheffield Metropolitan District Council 1983 b). For example local skill shortages will be identified and training resources directed towards these if possible. Apprenticeships in areas subject to declining private sector funding will be supported. Appropriate MSC placements will be created. Major efforts are likely to be made to support the particular needs of women, ethnic minorities, and the young, groups which traditionally have received little help from orthodox training programmes. Such help will take the form of educational, training and employment creation projects. An authority itself is likely to consider its own internal training and educational arrangements. Efforts may be made towards pushing local educational establishments into an educational and training programme which caters adequately for the differing needs of various client groups. Increasingly too some authorities will boost facilities intended to support the unemployed so often neglected in the training debate. This will involve the creation of unemployment centres, the dissemination of welfare rights, social support, assisting in the formation of co-operatives and community enterprises, specific retraining programmes and so on.

The creation of local labour market strategies has much to commend it. Overall objectives can be identified, resources

can be allocated in a rational manner and economic development can be integrated into labour market planning. It would
be idle to pretend however that the implementation of such
strategies will be at all easy to achieve. The MSC will
become more market orientated and is unlikely to be interested
in many projects of a more 'social' nature. Local authorities
will be unable to replace the resources withdrawn from
training by the MSC and by private industry. The integration
of educational and training services will be difficult to
achieve. It may be hard too to modify training services as
new skill shortages are identified. Retraining may re-
shuffle unemployment. No matter how skilled too a labour
force might be, if aggregate demand remains weak people will
stay unemployed. Nevertheless the new determination on the
part of some authorities to intervene in training provision
is surely correct. They can respond most rapidly to skill
shortages; they will not forget the needs of specially
disadvantaged groups such as blacks and the unemployed; and
their insistence on providing in-depth training leading to
identified employment makes sense. It is a more appropriate
response than would be boosting inflexible, ill co-ordinated
national organisations undertaking little thought out
programmes which simply keep people off the unemployed
register for a period of time.

LOCAL AUTHORITIES AND EDUCATIONAL POLICIES

It is clear that educational policies can play an important
role in economic development and employment creation. As
a major area of local government expenditure they can indeed
be seen as offering opportunities for a wide range of
innovations many of which will have implications for employment even if only indirectly. The Association of Metropolitan
Authorities (1978) for instance has outlined ways in which
educational provision can be used to achieve certain social
or economic goals. It can help reduce urban disadvantage;
school facilities can be used for community and recreational
purposes; disadvantaged minorities can be made more aware
of their rights and opportunities; nursery schools can widen
economic opportunities for women; education generally betters
the quality of the labour force; and capital investment in
educational infrastructure provides much needed work for the
construction industry.

Whereas many local authorities would undoubtedly accept
the benefits that educational investment would bring, they
would no doubt too point out that enhanced expenditure in the
area appears unlikely in the mid 1980's. Central governments

have steadily reduced the relative proportion of national expenditure allocated to education for a number of years and as local expenditure becomes ever more tightly constrainted it seems improbable that educational budgets will remain even constant in real terms. This reduction in national investment has frequently been justified on the grounds of declining school roles. This seems myopic in the extreme. As a nation, far less is spent on educational provision, especially higher education, than virtually any other developed economy; stay-on rates for the post 16 group will rise as unemployment for this age group remains high; and educational provision cannot be reduced per capita because of overheads which have to be borne however large or small a class or school may be. It should be pointed out anyway that educational services will have a considerable impact on economic recovery generally. They employ teachers and ancillary staff; they better the educational and training standards of the labour force as a whole; and in an era of high and probably permanent unemployment they can offer some alternatives to those unlikely ever to be employed full time again.

Clearly these broader debates whilst undoubtedly of importance are beyond the direct influence of local government. Issues such as increasing educational expend-iture, or, the role of education in an era of high unemployment, or educational provision and its impact on the labour market, will ultimately depend to a large extent on national political choices. From the point of view of local government the area of educational provision which perhaps allows greatest scope for innovation is the question of education-industry links which will form the main focus of attention for the remainder of this chapter.

Education-Industry links

The transition between school and work, never easy, appears especially problematic in the United Kingdom. There is for example evidence that many school leavers are under-achieving academically, are minimally prepared for work, and suffer from inadequate careers services (GLC Labour Manifesto 1981). From the point of view of employers moreover there are substantial difficulties too. When companies are taking on apprenticeships there may be a problem in recruiting satisfactory school leavers, possibly because of a narrowing of skill differentials and the payment of full rates at 18 for many unskilled manual workers (Woodward et al 1980). In general indeed many employers apparently have a poor impression of school leavers (Woodward et al 1980). This appears to be due to factors such as poor educational attainment, absenteeism, lack of social skills, poor work attitudes and so on. Such attitudes may be unreasonably reflecting say, unrealistic employer demands, poor industrial relations, or poor corporate productivity. Nevertheless it was in part a response to employers' perceptions of school leavers that the MSC introduced schemes such as the Youth Opportunities Programme within which subsidised, trained and supervised posts were made available for the young unemployed. Interestingly enough, there is some evidence that both employers and young people were generally enthusiastic about the scheme and many trainees found permanent employment (Manpower Services Commission 1980).

Local authorities are obviously not in a position to put on comprehensive training programmes for the young. Nevertheless they have a role to play in terms of education-industry links. The statutory basis for intervention in this area has existed since the 1973 Education (Work Experience) Act. In addition in 1977 the Department of Education and Science, in Circular 14/77, asked local authorities to report on steps taken to promote contacts between educational establishments and industry. It appears in fact that a great deal has been undertaken in this area not simply by local authorities but by industrial training boards, the Schools Council, the Department of Industry, Chambers of Trade and Commerce and so on. Some brief indication might be made of the sorts of initiatives that have been developed, although bearing in mind the number of national and local organisations involved this will inevitably prove a partial view.

Careers services for example help to negotiate short work experience programmes with employers (Mason 1983). In authorities such as Bedfordshire the service initiates and co-ordinates teachers' secondments and work experience projects for final year students. In addition an Industry and Education Liaison Group has been established bringing together representatives from all aspects of the educational services and local industry in order that work experience placements, teachers' secondments and teacher-industrialist links are maintained, and material suitable for curricula is provided (Mason 1983).

Other developments which should be mentioned include the Schools Council Industry Project and the Standing Conference on Schools Science and Technology. The former with more than a quarter of LEAs in the country involved, helps promote a variety of educational-industry links. These include the appointment of teacher co-ordinators committed to working with schools, industrialists and trade unionists to help develop curricula, provide students with a better understanding of industrial society, put on teacher familiarisation courses, outline employment choices to pupils, engage unionists in debates with school children and so on (Schools Council Industry Project 1981). One of the better known and evaluated projects is the Wandsworth Industry Schools Project (1981). In the first three years of this scheme extensive efforts were made, to ensure close collaboration between parents, firms, trade unions, and schools, induction days were held to integrate pupils into work experience; teachers were seconded into industry; teaching packages were devised with local institutions of higher education; links maintained with careers services; and close contact maintained with employers, unionists and others with appropriate work experience. The Project as a whole has been funded by the Inner London Education Authority. Another mechanism through which industry-education links have been forged is the Standing Conference on Schools Science and Technology which has established a number of Science and Technology Regional Organisations (SATRO's) to, amongst other ends, help improve the teaching of science and technology and to provide practical help in bettering the co-operation between education and industry. Many are funded by local authorities.

Bearing in mind efforts which have been made since the early 1970's to improve the relationships between industry and education it might be imagined that great advances had been made in this area. Undoubtedly however there remain substantial problems which have been raised by a number of observers (Mason 1983; Templeton undated; Wandsworth Industry School Project 1981; Woodward et al 1980). A number of these should be indicated

(a) There are real problems from the point of view of schools and teachers. Should all pupils receive work experience or only so-me-? The latter will probably prove to be the case. But should the academically brighter pupils be seconded or others who may need the experience more? How is the experience to be evaluated? Examinations may be totally inappropriate. The development of teaching materials will not be easy and will anyway raise the question of whether appropriate working skills can be developed in one course, or whether an across the board change will be required. The latter suggestion obviously in turn brings forth the fundamental issue of the role of education. Is it to

provide a better educated, more compliant, labour force
or is it about developing personal attributes which
might make pupils more critical of prevailing economic
and social structures?

(b) Seconding teachers and students to industrial establishments might not prove especially successful. It may
make them more familiar with prevailing economic
circumstances and allow them to pass on this information
to pupils with unrealistic aspirations. But on the other
hand, placements may be for too short a time, the
experience may not in fact be passed on to pupils in a
meaningful manner, and there is obviously no guarantee
that heads and others in more responsible positions
within schools will welcome appropriate changes to the
curricula that such secondments may well induce.

(c) It is by no means certain that pupils benefit all that
much from work experience schemes. Placements may be
poor, genuine experience limited, and the whole exercise
of minimal value. The experience may enhance social
skills, and help develop a pupil's personality. But it
is not at all certain that it will improve employability.
This will tend to occur rather more when genuine training and educational provision for the 16+ age group is
provided, if possible linked into specific job outlets.
Here the ITEC schemes organised between authorities
and the Department of Industry which provide substantial
training in micro-electronics and computer technology
for the young appear more appropriate. In the longer
run however if youth unemployment is to be moderated
this is more likely to be achieved through policy
innovations such as youth employment quotas imposed on
companies, job creation programmes or the widespread
development of maintenance grants for the 16 to 18 age
group which has been implemented by a number of
authorities such as Newcastle and Sheffield. This last
development can help keep children from socially and
economically disadvantaged households in higher education and/or training to their benefit and indeed to the
economy generally.

(d) Employers may express little interest in education links,
seeing these as likely to create additional costs with
few direct benefits to the company. Equally so employers
may impose unrealistic demands on the educational system,
or not recognise that they should pay for some training
and educational facilities which improve the standard of
their labour force. It seems quite clear too that what-

ever the benefits of industry-education liaison, central
government is unwilling to enforce such co-operation.
As the Cooper Report (1981) to the Secretary of State
argued, increased co-operation between industry and
education was to be welcomed but any centrally implemented co-ordination would likely dampen local
enthusiasm and be resisted by industry. Local
authorities might thus see this as an area where
greater intervention is both required and justified.
Whether however all authorities would want to align
curricula more specifically to the needs of an
identified industrial sector appears unlikely when job
opportunities there may be limited, even non-existent.
For more interventionist authorities education, training and employment will form a continuous process.
There is little point in radically re-orientating
educational standards towards specific industrial needs
if industry cannot ultimately provide suitable employment.

A CONCLUDING STATEMENT: TRAINING PROVISION AND EDUCATIONAL
SERVICES

This chapter has provided a brief overview of the role of
local authorities in labour market initiatives. In many
respects it is not an easy area for evaluation because of the
myriad of initiatives that have been devised and because of
central government's continued activities in the field,
sometimes operating in tandem with local government, sometimes not, But hopefully some indication of local
government's approach towards labour market planning has
been provided. At this juncture three final points ought
to be made. First it is important to stress the complexity,
even confusion, that surrounds areas such as training and
education. Many agencies may be involved, often with
conflicting ends and means. Work experience schemes for
school children for instance can be perceived in very
different ways. Are they to provide employers with better
labour forces, to give pupils a more thorough understanding
of society, or to suggest that schools are in some ways
attempting to dovetail their activities into contemporary
society? A second and related concluding point that should
be raised is the over-riding need for a co-ordinated approach
to training especially. Too many agencies are involved, with
little central direction and support, and with minimal
integration between economic planning and development on the
one hand, and retraining on the other. Too many responses
appear reactive, pragmatic and temporary. Central government

needs to plan for the labour market as a whole. What skills,
will be required where and when? How will these demands be
met? How can local authorities and other interested parties
be brought together into an integrated programme? And what
is to be done for those left high and dry by the recession?
And the third and final point to be made here is that training
and educational provision have to be seen as part of an
entire package which also incorporates the most important
element of all: employment. Labour market intervention is but
one part of a strategy which many interventionist authorities
wish to pursue. It must complement other initiatives,
discussed throughout the book, which will collectively boost
output, enhance job opportunities, widen political and
economic control for local communities, and improve the
material circumstances of the socially and economically
deprived.

13 Local authority economic intervention: the legal and financial framework

Although there has been some consideration of legal and financial issues throughout the book it seems appropriate to explore these in a more explicit manner here because of their crucial importance. Intervention in economic development and employment creation has expanded enormously in recent years. There remain however legal and financial constraints restricting expansion in this policy field. Indeed perhaps the most pertinent area for debate in terms of local government economic activity is the, at times notably successful, determination of some authorities to use whatever powers are available to pursue their economic and employment objectives. These innovations will form a major focus of attention in this chapter. However some attempt should too be made here to outline the ways in which local government has used both EEC and central government assistance to further local economic and employment policies. These developments cannot be evaluated in any great detail here because inevitably they raise broader questions about international economic agreements and national economic policy which must be beyond the scope of this exercise. Nevertheless the determination with which some local administrations have sought out financial resources beyond their own immediate control makes some mention of such undertakings necessary.

LOCAL GOVERNMENT ECONOMIC INTERVENTION AND THE EEC

In the past three separate sources of EEC funding in particular, have proved useful for local authorities attempting to moderate the scale of economic recession. The European Regional Development Fund has been used widely in the Assisted Areas for example to fund, usually 30%, of infrastructural projects. South Yorkshire County Council for example has used this fund to assist in the development of the South Yorkshire Navigation (Briant 1979). In coal and steel areas loans have been made available through the European Coal and Steel Community. These can be used for local authority housing provided some such dwellings are allocated to those working in steel or coal. More important in this context however, loans can be used for helping to create new jobs for those made redundant from contractions in the two industrial sectors concerned.

A second series of initiatives that ought to be mentioned in terms of the EEC are various developments promoted by British Steel Corporation (Industry) Limited. This organisation was created in 1975 to help generate new jobs in those areas most affected by steel redundancy. By 1984 BSC (Industry) was undoubtedly offering a particularly attractive package designed to encourage new firms to be created or existing ones to expand in its Opportunity Areas (BSC Industry 1984). In the most favoured of locations assistance can include regional development grant, of which more below, regional selective assistance on commercially viable projects, grants from some local authorities to cover rates, wages or consultancy fees, derelict land grant, government guaranteed loans under the Small Firms Loan Guarantee Scheme, BSC Industry Loans, the provision of cheap premises by organisations such as local authorities and the English Industrial Estates Corporation, benefits such as exemption from rates and development land tax in enterprise zones, and relevant EEC assistance. This last element consists of favourable loans from the European Coal and Steel Community which for firms with good security can be less than half true commercial rate. In such a case however jobs have to be created for ex-steel or coal workers. Somewhat less favourable conditions govern loans from the European Investment Bank where however no new jobs need be created. Bearing in mind this plethora of potential financial assistance and the existence of local Business Opportunity Teams to provide relevant financial, technical and managerial advice it seems apparent that BSC Industry using its own resources, and those available from the EEC and elsewhere, has articulated an especially attractive set of incentives that may have considerable implications for areas not so favourably treated.

A third main area of EEC financial assistance relevant to the economic development and employment creation field is the Social Fund. This has been used in conjunction with local authority funds for training and retraining purposes. In particular groups such as the disabled, the under 25's unable to find satisfactory employment, those made redundant from

industries subject to rapid technological change and ex-
agricultural or textile workers have all benefited through
Social Fund support. However perhaps a more interesting
development has been the use of the Fund for direct employment subsidies. By 1984 more than 30 authorities provided
direct employment subsidies to private sector firms
(Botham 1984). Up to 50% of an authority's eligible
expenditure on wage subsidies paid to private sector firms
for recruitment of additional employees may be paid. There
are two definitions of eligible expenditure. For all
authorities a one year subsidy will be paid provided that
the new recruit is unemployed and under 25. In 1982 however
this subsidy amounted to only about £8.65 and authorities
tended to provide far more than 50% of the overall subsidy
(Botham 1983). By 1983 about £700,000 had been received
through the Social Fund for a planned 1,330 jobs.

A second employment subsidy scheme is available to
authorities in Assisted Areas with the Social Fund paying
up to 15% of the additional employees gross wage for up to
six months providing that for firms with fewer than 25
employees the new recruit was previously unemployed and that
for larger firms the new recruit was from a priority group
such as the disabled, from an ethnic minority or from the
long-term unemployed.

Botham's analysis of this latter employment subsidy is
relevant here (1983; 1984). Some authorities such as
Barnsley have devised small targets of 50 jobs. Others such
as Strathclyde are aiming at 2,000. The latter authority
unlike many others has delegated decisions relating to the
subsidy to officials in an effort to achieve a rapid
response to relevant requests. Some such as Cleveland have
attempted to reduce deadweight spending by trying to target
subsidy on jobs which would not otherwise have been created
without the subsidy. Merseyside County Council links the
scheme to investment in premises, plant and equipment as
part of a general package of assistance to small firms in
that gross wages of any additional employees will be paid up
to a maximum relating to a firm's investment value. Other
relevant points to emerge from Botham's work are that some
authorities such as Strathclyde have achieved job targets
whereas others, more selective in their approach, for example
Cleveland, have not. The recruitment of long-term unemployed
has proved a problem in that larger firms in particular have
not taken as many as was anticipated. Half of Strathclyde's
subsidy has gone to manufacturing firms but a considerable
proportion, about a quarter has gone to construction and

retailing companies which might merely displace other jobs in these sectors elsewhere in the region. Similarly disquieting, certainly in Greater Manchester, the urban core with more than a third of the conurbation's unemployed received less than 15% of the subsidy.

Nevertheless with more than £100 m offered between 1980 and 1983 local authorities will continue to see the Social Fund as a potential source of financial assistance and one that, unlike many other areas of economic intervention, is concerned with employment subsidy rather than enhancing productive efficiency. New arrangements for EEC employment subsidies suggest that the overall principle of support will be maintained and that increasingly it will be targeted on youth unemployment in the regions.

Local authorities ultimately of course may have only lobbying powers over the direction of EEC policy but for three obvious reasons an increasing number will be seeking out EEC funds: for most schemes local authorities must at some time be involved in the implementation of the relevant project; assistance can be used to boost and complement limited public and private sector finance available for economic development; and the EEC offers some degree of independence from central governments, neutral or even positively hostile to local authority economic intervention. However it should be remembered too that competition for EEC assistance is severe, that many forms of assistance only apply to authorities in the regional Assisted Areas; and that EEC grant may in some cases simply be claimed back by central government as reimbursement for existing regional grant.

LOCAL AUTHORITY ECONOMIC INTERVENTION AND CENTRAL GOVERNMENT

In general, national economic policy will prove of much greater significance in structuring local economies than will innovations emanating from local government. Proposals governing the scale and distribution of public expenditure, fiscal and monetary strategies, subsidies, international trading agreements and so on can prove crucial in determining the fates of local employment prospects. Because of the sheer complexity of national economic policy it is apparent that discussion here must concentrate on those national organisations or administrative arrangements which have been manipulated in some way by local government to foster local economic activity. In many cases control of such organis- ations remains quite evidently with the centre. At times indeed the objectives assumed by central government agencies may run counter to those espoused by local administrations. Nevertheless because of the scale of resources that may percolate through to certain authorities some mention ought to be made of four types of national intervention: regional development agencies; regional policy; training initiatives and inner urban policy.

(a)   Regional Development Agencies

The 1974-79 Labour government created three development agencies as part of its industrial strategy. Of these the National Enterprise Board has disappeared and the Welsh Development Agency has proved far less interventionist than has its Scottish counterpart. The Scottish Development Agency, established under the 1975 Scottish Development Agency Act, has however been perceived as a model for guiding the evolution of regional development organisations through- out the country if this were ever to become a realistic political option.

The scope of the Agency's activities was considerable by 1983. Over 1,500 firms had received financial assistance, thousands of small firms had been assisted in some way, and almost 50,000 people were employed in the 1,000 or so industrial units leased by the Agency (Scottish Development Agency 1983). A variety of objectives are assumed in the corporate strategy. They include support for growth sectors, notably electronics and bio-technology, improving industrial efficiency, and the development of Scottish entrepreneurship. Many of these objectives may assist in the regeneration of local economies although may involve little direct local government action. In some cases however, as with the creation of science parks at Garscube in Glasgow and at Aberdeen, there has been a formal agreement between the Agency, local authorities and local academic institutions.

For many Scottish local administrations however the most pertinent of the Agency's activities remains its area development. Wannop (1984) has indeed argued that the area dimension of the Agency has become one of the major objectives of the organisation. In part he argues this reflects a reduced regional policy and the acute problems apparent within parts of West Scotland in particular. In the event whatever the reasons for the promotion of area development, Gulliver (1983) suggests that for the eight area projects with a defined operational time-scale, almost £90 m had been spent by the Agency by March 1983. Almost 500 new companies had been created in the areas concerned employing about 7,000 people.

In practice three discrete types of area development have emerged. Reactive task forces have been established, in Clydebank for example, to deal with major closures, in this case of the Singer plant. Primarily action has concentrated on the creation and leasing of new industrial and commercial infrastructure, and financial assistance for new and expanding companies on what is here an enterprise zone. A second approach is the integrated project where programmes are defined and resources allocated in combined local authority/Agency schemes. The best known of these is undoubtedly the Glasgow Eastern Area Renewal project. Created in 1976 GEAR reflects the co-ordinated activities of a number of local and central government organisations under the overall management of the SDA. The overall scheme has been seen as generally successful especially in terms of residential and environmental improvements. Economic development has not proceeded so successfully although training, counselling and employment subsidies have been developed and over 3,000 new jobs have been created in 900,000 square feet of floor space. By 1983 over £200 m had been invested in the area by the major participants, over £40 m of which came from the Agency itself.

The third type of area development project is the self-help initiative of which ASSET, the Ardrossan, Saltcoats and Stevenston Enterprise Trust, is one example. The approach here is for the Agency to encourage local authorities to plan and to implement integrated development programmes for which some support will be forthcoming. In the case of ASSET for example a one-door counselling service, environmental improvements and industrial development have been introduced using the combined talents of public and private sector organisations.

The creation of the Agency has proved of considerable importance in terms of local economic development within the country. With the area development proposals in particular it is apparent that substantial public sector intervention will take place. In the eight main development areas almost £370 m of public sector expenditure is planned with £160 m emerging from the Agency and much of the rest from local authorities concerned. Whilst the scale of this support cannot be denied such activity should not be regarded as entirely desirable. First such expenditure might anyway have occurred had not normal local authority spending been so severely reduced. Secondly some at least of the expenditure was planned anyway and cannot be seen as 'new'. Thirdly some areas have benefited to the detriment of others. And fourthly as central government organisations such as the SDA

replace local government as primary agents of economic
intervention so central government increases its control of
local expenditure and at the same time so local authorities
lose interest in their abilities to intervene in their local
economies.

(b) Regional Policy

Brief mention ought to be made of regional policy since
although local authorities have had little to do with its
development and implementation it has nevertheless had a
considerable impact on local economies. Throughout the post
1945 period central government imposed controls on companies
wishing to expand in the generally more prosperous South
and Midlands. At the same time incentives were available
for companies wishing to expand in the Assisted Areas. These
incentives were expanded throughout much of the post-1945
period with a particularly important boost being provided in
the 1972 Industry Act. As a result of this Act and allied
pieces of legislation a number of policy instruments came to
dominate regional industrial policy in the 1970's and early
1980's. These included a mandatory regional development grant
for capital investment undertaken by manufacturing companies
and regional selective assitance for general capital
purposes such as removal costs and interest payment grants,
for viable projects creating or retaining sufficient jobs
where most of the payment was to be met by the applicant.
In addition the regional dimension was boosted by the
construction of factories by the English Industrial Estates
Corporation, and through Section 7 of the 1972 Local
Employment Act, 30% grants were made available for the
provision of, or improvements to, basic services such as
transport, heating, lighting, sewage and power where this
would contribute to the development of industry. Finally
under Section 8 of the 1972 Local Employment Act derelict
land grants were made available to cover the acquisition
and improvement of land incapable of beneficial use without
treatment where such action would contribute to the development of industry. Although there have been variations in
grant level, local authorities in the Assisted Areas
have usually received 100% derelict land grant and
increasingly inner city projects of a combined public-private
sector nature have been similarly treated.

Although there has been considerable comment and
criticism of regional policy (Gudgin, Moore and Rhodes 1982;
Regional Studies 1984) it seems probable that about half a
million jobs have been created in the Assisted Areas as a

result of it. In times of economic expansion larger
companies have been prepared to invest in new plant and
equipment partly because of financial incentives available.
On the other hand the costs have been estimated at £35,000
per job in 1982 figures (HMSO 1984). The West Midlands in
particular can now no longer be seen as an over-
heating area from which companies should be encouraged to
move. There has been little attempt moreover to link
overall regional expenditure undertaken by central government
departments such as Transport, Industry and Environment into
appropriate physical development plans such investment
logically requires.

Whatever the shortcomings in traditional regional policy it
became apparent by 1984 that it was to be rationalised and
down-graded (HMSO 1984). It is likely for instance that
fewer areas will retain Assisted Area status, that projects
will only receive regional grant if they create or expand
production and if they enhance job opportunities.

The evolution of regional industrial policy and probable
modifications in the system appear to contain a number of
implications from the point of view of local authorities.
First local government's impact on the implementation of
regional policy has always been limited and frequently
consisted largely of lobbying for Assisted Area status. To
the extent that since 1979 the proportion of the UK's working
population within the Assisted Areas has fallen from about
44% to about 28% there may be little return for those efforts
and in future there appears little to be gained for many
authorities in lobbying for designation. Secondly because of
the marked reduction in central government spending overall
on regional industrial assistance in recent years, and
especially in 1983/84, many authorities will no doubt
become increasingly interventionist in the economic and
employment policy areas to counteract diminishing industrial
support from the centre. Thirdly regional policy has also
clearly shown that, particularly in times of economic
expansion, larger companies will establish branch plants in
Assisted Areas. Economic recession will equally however see
many such organisations prepared to close peripheral
operations in the regions. To more radical authorities it
is evident that longer term economic prospects are better
served by supporting indigenous socially owned, companies,
and through insisting on some agreement with companies
receiving public support to cover issues such as jobs,
investment, working conditions and so on.

(c)   Training Initiatives

Mention has been made in various parts of the book of
training initiatives undertaken by local authorities.
Clearly the context within which local authorities implement
their proposals in this area is very much framed by the
policies of organisations such as the Manpower Services
Commission. For example consultative guidelines issued by
the MSC in 1981 (Manpower Services Commission 1981) argued,
amongst other points, that a training strategy should be
economic, geared to the needs of the economy and should
largely be implemented by firms themselves, with the MSC
acting as a catalyst attempting to secure necessary local
and national changes. These changes might include some
speculative occupational training for the unemployed or those
wishing to establish their own companies but only where
economic circumstances suggested that such training would
enhance local production. In essence therefore, certainly
for adult training, the emphasis has shifted towards the
selective and economic and away from a comprehensive approach
designed to boost training skills across the board. For
example there have been attempts by the MSC to boost training
in certain areas or sectors where a skill shortage has been
identified. A more comprehensive approach has however
emerged in the MSC's policies towards youth training through
its Youth Training Scheme. The specific problems of the
long-term unemployed have also been recognised by the MSC
in that its Community Programme is a year long project
designed particularly for this sector of the labour market.

   Bearing in mind the resources and influence of the MSC it
is not surprising to see local authorities co-operating with
it in the training and job creation areas. Manchester, for
example has sponsored projects suitable for the Community
Programme (Kitchen 1983). Many local councils have become
managing agencies for the Youth Training Scheme. The Greater
London Council in association with the MSC, the Department
of Industry, the Inner London Education Authority and others
has sponsored a whole range of training centres, of
initiatives designed to reduce frictional unemployment, of
programmes intended to improve the economic position of women,
and ethnic minorities (Greater London Council 1983).

   Despite the willingness of authorities to work with the
MSC it is evident that many would raise substantial
criticisms of the policies adopted by the Commission (Greater
London Council 1983; Sheffield Metropolitan District 1983 b).
Wages paid on many schemes are seen as too low and genuine
training limited. Too much emphasis is placed on the

willingness of the private sector to train employees. The
position of the economically and socially disadvantaged is
largely ignored. Professional trainers are often poorly
equipped to undertake their functions. And in general
there remains a conviction that compared with most European
countries training is too fragmented, inadequately funded
and too readily divorced from national economic policy.

(d)   Inner City Intervention

Since the late 1970's the largest of English cities have
received additional economic assistance through centrally
devised inner urban innovations. It needs again to be
stressed here that this book is primarily concerned with
locally implemented programmes. Hence although some
mention ought to be made of inner city intervention because
of the resources and powers intrinsic to that innovation,
this will inevitably be of a brief nature. Much more
detailed information can be found elsewhere (Lawless 1981,
and forthcoming).

Four major initiatives ought to be mentioned here. The
first, the partnerships, were introduced in the late 1970's
and were designed to bring central and local government
together in the development of agreed, co-ordinated
programmes of action for the seven most deprived English
inner city areas. Enterprise Zones were devised by the
Conservative government elected in 1979. They were to
consist of a few hundred acres wherein rates would not be
levied and other financial and physical advantages would
apply. Over 20 had been designated by 1984. The third
initiative the Urban Development Corporations were created
by the same Tory administration for the docklands of London
and Liverpool and are in effect powerful, centrally
appointed and funded, developed agencies. Finally urban
development grants have been established whereby central
government will support locally co-ordinated projects which
indicate that local authorities concerned have been able to
'lever' out private sector resources for the implementation
of commercial, residential, retail or industrial schemes.

By 1984 it might therefore well be assumed that the major
urban authorities had benefited considerably from the inner
city programme. Resources are running at around £350 m
per annum. Many projects have an economic bias. There has
been substantial investment in areas such as new infra-
structure, new industrial estates and financial support to
companies as an apparent result of the urban dimension.

In reality things are rather different. Some of the
initiatives such as the partnerships have not invested anything like as much as had been imagined in the economic and
employment creation fields. Rather more instead has been
directed towards social, community and recreation areas
certainly in the early years of the programme. More
disturbingly the cities have not gained additional financial
resources. Far more has been taken from orthodox forms of
central support for local authorities than has ever been
returned through the urban programme. Indeed to many of the
larger cities it must appear that the main purpose of the
entire approach is to re-allocate resources away from local
to central government control thus allowing, as for example
in London's Docklands, the centre to implement detailed
policies in terms of both production and consumption that
are at odds with the aspirations of local authorities
involved. And finally despite the resources allocated to
economic intervention within the inner city perspective as a
whole this has not been paralleled by particularly innovative
policies. The economic programmes supported by, say, the
partnerships or implemented in enterprise zones do not
differ substantially from those undertaken by more interventionist local administrations. And it is to their financial
constraints that we should now turn.

LOCAL AUTHORITY ECONOMIC INTERVENTION: FINANCIAL RESOURCES
AND CONSTRAINTS

Mention has been made in various sections of the book of the
major financial constraints and opportunities which govern
local authority intervention in the areas of economic
development and employment creation. Some of the issues
raised by the idiosyncracies of legal constraint are somewhat
byzantine. But others, notably the contentious question of
Section 137 of the 1972 Local Government Act, remain central.

Before however embarking on the vexed issue of Section 137
an indication should be made of the sorts of powers
available to local government in their efforts to assist,
and intervene within, economic development. For example
under Sections 2 and 3 of the Local Authorities (Land) Act
of 1963 local authorities can acquire land for development,
undertake works on land, and provide loans for up to 75% of
the valuation of the capital value concerned. The power to
provide loans and also grants was widened in the 1978 Inner
Urban Areas Act as is discussed in Chapter 6. Briefly however
in those urban districts so designated by the Secretary of
State for Environment loans up to 90% of the mortgage

security may be made available for the acquisition of land, or the carrying out of works on land; loans and grants may be made towards the costs of establishing co-operative or common ownership enterprises; in industrial improvement areas grants may also be provided for environmental improvements, or for the conversion, improvement or modification of commercial or industrial buildings; and in the partnership areas with the worst inner urban problems, rent and interest relief grants are available and so too are two year interest free loans for site preparation. Financial assistance for industrial concerns may also be possible under Section 123 of the 1972 Local Government Act which permits free or reduced industrial rents on land let by a local authority, on short-term tenancy or with the agreement of the Secretary of State.

Other powers have, or in 1984, still do govern aspects of industrial development. The 1975 Community Land Act for instance allowed local authorities wide powers to acquire land which in their opinion was suitable for development. Although this Act was subsequently repealed by the Conservative administration elected in 1979 other powers notably Section 112 of the 1971 Town and Country Planning Act, later modified in the Local Government Planning and Land Act (1980) permit local authorities to acquire, sell or develop land, say, in the interests of proper planning or where this may be necessary for the relocation of industry. 50% of the net capital loss of a project may be paid by central government. Powers also exist within Section 122 of the 1972 Local Government Act to allow local authorities to appropriate land from one use to another. This can prove useful where for instance land originally acquired for housing purposes is no longer required for that use but would be suitable for some form of economic development.

For more interventionist authorities the powers listed above do not allow for the sorts of policies which are perceived as crucial for the regeneration of local economies or at least a moderation in the rapid rate of decline. For radical administrations it has proved important to pursue wider powers and appropriate additional sources of investment. Perhaps three such approaches can be identified: local acts of parliament; municipal enterprise; and Section 137 of the 1972 Local Government Act.

(a)   Local Acts of Parliament

Particularly in the 1970's a number of local authorities
attempted to obtain private acts of parliament to deal with,
amongst other issues, industrial development. One well
documented case is that of Tyne and Wear (Rogers and Smith
1977). In this case the authority attempted to acquire wide
ranging powers to cover, for instance, site preparation, the
provision of unsecured loans on plant and machinery, and the
allocation of grants for interest and rent relief. Many of
these powers were in the event allowed and this undoubtedly
proved of value to the County in its economic planning in
the late 1970's. However to some extent the powers themselves became less relevant because of the 1978 Inner Urban
Areas Act which, in some respects at least, closely mirrored
the Tyne and Wear Act and which thus provided to all the
more deprived English local authorities somewhat similar
powers. Moreover one crucial power requested by Tyne and
Wear, that of equity investment, was disallowed in the Lords.

(b)   Municipal Enterprise

Municipal enterprise as a whole is discussed in Chapter 10.
Mention ought to be made here however of the attempts by
authorities such as Wandsworth to expand into the direct
municipal production and trading (Wandsworth London Borough
1976). In the mid 1970's the then Labour authority of
Wandsworth explored the whole area of municipal enterprise
and concluded that there were considerable deficiencies in
relevant legislation. In particular the 1970 Local
Authorities (Goods and Services) Act allowed authorities
powers to enter into agreements with other authorities, or
public bodies, to supply goods or materials, provide
technical services, use vehicles, undertake maintenance works
and so on. Indeed Wandsworth was itself at that time being
supplied in a variety of goods and services by the Greater
London Council's Supplies Department. Crucially however
there was no power within relevant legislation to allow the
Council to use a factory, even one in its ownership, for
production. Certainly at that time Wandsworth saw this as
a marked weakness in the legislation and lobbied for
appropriate changes. These have not occurred. Nor do they
appear probable in 1984. Certainly the Conservative government elected in 1983 would be unlikely to countenance such
developments. It has indeed expressed considerable disquiet
at the use of Section 137 of the 1972 Local Government Act
which has undoubtedly become the fulcrum for local authority
financial intervention.

(c) Section 137 and Pension funds

The 1972 Local Government Act introduced a number of powers
that in the event have been used ingeniously by local
administrations. Section 111 for instance permits a local
authority 'to do anything which is calculated to facilitate,
or is conducive to, or incidental to the discharge of any
of its functions'. In retrospect however it has not been
the use of this somewhat permissive power that has facilitated the most expansive employment creation schemes but
rather the application of Section 137 of the 1972 Act which
permits an authority to 'incur expenditure which in their
opinion is in the interests of their area or all or some
of its inhabitants'. The Act limited the product from the
rate to 2p in the pound but also gave the Minister powers to
alter this rate which is a facility that could be used
seriously to hinder certain employment creation initiatives.

The central importance of Section 137 has been outlined
by Lyons (1983). He points out that it usually supports
more than half of many local administrations' expenditure
in the areas of economic development and employment creation.
It has been used for example to establish employment
departments and economic development units such as those of
the GLC or the West Midlands, to fund co-operative development agencies discussed in Chapter 7, to provide grants and
loans to local industry and to provide the most significant
financial basis for enterprise boards.

Some other funds may it is true be available for economic
development. The urban programme will prove useful for
authorities with specified inner city problems. The 1974
Superannuation Regulations moreover allow some authorities
to invest up to 10% of funds in unquoted securities
although such a policy must not compromise the interests of
members of the fund. When the idea of enterprise boards were
first canvassed there was considerable optimism that local
authority pension funds, which are governed by a membership
board comprising councillors and statutory financial experts
under the framework of the County Councils, would become a
major source of funding. South Yorkshire County Council had
anticipated this idea in the mid-1970s by establishing a
scheme for investing in local industry through their pension
fund. Strict concern for the economic viability of the
fund however dictated borrowing terms that were no more
attractive to industry than schemes offered by the banks and
the project therefore gained little interest from local firms.
West Yorkshire County Council have found similar difficulties
in their policy of providing large loans to industry through

money lent jointly by their pension fund and the Midland Bank. West Midlands County Council had planned to fund the Enterprise Board through pension fund money but this scheme has also foundered due to a lack of enthusiasm among all the District authorities participating in the fund as to the value of such an initiative. The Enterprise Board is however hoping that in the near future it will receive investments from a number of London based pension funds.

Enterprise Boards To many working in the area of local authority economic intervention the enterprise board concept is certainly one of the most exciting to emerge in recent years. Typically enterprise boards can be seen as institutions 'seeking to put together financial packages including loan, equity or preference shares but with an emphasis on capital growth through equities with participation in profits wherever possible (Mawson and Miller 1982, p 28). Although this may describe the general framework of these organisations they differ widely in the scope and style of their investments and ambitions.

Geoff Edge who did much to establish the first Enterprise Board within the West Midlands County Council has observed that their basic role is to provide finance to industry through the provision of equity or long term loans. He points out that this form of finance is in short supply in Britain.

'British banks, perhaps as a consequence of Britain being an international financial centre, concentrate on the provision of short term finance either in terms of overdraft facilities or short-term loans. It can be argued that what is needed by British industry is the provision of long term finance especially equity capital. Unlike the situation in Britain companies in Japan and West Germany frequently have banks as substantial equity holders'. (Edge, 1983, p 156)

Given this form of finance a company will be far less vulnerable to the problems created by sudden increases in interest rates and as a result its burden of debt. This economic argument is not however the only justification for establishing enterprise boards. Mimms and Thornley who were also responsible for helping to design the West Midlands Enterprise Board observed before its creation that the Board and through it the local authority could gain greater control over a local economy, influence corporate decision making, and ought ultimately to obtain a return on its investment through dividends and sales, whilst not becoming too closely tied to the day to day management issues of the company concerned. (Mimms and Thornley, 1978).

The largest and most comprehensive Enterprise Board in
1984 was the Greater London Enterprise Board (GLEB) founded
in 1982 by the controlling Labour Group of the GLC along
guidelines published in their 1981 election manifesto. Its
overall function is to develop London's economy and create
jobs within the policy framework laid down by the Industry
and Employment Committee of the GLC. It is however a private
company limited by guarantee which is controlled by a Board
of 9 directors appointed by the GLC. The Chairman,
Sid Staden, is Regional Secretary of the London Area of the
Transport and General Workers Union. GLEB is financed under
Section 137 and the 1983/84 GLC budget proposed a £27 million
revenue and £33 million capital input. The organisation
employs, under the leadership of its Chief Executive, a
staff of some 70 individuals who deal not only with investments in firms but also with purchasing industrial sites and
property. GLEB has rapidly become one of the largest owners
of industrial property in London concentrating on areas in
need of redevelopment which do not attract enthusiastic
investments from the private sector. In the area of
industrial development investments are usually made in
medium sized firms with at least 40 employees. Exceptions
are made in respect of small co-operatives which are helped
by GLEB under a strategy to stimulate this form of ownership,
and to firms established by minority groups. Investments
are made not only with reference to their economic viability
but to their social consequences in respect of the number of
jobs they can save and the extent of depression in the area
in which the company operates. Any firm receiving loans or
equity funding must conform to a code of practice in
relation to working conditions, recognition of Trade Union
rights and other forms of good working practices. By the
end of December 1983 GLEB had approved investments totalling
£18.6 million in support of 142 projects and was able to
argue that as a result it had saved or created almost 2,000
jobs.

Other enterprise boards are similar to GLEB in respect of
their basic structure as companies limited by guarantee
controlled by boards of directors appointed through their
local authority and in practice willing to follow broad
policy guidelines laid down by the controlling party group
within the authority. They are also largely funded through
Section 137 monies although the West Midlands Enterprise
Board is beginning to attract investments from pension funds
and the Northampton Enterprise Agency has a small fund
provided by private firms to aid small businesses. The

Lancashire Enterprise Board which claims to make a profit
can as a result begin generating its own revenue. Enterprise
boards are also similar in that they take a generally
business-like approach towards achieving their aims.
Normally investments will be directed to commercially viable,
well managed firms and detailed studies are made before funds
are allocated to particular projects in order to ensure that
a reasonable return can be obtained from the investment.
Employees of enterprise boards in contrast to many, though
not all, economic development units or employment committees
are usually experienced in business and management work.
On occasion poor investments have been made but enterprise
boards such as the organisation in Lancashire can also
point to considerable commercial successes although it is
as yet too early to make any definitive pronouncement on the
financial efficiency of institutions concerned primarily
with making long-term investments.

The similarity in the structure and economic purpose of
enterprise boards reflects their common role of acting as a
vehicle through which local authorities can fund local
businesses whilst escaping the strictures of ultra vires.
They nevertheless differ considerably as regards the scope
of their activities and the extent to which investments may
be tied to strictly commercial criteria. The West Midland
Enterprise Board for example in contrast to GLEB is solely
concerned with providing capital for medium-sized industry
and does not involve itself with property development or
funding co-operatives. Both these functions are handled
directly by the County Council through its Economic Development Unit. The Board does not analyse the social value of
investments in terms of jobs created but has been more
assiduous than GLEB in acting as a device through which local
industries may be restructured on a coherent basis. Particular effort has been placed in aiding some of the more viable
foundry firms within the West Midlands in a deliberate attempt
to restructure what is a declining industry through more
positive and direct action that could be achieved by pressure
and persuasion. A similar policy has been followed by the
Lancashire Enterprise Board in respect of the fishing
industry. This organisation however differs from the West
Midlands Enterprise Board by having an interest in purchasing
and refurbishing industrial property. The West Yorkshire
Enterprise Board established by the Metropolitan County
has a similar policy to the West Midlands in that it supports
medium-sized industries but it differs in being less
interested in imposing demands on participating companies in
respect of working practices and has made little attempt
to restructure particular industries leaving this task to

the County's Economic Development Unit. In contrast to these
organisations the Northampton Enterprise Agency established
in 1983 concentrates on funding small firms on the grounds
that its relatively small resources are best spread evenly
and equitably around the County. The Agency also has close
associations with the local Chamber of Commerce and a number
of large manufacturers within the County and correspondingly
makes no demands on the firms in which it invests other than
ensuring their commercial viability.

The differences between enterprise boards is a reflection
of the extent to which local authorities are eager to pursue
the various elements of their possible functions as outlined
by Mimms and Thornley (1978) and Edge (1983). The West
Yorkshire and Northamptonshire organisations are examples of
enterprise boards which are predominantly concerned with
providing financial aid for local industry in partnership with
the private sector. The West Midlands Enterprise Board and
GLEB have in contrast a far more radical political
philosophy and consider their organisation not only as a
resource for funding local industry and commerce but for
ensuring that whenever possible and appropriate, reorganisation can take place in the patterns of management and
industrial sector organisation within their community. The
Boards therefore enable local authorities to become a direct
participant within the capitalist process so that through
such direct involvement they may steer the economic system
into adopting practices and strategies that retain jobs and
ensure good working conditions. The enterprise board
structure also enables left wing councillors to keep themselves at arms length from this process of interaction with
capitalism by leaving the detailed work of investment to the
experts and retaining for themselves the power of determining
an overall strategy for the economy.

It is clear that for many authorities some form of enterprise agency becomes increasingly necessary if economic
intervention is to develop. They can provide a more
immediate and sensitive response to local economic decline
than can, say, regional policy. They can help sustain
public-private sector combined initiatives. They can boost
local investment particularly in medium to large sized
companies where equity investment is especially difficult to
obtain. They can encourage co-operative and community
enterprise and ensure that more deprived groups and
individuals are placed in a better position with regard to
the employment market. They can ease the application and
manufacture of new technologies. They clearly too are
necessary in that there has been a veritable flood of

231

applicants. They create jobs at perhaps one-third the cost of, say, the Nissan factory in the North East. But because they allow local authorities a wider say in economic issues and a larger role in industrial intervention it is clear that they have not been well received by central government.

Lyons (1983) has outlined the convoluted attempts by the Conservative administration elected in 1979 to reduce the powers of local authority intervention in the economic development and employment creation fields. The reasons for this appear ostensibly to be central government's concern that local authorities will simply compete with each other with little or no overall benefit and that areas such as the inner cities and the declining regions will lose out (Department of the Environment 1982). Bearing in mind the determination with which more interventionist authorities have insisted on avoiding an expensive public auction these arguments appear irrelevant and may simply hide a determination on the part of a Tory central government to reduce the powers of Labour councils.

In the event however although efforts were made in the Local Government (Miscellaneous Provisions) Bill to reduce local authority powers by for example limiting local government assistance to smaller firms and lowering the 2p to ½p rate for many authorities, the resultant Act passed in 1982 clarified and supported the existing use of Section 137 largely due to the influence of the Lords. There remain however real areas of uncertainty. It appears that Section 137 can support enterprise boards and their activities and through revenue rather than more tightly controlled capital resources. On the other hand Section 137 cannot be used to extend or to modify an existing power which creates problems for those authorities, more than thirty in all, that obtained private act of parliament between 1963 and 1973. Equally so, as district auditors increasingly apply criteria such as economy and efficiency to local government expenditure so the use of Section 137 may become less certain (McSweeny 1984). Interestingly enough however early in 1984 it is not certain what will happen to enterprise boards established by the metropolitan counties and the GLC which are due to disappear in 1985. As these boards build up industrial and property portfolios, and as additional funds are attracted from pension funds, the market, and elsewhere, so it will become that much harder to dispense with them. Perhaps ultimately there will prove to be a crucial dilemma for any anti-collectivist Conservative government: enterprise boards may reflect an unacceptably high degree of public intervention in the market, but on the other hand they create jobs far more cheaply than does regional policy, they assist local companies, they have attracted considerable financial support and they are successful. It will be of more than idle interest to see which way central government moves on this because for many local authorities direct investment into local production represents the logical development in their thinking.

Part III
Some evaluations

14 Local authority economic intervention: viability, equity and effectiveness

An overall assessment of local authority economic intervention is attempted in the final section of the book. In the last chapter emphasis will be placed on political considerations which have governed and stimulated the development of this policy area. In this chapter the emphasis will be placed on more orthodox economic assessments of the viability, scope and effectiveness of local government economic intervention. Later in this chapter attention will turn towards efforts made to identify the costs and benefits intrinsic to intervention. Initially however some mention should be made of the limits that either directly or indirectly constrain the activities of local authorities in terms of economic development or employment creation.

THE LIMITS TO INTERVENTION

Throughout the book mention has been made of economic, political, legal and financial constraints that impinge on local authority economic intervention. Nowhere, however, has a comprehensive assessment been made of broader issues which will inevitably guide or constrain economic intervention. Four factors ought to be given some consideration here: national economic policy; trends in the labour market; spatial issues and the primacy of the market.

a) National Economic Policy

Central government's economic policy will always have a far greater impact on local government prospects than will the actions of authorities themselves. It is clearly not possible here to delve in any depth into these issues which have anyway been raised elsewhere (Fothergill and Gudgin 1983; Gudgin, Moore and Rhodes 1982). Briefly however, Britain's economic performance has been poor even within the world recession of the 1970's. The recession probably triggered by the large increase in oil prices in 1973, caused eventually many governments within the developed world to cut public expenditure which would otherwise have risen as unemployment grew and tax revenue fell. So many countries ultimately engineered severe economic slumps that the world system as a whole fell into a virtual crisis and attempts by individual countries to adopt expansionist Keynesian policies proved impossible to implement.

Not that there was ever much danger of them being attempted in the United Kingdom. The awful state of the economy by the late seventies was to some extent hidden because of oil exports. But the underlying trends within the real economy point to a potentially disastrous economic status by the end of the eighties. Exports have continued to grow slowly and imports rapidly such that the traditional surplus in manufacturing goods had disappeared by 1983. Investment and output have consistently remained generally low relative to international competitors although in some sectors where investment has been enhanced productivity figures comparable with European rates have been achieved.

But whatever the underlying problems of the economy inherited by the incoming Conservative administration elected in 1979 there can be little doubt that the scale of the recession was disastrously accentuated by the policies of that administration and of its successor elected in 1983. High interest rates designed to reduce, a partly self-induced, inflation, combined with a dramatically overvalued pound had the most awful effect on manufacturing exports and output. The latter fell fully 17% between 1979 and 1982. Tight public expenditure programmes severely curtailed necessary infrastructural investment and created grave problems throughout the public sector. Local authorities found themselves in the invidious position of having to cater for the same, or enhanced, need, with far less support from central government. Even the major cities identified as having the most acute social and economic problems received between 10% and 20% less from central government between 1979 and 1982 (Association of Metropolitan Authorities 1982). Housing investment and regional support were more than halved in the first three years of the Tory government elected in 1979. The vast proportion of independent observers might well argue that a programme of public works must be implemented, that the pound must remain realistically priced, that central government must intervene in areas such as industrial investment and research, and that some selective import controls are essential, but as long as central economic policy remains wedded to ludicrously anachronistic principles so such exhortations will prove in

vain. And so too will local authorities find their efforts at
economic intervention more essential but also more marginal to
the problems their economies face.

b) Labour Market Trends

Labour market trends will obviously be influenced by central
government policy. Unemployment, retraining, job creation
schemes and so on will all affect the labour market. However
it may well be that certain trends are likely to occur or
accentuate irrespective of central government intervention.
These will have to be taken on board by local authorities in
their attempts to intervene within their economies. The
implications of some trends are in fact disturbing. They
cannot however be ignored.

The decline of manufacturing employment for instance has
not moderated. By the early eighties less than one-third
of the total working population was employed in manufacturing.
It seems hard to envisage circumstances wherein this proportion is likely to rise. So many of the incentives, for
example, provided by both local and central government to
manufacturing industry will hasten the replacement of labour
by capital. As Massey and Meegan (1982) have shown, industrial
sectors facing expansion or contraction are likely eventually
to rationalise, invest, and reduce labour requirements.
Industrial investment into plant and equipment will simply not
create additional jobs. There is indeed a clear and vital
distinction to be made between economic development, which of
itself may well be necessary, and employment creation which
may well require very different policies. Many of the
initiatives which have been examined in this book are really
about economic development, particularly in manufacturing
industry. Some additional jobs may be created here because
of enhanced output or the substitution of local for imported
products. In general however the creation of jobs will depend
on policies such as boosting leisure and tourism, environmental
improvements, but particularly by public works programmes
which can only be implemented on the appropriate scale by
central government. Such programmes will become ever more
necessary as the gap between economic growth and employment
creation increases. Evidence from the early 1980's suggests
that economic growth will need to be of the order of at least
3% pa, hardly ever achieved on a sustained basis in the
United Kingdom, before unemployment even begins to decline.

Because of the secular decline in manufacturing employment
it is inevitable that attention should turn to service
employment where jobs have been created in both the public and

private sectors in recent decades. The long term prospects
do not however look encouraging (Harris and Taylor 1978). Much
of the post-war expansion in public sector service jobs was in
areas such as health, education and social services which have
endured considerable expenditure cuts post 1976, and especially
after 1979. In the private sector any expansion seems likely
to be concentrated in specialised professional and managerial
sectors. Much service employment serves the local populace
and may thus not be capable of dramatic expansion anyway. And
of course the service sector, just as much as manufacturing
will become increasingly subject to new technologies and
processes. In some respects sales, servicing and management
of these will create jobs. On the other hand there will be
substantial job losses in more routine clerical sectors and
the overall impact may well prove negative in terms of job
creation. It is true that there will be greater demand for
leisure and recreational services by those in work, but
employed fewer hours, and by the unemployed. But local
authorities by themselves may be unable substantially to
enhance leisure and recreational services unless their capital
and current expenditure is increased by central government.
In essence for both service and manufacturing employment
longer term trends can be identified which highlight both the
necessity and the marginality of local intervention. Secular
trends in the labour market may simply overwhelm the efforts
of many local administrations.

c) Spatial issues

Although this book is concerned with local authority economic
intervention throughout the country relevant spatial issues
cannot be ignored. In particular it appears that some
authorities will find themselves in a relatively advantageous
geographical location which attracts new investment or retains
existing development whereas others will face not simply the
problems associated with an acute international recession and
disadvantageous national economic policy but additional
difficulties intrinsic to their location within the country.
Much of the most important work here has been undertaken by
Fothergill and Gudgin (1982).

In brief they suggest that certain factors begin to explain
why parts of the national economy are likely to grow more
rapidly in the future than are others. In particular, regions
with an over-representation of declining manufacturing sectors,
with little service employment, with bigger cities dominated
by older, larger plant and with poorly educated workforces
are likely to sustain substantial job losses. Alternatively
those regions in the south of England with a settlement

240

structure consisting of smaller towns and with a better
educated labour force living in an environment generally
perceived as more attractive are much more likely to attract
new industrial and service employment. There is unlikely of
course to be a great deal of mobile employment of any
description in the near future. But what there is appears
increasingly likely to be sited in two growth zones: the
M4 belt, and the Cambridge, Milton Keynes, Northampton area.
Moreover as technological change quickens it does seem
probable, although forecasting here is inevitably complex,
that the regions dominated by older industrial sectors will
be adversely affected by additional difficulties (Goddard
and Thwaites 1980). New products are unlikely to be made in
these regions, new manufacturing processes will reduce labour
and skill requirements in traditional industries, and many
routine service functions will be decentralised from the
larger cities to cheaper premises in smaller towns.

The prospects for the older cities and indeed whole regions
such as the North West and the North East appear singularly
bleak. The dramatic decline in employment particularly in
basic, traditional industries has been little short of horrific.
The consequences of this process have been documented
elsewhere. Miller (1982) for example in examining the impact
of unemployment in Newport, South Wales, concludes that high
unemployment has an impact across the board. Less is spent on
local services, retailing and leisure activities; health
problems, especially stress and anxiety are accentuated;
marital problems increase; and crime rates rise.

Faced with the economic and social consequences of such
decline it is inevitable that many of the older cities and
towns have attempted to re-industrialise. Much of this book
has dealt with the efforts especially of the older communities
to reinvigorate their industrial sectors. Robinson and
Sadler (1984) have similarly explored the attempts in Consett
in the North East to re-industrialise a town devastated by
the closure of a steelworks. Interestingly enough however
here the authors conclude that although heroic efforts have
been made to create new industrial employment the sheer scale
of job loss makes this at best a partial policy response.
Others have made the same point. Eversley (1980) for instance
suggests that the strategy least likely to create urban
employment is that which concentrates on new industrial
investment. Far more jobs will be sustained in areas such as
tourism, routine service jobs, financial services, education
and possibly retailing. Clearly not all of these sectors will
provide well paid permanent employment. Many will provide
at best part-time underpaid labour. New employment here too

may displace jobs elsewhere. This strategy of concentrating on non-industrial sectors moreover will be marginal compared with the changes in unemployment that central government could make through, for example, public works programmes designed to improve housing and urban infrastructure or through nationally implemented socio-economic changes to the labour market, such as earlier retirement, work sharing, job creation, retraining and so on. Nevertheless the larger older cities, whose employment strategies have formed to a large extent the basis of this work, cannot avoid one fundamental conclusion: it seems inconceivable to imagine that new industrial employment can be created on a scale sufficient to replace those lost from declining basic sectors. For those administrations in the older industrial regions this will be a bitter pill to swallow but every conceivable economic, social and technological indicator suggests this to be true.

d) The primacy of the market

Local government can only alter economic output and employment at the margins. The vast proportion of new industrial, commercial and retail development is under the control of either the private sector or state capital or combinations therein. The determination on the part of both private and state capital to seek out profitable locations, maintain the most profitable of plants, rationalise output in recession and generally to pursue the ends of efficiency and competitiveness, has clearly had a marked impact on the British economy as a whole and on the more deprived older regions in particular (Scott 1982). Few if any controls exist on companies wishing to expand, contract, close, or relocate within the United Kingdom or abroad. Local authorities have to operate quite simply within an economic environment that imposes minimal controls on the private sector and increasingly insists that nationalised industries adopt market principles.

Whatever the merits of this situation it imposes considerable constraints on local administrations. The major trends in both the national and the local economies may largely be beyond their influence, even cognisance. As an earlier chapter has indicated, the willingness of some more interventionist authorities to use Section 137 and relevant local government pension fund regulations to invest directly into their local economic base has increased, in some cases dramatically, the capacities of local government to intervene in economic development. It may well be too that additional funds will come the way of local government inspired enterprise boards from pension and insurance companies as an

increasing number of regionally based institutional investors
become more aware of the direct consequences to their own
fortunes of untrammelled economic demise.

Such trends must not be overestimated. Local government
intervention in economic issues will remain marginal overall.
Some authorities indeed because of their determination to
assist establishments producing desirable goods in socially
organised units may marginalise still further their impact on
local employment prospects. Inevitably indeed, the constraints
due to external factors or internally devised objectives
raise the question of whether local authority economic
intervention is worth the effort at all. To many observers it
certainly is (Mawson and Miller 1982; Morley 1981;
Self 1983). Central government appears to have written off
too many of the older cities and regions to rely on its
beneficence; local authorities may be in the best position
to respond to prevailing economic trends; local government
funds may be especially useful in attracting forth additional
private sector investment, a vital factor in an era when so
many projects are on the margins of profitability; local
government may anyway be unwilling, and rightly so, to preside
over catastrophic collapse without in any way attempting to
reverse the decline. Whilst accepting, nevertheless, the
need for local authority intervention in terms of economic
development and employment creation there remain however
certain issues that require amplification. Who benefits from
local authority action? How much does such intervention cost?
Are some forms of intervention more effective than others?
It is to these and allied issues that we should now turn.

THE COSTS AND BENEFITS OF ECONOMIC INTERVENTION

Assessing the costs and benefits of any policy area in the
public sector is fraught with problems. For example, some
authorities may only be interested in creating co-operative
establishments producing socially desirable goods and employing
people marginalised by the market. Orthodox economic
assessments would be inappropriate here. It is not so much,
say, the cost per job that is relevant in this case but the
social benefits to the community and the individual concerned
which may be impossible to quantify. For these sorts of
reasons an attempt has been made in this book to divorce more
orthodox economically based evaluations of local authority
intervention which will be discussed in this chapter and
socio-political considerations which will be raised in the
last section of the book.

More orthodox assessments of local authority economic
development and employment creation have raised three major
areas for debate: the costs of intervention; the effectiveness of different types of intervention; and the equity
issue of who benefits from local authority action in this
policy area.

(a) The overall costs of intervention

Although varying approaches to intervention have proved
markedly different in terms of costs and benefits to local
authorities as will be discussed shortly, some overall
assessment of the costs of intervention per job may prove
useful. This is a complex process. Some indication ought
here to be given of the factors which would need to be taken
into account in the building up of a balance sheet outlining
the costs and benefits of intervention. Not all of the items
here will prove easy to quantify and not all factors will
apply to all equations but a simple totting up of jobs
apparently created or retained by local government intervention will not do. One obvious reason for this is that the
determination to create or retain jobs is increasingly no
longer the sole prerogative of employment or industrial
departments. Social services, education and housing departments, for instance, are increasingly recognising the central
importance of employment issues (Lomas 1981). But to assess
the total impact of all local authority departments and
services may prove complex in the extreme.

Nevertheless some indications of the costs of direct
intervention can be made. These include obviously the costs
of the initiatives themselves whether they be the acquisition
and development of land, loans, grants, environmental
improvements and so on. Additional costs clearly include
management costs of infrastructure remaining within the
control of the authority, and the administrative costs of
industrial promotion or employment departments. Benefits
accruing to an administration as a result of intervention
might include an increase in industrial production and
employment, the retention of companies unable to raise
capital at market rates, the levering of additional private
sector assistance as a result of pump-priming public
investment, and a boost to the service and construction
industries as a result of industrial expansion.

This simplified assessment of costs and benefits
inevitably hides a myriad of complexities (Willis and Whisker
1980). It is net and not gross job creation for example
that matters. 'New' industrial, retail or commercial jobs

may simply be replacing employment elsewhere. Enhanced
production as a result of public subsidy may simply reduce
output in non-subsidised firms. Moreover public support for
capital investment may of course simply result in the
substitution of capital for labour which could hardly be seen
as reflecting the objectives of most authorities wishing to
intervene in this area. Clearly subsidy may however boost
output in companies resulting in an increased demand for both
labour and capital. Whether the output effect will prove
greater than the substitution effect will vary from company
to company, sector to sector. Nevertheless authorities ideally
should be supporting companies which can boost output and
employ additional staff at no cost to local competing
companies. Ideally such companies should be producing either
new goods or services or replace those imported from abroad.
It is unrealistic to imagine in practice however that a great
deal of assistance will be directed to such establishments.

Additional evidence of job creation resulting from public
subsidy has emerged from evaluations of enterprise zones
(Catalano 1983; Tym and Partners 1984). Usually the subsidy
pertaining in the zones will be far greater than those
normally available to local authorities. In particular the
waiving of rates and 100% building allowances represent
considerable subsidy. Nevertheless the evidence suggests
that public subsidy in the zones was of little significance in
the overall development of the zones. Most of the jobs
apparently created in the zones between 1981 and 1983 would
have occurred anyway irrespective of public subsidy; most
jobs would have been located within the immediate area of
the zone concerned; and little in the way of increased
production occurred as a result of zone designation. Hence
in the case of enterprise zones where more intensive forms of
subsidy apply than virtually anywhere else, this seemed to
have minimal impact in terms of net job creation. Most
subsidy was in effect autonomous in that enhanced production
or job creation would have occurred irrespective of the
inherent advantages of the zones.

Many urban Labour authorities would certainly accept this
and suggest that genuinely new output and employment can
nevertheless be created which will not adversely affect other
existing companies or other administrations. This can be
achieved by producing new goods and services or by substituting
indigenous for imported products. Even then opportunity costs
need to be taken into consideration. Would land be better
used for housing rather than employment for instance
considering the likelihood of permanently higher unemployment
levels? Would investment into production be better spent on,

say, environmental improvements or residential rehabilitation where, at least in the short term, labour input is high? And ultimately of course would authorities be better leaving the money in the local economy rather than enhancing their rate calls to implement interventionist economic policies? Interestingly enough, where work has been done on this last crucial issue it appears certainly to be the case that the employment benefits are much higher from direct public spending than would be the case with lower rate calls (Cameron et al 1982). It may be of course that some companies do migrate from more highly rated authorities to lower ones but this is unlikely to prove significant and is somewhat illogical in that rates represent a relatively small proportion of outgoings for many companies which anyway benefit from higher social wages pertaining in more interventionist administrations.

Finally, in this section some indication might be made of the costs of creating or saving jobs assumed by public sector organisations. The Greater London Enterprise Board (1984) for example suggests a gross overall figure of about £12,000 in 1983 prices. This is somewhat higher than parallel figures elsewhere. Mawson (1982) indicates that the costs to the West Midlands Enterprise Board of every job created or retained amounted to £2,500 in 1982 prices. The exact costs anyway do not really matter. Two other points seem far more relevant. First, when the average cost for those on the employment register is usually estimated to be about £5,000 pa to the Treasury through lost taxation and social security payment, it seems extraordinary that central government should not use some of the £17 billion allocated for unemployment benefit in 1983/84 for job creation measures. And secondly, whatever the per capita costs of local authority job creation they have proved far less expensive than have centrally implemented policies such as enterprise zones and regional policy. For example in 1982 prices the government estimates that at its peak of intensity in the 1970's regional policy created jobs at a cost of £35,000 per employee (HMSO 1984).

(b) The costs of differing development policies

Because of the sheer range of initiatives undertaken by local authorities in their efforts to boost economic development, the most sensible approach to evaluation is clearly one which examines differing innovations separately rather than lumping them together in a rather meaningless whole. Detailed work has been done on this area (Bovaird 1981; Cameron et al 1982; Gough et al 1981; Jurue 1980; Storey 1983). One

obvious problem is the designation of criteria by which
initiatives should be evaluated. Bovaird (1981) whilst
highlighting the callow nature of the evaluation debate as a
whole, suggests that assessment might proceed according to
the degree to which employment initiatives meet certain
defined objectives. Even here however assessment can be
difficult in that whilst some authorities may be interested
simply in jobs created, others may be attempting to satisfy
somewhat more amorphous goals such as employing those
marginalised by the market. This latter criterion clearly
raises issues of socio-political nature and as such will be
dealt with in the last chapter. The point should nevertheless
be made here that evaluation of local authority economic
intervention is far from a refined art, and remains one
wherein the very assessment criteria to be used are
contentious.

Bovaird (1981) whilst accepting these, and similar,
problems suggests nevertheless that evaluation should proceed
according to two sets of criteria: the degree to which
initiatives are self-financing and the cost-effectiveness of
intervention.

(i) The self-financing criterion. Bovaird (1981) argues
that there are a number of initiatives which local authorities
can undertake which are clearly self-financing. This is
especially true of land assembly and servicing where
authorities may have spotted market gaps, or where lower
profit margins would be accepted by the public sector than
would be the case with the private. In general in fact
unless there is a clear surplus of industrial land, this
appears to be a policy area where intervention can be self
financing. In the past this was probably true for the
provision of industrial units as well. Local authorities
significantly expanded their activities in this field in the
1970's especially in terms of smaller units. This probably
did satisfy a demand that existed because of the traditional
reluctance on the part of the market to invest in what may
become rapidly outdated infrastructure. However estimating
the true self-financing nature of this approach is difficult.
Costs may include relatively expensive land compulsorily
acquired years ago for residential uses now no longer
required. In addition industrial units are often leased out
with rent relief which will obviously reduce initial returns
from the development. In any case industrial building
allowances introduced in the 1980 Finance Act stimulated a
plethora of private sector developments which should encourage
authorities to reconsider their role in this area. If the
private sector can satisfy demand local government should seek

out alternative opportunities for intervention.

It seems unlikely that many financial aids will prove self-financing. Loans at less than market rates, grants, support for cooperatives and so on will probably involve net expenditure. It is often by no means certain that firms so assisted moreover would not have been able to raise financial support from elsewhere or that aid has much effect on output or employment. Equity financing may prove self-financing depending on the nature of firms receiving support from an authority or enterprise board. Early evidence in terms of the latter suggests indeed that enterprise boards will prove profitable if investments are made according to economic rather than political considerations. Finally in terms of the self financing nature of local authority initiatives, Bovaird (1981) points out that one planning amendment might easily be implemented at little or no cost. The often held assumption that warehousing provides fewer jobs per unit area than does industry certainly is not always true in the West Midlands at least. More sensitive planning controls might thus well be introduced to differentiate between warehousing projects providing little employment and others creating as much as equivalent sized industrial projects.

(ii) The cost effectiveness of initiatives. A second criterion suggested by Bovaird (1981) by which innovations can be assessed is the cost-effectiveness indicator. Costs here are those borne by the authority and effectiveness is determined according to jobs saved or created. He suggests that there are four classifications: low cost, high effectiveness; high cost, high effectivness; low cost, low effectivness; and high cost, low effectiveness.

Bovaird (1981) suggests that advice and information services can prove both low cost and highly efficient. This is because information concerning land, available premises, financial aid and so on is often readily available anyway to a local authority and can easily be assembled at one centre. There appears to be a demand for such services, especially on the part of small firms. It may well be too that these kinds of sign-posting activities frequently direct employers towards financial, technical and managerial services located in either central government departments or the private sector or local educational establishments. The actual provision of assistance would thus not fall on the authority concerned. On the other hand it is by no means clear that many firms requesting information about financial or other assistance actually implement expansionist proposals and most enquiries from firms beyond an authority's administration do not result in the subsequent relocation within the authority involved.

High cost high effectiveness innovations tend to relate to labour subsidy and training. Botham (1984) establishes an economic justification for employment subsides. Firms are unlikely to take on additional labour, even when subsidised, unless this results in increased output. Since output tends to increase most rapidly in sectors with a high price elasticity of demand, and this condition tends to occur most frequently in companies selling abroad or competing with foreign companies domestically, the subsidy can help reduce balance of payment deficits. The inflationary effects attendant upon this type of expansion are relatively low too because of a reduction in production costs and because the costs per job are less than would be the case with other forms of reflation.

Both the firm and the individual benefit moreover in that the former is able to raise its capacity and thus protect jobs elsewhere in the company and the latter gains more valuable experience than would be the case with most other forms of job creation. Equally effective, if again expensive, are retraining programmes undertaken by authorities where gaps in provision can clearly be identified which impede the expansion of the local economy. Such retraining programmes can help retain companies within an area, encourage their diversification or intensification, stimulate the creation of new companies, and prevent inflationary pressures occurring in sectors experiencing skill shortages.

The third classification identified by Bovaird is that encompassing low cost, low effective initiatives. Here two major innovations are identified: land allocation and advocacy of the local area. In the case of the former, using empirical evidence from the West Midlands, it appears that much industrial development has occurred on land zoned for alternative uses and land zoned for industrial development in various development plans is frequently used for other purposes. Some firms have moved somewhat prematurely to industrial zones which have never fully developed and others successfully obtained planning permission for in situ expansions. A more flexible policy treating all applications on their merits may well thus be required. Advocacy for the local area may again prove of limited cost but is often poorly organised and may remain intellectually uncertain in that authorities are torn between stressing the weaknesses of the area, thus highlighting the case for national assistance, whilst simultaneously emphasising the strengths of the local economy in any national recovery.

The final classification here is high cost low effective
initiatives. Three are identified by Bovaird (1981).
General promotion of one authority to the detriment of others
does not increase national output if firms simply migrate to
take advantage of public subsidy. Preferential local
purchasing policies may accentuate inefficiencies unless
local firms are equally efficient as companies displaced.
There may here anyway be strong economic and political grounds
for substituting local suppliers for foreign ones even if the
latter prove marginally cheaper. Some forms of direct
employment by authorities may prove expensive too. Employment
subsidies may be better spent in the private sector rather
than the public since extra private sector output can more
easily boost additional employment, and profits created by
subsidised staff will help pay wages. On the other hand of
course many aspects of public sector activities such as
direct labour organisations do earn monetary returns.

The evaluation techniques developed by Bovaird (1981) and
briefly expounded here are clearly somewhat crude. In one
sense that is a constraint which afflicts many attempts to
evaluate public policies where objectives and outcomes may be
difficult to define accurately. Nevertheless these sorts of
exercises are of value. In particular they ensure that
efforts are made to identify objectives, and they force
authorities to consider the degree to which initiatives are
self-financing and cost-effective. This latter point is
crucial because of the limited resources available to
authorities at a time when an increasing proportion of some
forms of intervention will be funded by the private sector,
occasionally by central government, or by various public-
private sector partnerships. If these organisations undertake
some forms of economic development it may well be in the
interests of authorities to concentrate on innovations
designed, say, to employ those marginalised by the market.
In these areas there is unlikely to be much competition.

(c) Equity Issues

One final issue ought to be mentioned in this overall effort
to identify costs and benefits of local authority economic
intervention. The question of equity is central to
interventionist strategies adopted by many of the more radical
authorities. To many of these administrations the mere
process of economic development is a necessary but not
sufficient policy objective. The disadvantaged must benefit
from such intervention. What evidence there is available
here is not however encouraging. Storey (1983) points out
for example that the determination on the part of so many

administrations to boost the small firm sector is not likely to help many of the unskilled since it is medium and larger establishments that employ so many of the unskilled that can actually find jobs. In this context it is perhaps fortunate to find that Gough et al (1981) in examining local authority-employer relations in inner London discovered that larger companies knew more about possible sources of local government assistance and made more demands on such aid than did smaller establishments.

Generally however there is little to suggest that local authority economic intervention has done a great deal to assist the most deprived. Cameron et al (1982) point out for instance that economic intervention in Tyne and Wear does little to help the acute employment problems of the inner city areas. This is not perhaps surprising bearing in mind the travel-to-work patterns in the region with many managerial and skilled workers living beyond the urban core. Perhaps too economic development of any kind should be welcomed in the more deprived urban areas where severe physical and other constraints limit the scope for expansion and encourage relocation (McIntosh and Keddie 1979). On the other hand faced with the scale of labour market disadvantage in inner urban areas where spasmodic employment, deskilling, and long term unemployment, for the young and old in particular, appear endemic (Cousins et al 1982) it cannot be surprising to find that for more interventionist authorities narrowly economic evaluations of intervention will not suffice.

15 A political evaluation

It has been stressed throughout this work that job creation initatives by local authorities involve political choices as well as more technical economic evaluations of strategies. By committing a council to pursue policies aimed at creating jobs its members demonstrate their acceptance of a particular set of attitudes as to the right and proper functions of a local authority. A number of local authorities have established a much more specific philosophy of the role and potential for local authority economic intervention. This chapter will outline the interconnections between political ideology and the choice of policies towards the local economy pursued by councils. It will also consider some of the theoretical implications of these policies for recent interpretations of the role of local governments in capitalist societies.

In Chapter 2, we identified three basic and idealised modes of political thought within local authorities today. These positions, the neo-liberal right, the centre and the socialist left, should not be too closely identified with the three major political parties in Britain. The majority of local authorities pursue policies that most closely conform to the centrist 'end of ideology' stereotype. Essential to this view is a broad acceptance of capitalism as the predominant but not sole means of economic organisation although certain elements of service provision should be owned and controlled by public sector organisations. In particular provision is made through public enterprise, in which local authorities play a part, to provide sustenance and some comforts to individuals who cannot survive within a free market economy. This mixed economy welfare capitalism was overwhelmingly accepted in the post 1945 years until economic depression and lack of growth motivated the Conservative and later the Labour Party to seek alternative ideologies.

Attitudes to the system of production, or in other terms class politics, are not however the only determinants of local government policies. Parochialism for example may be a significant factor that impels councillors, interest groups

and the electorate to push forward the economic interests
of their area regardless of the problems of more depressed
regions of the country. Policy may also be dependent on
the presence of particularly perceptive or innovatory actors
within the local community and their exposure to new ideas
and practices in local government. Limitations on policy
will also be imposed by political actors external to the
local polity and in particular the central government. It is
nevertheless of value as a heuristic device to place the
predominant packages of economic development initiatives
within an idealised ideological spectrum which is centred
around attitudes to the dominant system of production within
the country since this must be regarded as the most significant element of ideologies within the British State.

NEO-LIBERALISM

Although this book has described positive attempts by local
authorities to increase employment within their communities
a few have deliberately pursued policies that led to a loss
of jobs and deterioration of working conditions in specific
industries. These authorities include Birmingham City Council
which under Conservative control from 1982 to 1984 reduced
the number of its full time employees by 950 or the Wirral
Metropolitan District Council which has privatised its
cleansing services with a loss of 194 jobs and generally
worse rates of pay and conditions of service for those
workers who now provide the service under private management
(Bannon 1984).

The actions of these authorities are in part motivated by
neo-Liberal Thatcherist views that in their purest form
demand the withdrawal of local, or central government, from
activities that can be provided by the private sector. Few
if any local authorities in Britain pursue neo-liberalism
to its logical conclusion but those councils in which this
philosophy has a significant impact are unlikely to adopt any
positive measures directly to increase jobs in their
community although they will argue that the economic logic
of their strategies is to create full employment through the
operations of a free economy. Reduction in the number of
local authority employees, and privatisation of services will
lead to lower rates and greater scope for competition and
entrepreneurial initiative. It has been suggested
previously that there is little evidence to support the view
that lower rates benefit local industry or that publicly
controlled services such as direct labour organisations are
necessarily any less efficient or costly than private

sector provision. It is moreover clear that local
authorities permit generally better conditions of service
than the private sector,

THE KEYNSIAN CENTRE

Local authorities that broadly accept the capitalist welfare
economy of Britain can have no ideological objections to
local government intervention in the economy provided this
is on a modest scale. In as much as central government has
an important role in steering the British economy local
intervention is also acceptable provided that it does not
distort national objectives. The many local politicians who
abide by these views may not however take up the task of
economic intervention. In many cases it will simply not
occur to councillors or their officers that such work exists
or is practical. More significantly, and in line with
Keynsian theory, the health of the local economy can be an
important factor motivating intervention. If the economy
is in decline government should intervene to stimulate growth
but where there is rapid expansion and full employment it may
be necessary for government to intervene to damp down the
rate of growth to avoid economic ills such as inflation.
There is similarly at local level no need for councillors
to promote development in already prosperous areas since
this may result in unwanted pressures on local housing,
amenities and the environment.

Where the mixed economy is accepted and local unemployment
motivates the council to promote development, the strategies
used will be largely aimed at facilitating the growth of
industry and commerce regardless of its ownership, working
conditions and, except where pollution may result, its
product. The policies typical of these authorities include
the attraction of industry and tourists, the provision of
factory sites, premises and infra structure, and the supply
of loans, grants and advice to small and medium sized
businesses. Less frequently they may also offer their support
to industries fighting for government protection from overseas competition, arrange to purchase local products and
can be actively engaged in training schemes for industry and
commerce. On occasion they will form enterprise boards
possibly in association with private industry and on the
more radical leftward fringe will be more concerned to
retain the existing number of employees within the authority
than keep rates at a relatively low level.

These activities, with the possible exception of rating
policy, are all supportive of industry and strenuous efforts
are frequently made to avoid possible conflict between
local business and the local authority. Questions are
rarely raised about the policies of local industry
especially concerning their working conditions and concern
over their development policies is usually voiced only if
the firm is seeking to reduce its activities in the
community. On occasion where a large employer is to
disappear, as in the case of the steel industry in Corby or
Consett, strenuous efforts may be made to persuade the
industry or the government to retain the plant although this
action will not extend to a serious critique of government
economic policies towards the industry. In cases where
local authorities have been critical of industrial policies,
as in the case of WOOLTAC, councillors have not pressed
their objections when their comments are rebuffed by the
industry. There is therefore no attempt among these
authorities to force firms to follow particular working
practices, guide the development of the industry, or
suggest alternative methods of employment.

Although these authorities may have a similar ideological
stance and adopt policies supportive and uncritical of
industry they can differ considerably in their level of
activity and in the emphasis that they place on particular
policies. Bradford Metropolitan District Council has for
example created one of the most highly developed set of
employment creation policies which demonstrates an
entrepreneurial style similar to some of the much more
substantially funded new town development corporations.
Its Economic Development Unit co-ordinates and implements
a range of powers needed to secure industrial development
in the District. Industry is brought into the City through
established publicity techniques and also their imaginative
strategy of organising holidays and thereby building an
attractive image for the area. Factories, sites and infra-
structure can be provided for expanding firms and efforts
are made to overcome planning difficulties. A wide range of
grants are available for suitable firms and considerable
effort is made to publicise these schemes. Close liaison
is achieved between developing industry and the Economic
Development Unit which will not only provide advice and aid
but also ensure that support is delivered with a minimum of
delay. The whole package is designed both to attract new
firms to the area and to develop within the city industries
which through the use of new technologies are likely to
grow and survive in the late 20th Century.

In contrast to the approach of Bradford other authorities
may adopt less of an entrepreneurial new technology role
and be more inclined to aid existing traditional industries
than stimulate the relocation and growth of new high
technology companies. West Yorkshire Metropolitan County
Council, although it includes the District of Bradford
within its boundaries, adopts a low profile in respect of
the attraction of industry. It employs a lone I.D.O. working
within the Country's Economic Development Unit, who is mainly
concerned with liaison with the Regional Development
Association and the Department of Industry. The County
nevertheless offers a comprehensive range of grants for
industry, ranging from large firms, through its pension
funds, medium sized industry, from the Enterprise Board,
and small businesses. The authority is also highly
supportive of major employers in industries traditionally
associated with West Yorkshire such as woollen textiles.
Other authorities may demonstrate somewhat different
emphasis from these examples. Leeds is supportive of
community improvement and development schemes, whilst
Allerdale District Authority along with the County Council
of Cumbria has shown particular interest in environmental
and infra-structural improvements.

Differences between authorities that accept the Keynsian
mixed economy is in practice a matter of scale. Many
councils would probably adopt packages of policy similar to
those of Bradford or West Yorkshire if they devoted greater
resources and interest to employment creation. There are
however a large proportion of authorities which, like
Doncaster Metropolitan District, have for several years left
their share of local economic development to an I.D.O.
often working alone and without sufficient resources. In
these circumstances, however able the officer may be, there
can be few achievements to rival those of councils with
established economic development committees and development
units. There are finally, authorities both Labour and
Conservative controlled that may not only show little
interest in developing their local economies but also, due
to the short term interest of lowering rates for electoral
gain, reduce their own workforce. Birmingham District
Council when controlled by Labour from 1980 to 1982 lost
more council employees than the much more ideologically
motivated Conservative council that succeeded it. The
Labour council that has controlled the city since 1984
is however unlikely to pursue these policies, possibly
because of the influence of the more radical left.

These authorities were described in Chapter 2 as being
concerned not only to alleviate unemployment but to 'increase
the element of democratic control over industrial decisions'
and 'encourage new forms of social ownership' (Greater
London Council 1981 p 15). They are critical of the mixed
economy and may dream of a society guided by socialist
values in which if it is not possible to provide to each
according to their needs, at least allocates scarce resources
on a more equitable basis. Leaders of Councils such as
Sheffield, Greater London or Liverpool are however also
realists who are aware that they discharge major
responsibilities within a predominantly capitalist society
that will not change its structure overnight. Their
policies are therefore radical only in relative terms and
are far from revolutionary in the sense of attempting
rapidly to undermine existing social and economic relations.

Rather than seeking the overthrow of capitalism the
authorities of the radical left which are involved in
economic intervention are attempting to democratise business
control by permitting much greater numbers of individuals
to have some control over capitalist ventures. Support
is therefore given to co-operatives and businesses run by
minority groups, provided that the proposed ventures are
economically viable. Through enterprise boards these
authorities may also purchase equity control in companies
and development land. In an effort to make business more
accountable to employees and the community in which they
are situated, a variety of strategies, termed by the G.L.C.
popular planning, have been developed by these councils.
Research is carried out on behalf of employees and trade
unions, resources and advice are made available to workers
and communities in order that they can better understand
the policies of their companies and, if need be, challenge
their plans or prepare for the possible failure of an
enterprise. The local authority itself can also challenge
the policy of large companies and the government in order
to prevent closures and relocation of plant. They are also
aware of their own role as major employers and consumers
and strongly oppose pressures to reduce their workforce or
privatise services. Instead they seek to use their purchasing
power to ensure acceptable working practices among their
contractors and suppliers.

The ideological perspective of the radical left leads to a
rejection of a number of strategies that are mainstream
practices with councils which are uncritical of the prevail-

ing economic system. In particular they are not enthusiastic about attracting industry into their area if this entails further privation for regions already suffering serious unemployment. Emphasis is placed more on creating or saving jobs rather than shuffling around the distribution of a decreasing pool of work. Little enthusiasm is also shown for firms that adopt harsh conditions of employment or manufacture socially destructive products such as armaments.

Although left wing authorities undertake a number of distinctive employment creation policies which imply a critical view of the prevailing economic system they also carry out, and in several cases have initiated, strategies that are widely adopted by more conservative councils. They are for example pioneers of enterprise boards which are active within both radical and more consensus minded authorities. It would also be misleading to give the impression that all radical authorities pursue economic interventionism with equal enthusiasm or that those which are most active adopt similar strategies. Despite its challenge to the government over rates and its infusion of Militant tendency councillors, Liverpool City Council under Labour control has for example developed few initiatives to alleviate the loss of jobs from the private sector within the city and has devoted its attention to employing more local authority staff through increased services.

Three authorities are usually identified as the outstanding advocates of radical strategies for economic intervention: West Midlands County Council, Greater London County Council and Sheffield District Council (Boddy 1984). These authorities undoubtedly deserve a pre-eminent position in the development of policies for employment creation, although they are not the only radical creators of employment with some London Boroughs such as Hackney following this tendancy. They also have distinctively different approaches to the task.

The West Midlands County Council has a more entrepreneurial approach than either the G.L.C. or Sheffield with an interest in developing jobs in high technology through the promotion of science parks, and, through its Enterprise Board, in funding medium sized private firms. The Council is much less inclined to pursue political campaigns to prevent closures or to impose compliance on specified working conditions. In these respects the local authority has a similar view to West Yorkshire County Council albeit on a somewhat larger scale and both these authorities would probably be placed close to the radical, centrist border, along an ideological class orientated scale. The West Midlands nevertheless has a number of radical credentials through its work in advising employees and trade unions, encouraging socially useful products and the work of its Enterprise Board influencing the structure of local industries.

The G.L.C. has in comparison with any other local authority much greater ability to raise revenue through the application of section 137 of the 1972 Local Government Act and through this largesse is able to establish a substantial industrial role which is implemented principally by its Enterprise Board. The authority is however concerned that as it funds industry it also ensures that assisted companies are subject to full or partial control by the Council and conform to acceptable working conditions. Through its concept of popular planning the authority is particularly interested in obliging firms to be sensitive to local needs and has even developed international links between workers to help prevent redundancies within the metropolis.

Sheffield City Council is in comparison with the G.L.C. and the West Midlands County Council much more given to pressure group campaigns in order to prevent business closures rather than creating new jobs through funding new or growing businesses. Considerable work has for example been put into research and campaigns concerning the policies of the British Steel Corporation. The authority has also developed a scheme to ensure that contractors and suppliers conform to specified working conditions whilst the Council itself is in the forefront of campaigns against the privatisation of services. In these respects Sheffield has probably the most politicised strategy to save jobs and although its Employment Department can and does provide funds for co-operatives and conventionally owned private businesses many of its members are far from convinced that they should be involved in subsidising the private sector. Unlike the West Midlands or the G.L.C. Sheffield has not established an enterprise board.

These radical authorities are viewed by their political opponents as irresponsible organisations imposing high taxes on local industry and wasting funds on futile class orientated gestures rather than supporting productive forces within the country. Despite their differences in strategies these authorities clearly have a common interest in extending industrial ownership and controls over business.

259

They have however also in common shown little enthusiasm for following traditional socialist strategies of ensuring the collective ownership of the means of production.

The writings of Shaw, the Webbs or G.D.H. Cole concerning municipal or syndical ownership have been largely forgotten by present day Labour Party activists. Through their Enterprise Boards, the G.L.C and the West Midlands can and on occasion do, purchase equity in companies but this is not carried out with any systematic intention of expanding local government ownership of profitable enterprise. Sheffield is even less interested in buying control of firms. All three authorities along with several other Labour controlled councils have fought to prevent the privatisation of public assets but apart from a few curiosities and small scale schemes as reported in Chapter 10 none have attempted to test the limits to which it is possible for local authorities to acquire local industries and services as directly controlled elements of the local authority. This reticence to municipalisation may well reflect a reluctance by politicians and politicised local government officers to take on the risks involved in ownership and management. From a socialist perspective the tendency of their policies is however moving them in a direction which has, in terms of pure theory, been soundly rejected by most politicians of the British left. Rather than achieve socialism through the gradual ownership and control of industry and commerce by democratically responsive public bodies they are like Gaitskill and Crossland rejecting Clause IV in favour of the Swedish approach of controlling private capital through redistributive taxation and close regulation of capital investment and working conditions.

This survey of local authority economic policies should dispel the image that the authorities of the left are irresponsible revolutionary cliques. Far from pursuing revolutionary or futile aims they have developed imaginative portfolios of schemes that are supportive of capitalism in Britain. Unlike more moderate authorities, radical councils have however had the unpardonable affrontery to suggest that all may not be well within the mixed economy and that unbridled capitalism can have disastrous social and economic consequences. Support for a co-operative does not undermine capitalism but rather widens the extent of ownership of the means of production. The arguments put forward by the most campaign orientated authority, Sheffield, in favour of an alternative strategy for steel are based on a position, that points to the relatively more successful policies of European nations which have provided greater subsidies for

the industry. These are the arguments of Keynsian rather
than Marxist economists, concerned with the immediate
restoration of jobs within a capitalist society rather than
long term fundamental restructuring of the British economy.

THE POSITION OF CENTRAL GOVERNMENT

Although there may be few local authorities that practice a
thorough neo-liberal ideology this position will in the
immediate future seriously affect the development of local
economic intervention through the policies of the
Conservative central government led by Mrs Thatcher. There
is ideologically little sympathy within the Thatcher
cabinets for local authorities in general let alone their
interest in promoting employment. The government has since
1979 put forward several measures which have hindered these
policies.

In 1980 partly in response to local authority association
pressures for greater powers of economic intervention, the
government set up a review body for this area under the
chairmanship of the Chief Planner Sir Wilfred Burns. The
subsequent report provided a number of ideas on how to
codify local authority powers to develop their economies and
prompted in March 1982 a Green Paper from the Department of
the Environment which sought to curtail their powers to fund
industry. It was suggested that the section 137 precept
should be only ½ pence in the pound for all but inner city
areas where it would remain at 2 pence. Grants should
however only be given to firms with less than 25 employees
and special acts giving authorities powers to finance
industry would not be renewed. The proposals would have
seriously damaged the ability of large authorities such as
the G.L.C and the West Midlands to operate enterprise boards.
The proposals formed part of a Local Government (Miscellaneous Provisions) Bill which was resolutely attacked by the
local authority associations which had been hoping that an
increase in their powers would result from the Burns report.
The protesters were largely successful and the Bill, like
many others concerning local government, was amended in the
House of Lords to give local authorities somewhat greater
freedom to use section 137 monies to aid industry than had
previously been the case by specifically stating that the
rate could be used to fund loans and grants to industry.
The Act also ended up by providing a more generous system of
calculating the product from the 2 pence rate and also
extended the effectiveness of local acts due to terminate in
1986 by a further two years. Despite the failure of the

government to restrict the use of section 137 funds the
government has on several occasions attempted to restrict the
Greater London Council from providing substantial aid to
industry by curtailing the ability of the Greater London
Enterprise Board to purchase industrial property and the
proclivities of the Council for mounting large scale
publicity campaigns. More generally the Local Government
Planning and Land Act of 1980 severely restricted the
ability of local authorities to increase employment through
the expansion of direct works departments and has subsequently
encouraged privatisation of other local authority services.
Apart from specific attacks on local authority employment
one of the most damaging general effects of their policies
is the squeeze on the finances of local authorities in urban
areas. Councillors who feel obliged to cut back on spending
or at best maintain a stand still budget are unlikely to find
extra resources required to fund new employment initiatives.

A further potentially serious blow to local authority
economic intervention is the proposal to abolish the Greater
London Council and the Metropolitan Counties. It is clear
from this book that these authorities have been to the fore
in employment creation and their removal would break up
effective and innovatory economic development units. It is
at the time of writing by no means clear what will become
of these organisations, although Streamlining the Cities
assumes that since the employment creation function is open
to metropolitan districts the role can be continued by this
tier of local government.

It is however unlikely that all metropolitan district
councils will be able to replicate the work of the countries.
Even in South Yorkshire where all the district authorities
are firmly under Labour Party control they are not all
radical councils. Doncaster and Rotherham in particular
may well be reluctant to pool their efforts under some form
of agency arrangement to keep in being the present County
wide employment creation initiatives. In some other
metropolitan counties and London where there are some
entrenched Conservative led districts such co-operation is
even less likely. Without the development of some form of
joint working between local authorities in metropolitan
conurbations it will be difficult to sustain existing levels
of economic activity. Unless districts are allowed to
increase their section 137 precept to 4 pence in the pound
metropolitan areas will immediately lose half their
potential revenue for employment creation work and it will,
even at such a rate, be difficult for an authority such as
Hackney to sustain a system of funding industry in its area

that would replicate the work of GLEB. It may however be possible for a number of London boroughs or metropolitan districts to agree jointly to subsidise enterprise boards covering their territories although the resultant organisations are unlikely to be as large as their predecessors.

Abolition of the metropolitan counties will also seriously destroy the planning aspects of their economic policies. It would not be as easy for an initiative such as West Yorkshire's WOOLTAC to be sustained without the help of a county authority covering a regional industrial interest. The attempt by West Midlands County Council to re-organise the conurbation's foundry industry would probably be impossible were it to be conducted by several district authorities. There will finally also be a loss of expertise and possibly resources of information if established county employment creation units are broken up. It is as yet far from clear whether personnel employed in these organisations will find similar work in other authorities or be obliged to seek jobs in other forms of employment.

The future for local authority economic intervention under the neo-liberal Conservative Government is likely to continue to be strewn with stones and thorns. It would however be very difficult for the Government to legislate the complete abandonment of such strategies and attempts seriously to curtail the use of Section 137 funds have, as indicated earlier, failed. It is also probable that any government that sustains a neo-liberal policy will create and sustain high levels of unemployment and as a result the major motivation for local authority councillors to continue to develop policies to overcome the problems that unemployment creates within their communities will remain.

It is highly speculative in 1984 to suggest what a post-Thatcher future may reveal. If however either the Conservative, or Labour or Alliance parties acting either alone or in coalition move the ideological perspective of government back to a Keynsian position there will at least be less hostility towards local authority efforts to alleviate unemployment. It is however unlikely that such a government would press strongly for any increase in local powers. The position of any Labour Government is clouded by the question of what its prevailing ideology would be let alone any specific policy towards local authorities. Despite the popularity within the Party of local government leaders such as David Blunkett and Ken Livingstone and their presence in the inner policy committees of the Labour Party a coherent view of the role of local authorities in Britain has yet to emerge. At present there is little more than an overwhelmingly agreed commitment to remove many of the restrictions placed on local councils by the Conservative administration. It is however possible that once back in power the Party may again seek to use solely nationally imposed solutions to the problems of social and economic development rather than allow greater freedom to local authorities to pursue these aims.

THEORETICAL PERSPECTIVES

Even though the study of party programmes, such as they are, gives little indication of the future progress of local authority employment creation initiatives there are several theoretical analyses of the functions of local governments that provide possible answers to this question. Following the work of neo-Marxist theorists such as Manuel Castells, there is a considerable body of writers who argue that urban societies have developed to ensure the replication of the labour power necessary for the maintenance of capitalist production through the process of collective consumption. In other words urban society supplies through private and public institutions services such as education, cleansing and hospitals, that ensure that there is a healthy and sufficiently skilled workforce to keep the wheels of capitalist production in motion.

Peter Saunders has moved from this analysis of urban society to the position that the function of local government in urbanised capitalist society is to facilitate the process of collective consumption. Following theories advanced by O'Connor and Offe on functions and decision making processes within the state, Saunders argues that there are three major functions of the state. It has a direct role in maintaining the existing order of society through processes of coercion and legitimation. Stimulation of capitalist acquisition is achieved through a corporate relationship that exists between the state bureaucracy and the controllers of capital. The third function, the provision of services, that is the process of collective consumption, is to a large measure entrusted to units of local government which although created by the state are allowed a measure of discretion. The distancing of this function from direct state control is necessary since this activity is not directly beneficial to capitalists as it generates tax demands and also creates conflict between those individuals who rely on public services, such as council housing, and those who utilise privately supplied services. If however divisions between these two sectors create instability or the demands for public consumption undermine the process of capitalist accumulation the state will be able to restrain the activities of its semi-independent creation.

Saunders therefore argues that 'Local politics are essentially consumption politics and local campaigns around issues of consumption cannot be easily integrated into a nationally organised class-based movement centred on the politics of production'. (Saunders 1984 p 45). If this theory is valid then there is a limited future for local authority efforts to intervene in the processes of economic production. Saunders is nevertheless aware that in recent years there have been increasing demands for interventionist local economic policies but he regards these as somewhat minor activities that are unlikely to develop in the long term (Saunders 1981). It is also implied that radical authorities which see the possibility of advancing the cause of socialism through economic campaigns at the local level are misdirecting their energies.

The theory can be criticised on a number of grounds. Dunleavy (1984) suggests that it is empirically unsound given that different states have different allocations of functions between central and local government. He also observes that in the 19th Century local councils were extensively concerned with productive processes. It can however be suggested that the development of the corporate state linking private capital and the central bureaucracy is a 20th Century phenomenon and its growth is reflected in, for example, the 1945 Labour Government nationalisation of many municipally controlled utilities. It may also be argued that whilst it can be accepted that central governments may frequently be concerned with facilitating collective consumption they have increasingly ensured that this activity is the predominant function of local government and hence Saunders's implied pessimism over the progress of local authority economic initiatives remains valid.

A further avenue of criticism emerges from the work of public choice theorists such as Tiebout (1956) and Peterson (1981) who have established a model of local authority activity based on the unrestrained choices made by citizens who are collectively assumed to be highly acquisitive. Peterson classifies local authority functions as firstly allocational, in which communities provide services collectively required by the majority of the population such as roads, and more arguably schools, and secondly, as redistributive, entailing the transfer of taxation revenues from wealthier to poorer citizens for services such as public housing or social security. The creation of employment is classified in the third set of functions which are developmental and seek to increase the general wealth of the community. Local citizens will give little support to redistributive services that provide services at their expense to groups poorer than themselves but will be supportive of allocational and developmental services provided that they ensure value for money to their community. Under this model central government will therefore be left with the duty of providing welfare services, but can share allocational functions and development activities with the units of local government.

Public choice theory therefore suggests that local authorities will be active in the creation of employment provided that they can demonstrate to their electorates that the community is getting a return from its outlay in support of this activity. The argument has some merit in explaining the fluctuation of interest in economic intervention by local authorities in line with rates of unemployment. A wealthy community with high employment will get little value from campaigns to create further jobs. The theory also fits in well with the generally conservative pattern of local interventionist policies which when involving the allocation of large resources to businesses rarely take risks by supplying funds to insecure companies.

The public choice theories are not however as useful as that of Saunders in explaining the allocation of functions between central and local governments. Public choice theory assumes incorrectly as argued earlier, that the growth of cities is dependent on prevailing rates of taxation and that businesses will move from highly taxed to low taxed areas. There is also little account taken of the ability of central government to aid poorer communities in maintaining redistributive service provisions. It can nevertheless be argued that despite their inadequacies both theories provide some insight on the limits of local government policies towards their economies.

The state and the local community may be tolerant of local initiatives to create employment and to stimulate the economy provided that this is seen to operate on a value for money basis that does not undermine the facility of the state to indulge with business in corporate economic planning. It would seem irrational for a central government concerned with ensuring capitalist accumulation to object to local communities subsidising in a small way capital growth from the community when it appears that it is achieving a profit-

able return for both the capitalist and the community.
Restraints will however be imposed by the state if the scale
of such activity begins to undermine its relationship with
big business or by the community if the employment creation
strategies appear to be of little value to the locality.
Local authority economic intervention is therefore likely to
continue and even flourish as a relatively small scale
activity within communities facing economic hardship.

The preceeding analysis is clearly applicable to most local
authority schemes to create employment and in particular
their efforts to fund local industries or to promote the
development of a better physical environment for business
development. It is not however readily applicable to the
efforts of radical left wing authorities that seek to
mobilise public opinion and organise workers against the
policies devised by central government and big business in
respect to capital accumulation. These campaigns can be
sustained by local communities with little opposition from
their citizens since they are relatively inexpensive to
maintain requiring the co-ordination of economic experts,
workers in threatened industries and publicists who may
give their services free of charge, or are principally
employed by the local authority in other capacities. These
challenges to central economic policy are significant in that
they are an example, contrary to Saunders's theory, of locally
generated activity that presents a serious challenge to the
central class interests defended by the state. Considerable
tension will therefore be created should local authorities
be able successfully to maintain this form of campaign and
this will be exacerbated by the problems that may be faced
by the state in suppressing such activity. Inexpensive
campaigns based on the co-ordination of interests providing
help voluntarily is difficult to eradicate without destroying
many of the traditionally accepted functions and freedom of
local governments. If however such activity prospers it may
conceivably be a means through which the hopes of Fabian
writers such as the Webbs or Shaw may be realised. Local
authorities may be able to convince majorities to oppose
the central process of capitalist orientated corporate
decision making on the economy in favour of more democratic
socialist solutions.

Bibliography

Adams, G., 'Tourism as a Means of Development', in
Duffield, B. (ed), Tourism : A Tool for Regional
Development, Tourism and Recreation Research Unit,
University of Edinburgh 1977.

Advisory Council for Applied Research and Development,
Industrial Innovation , (Cabinet Office) HMSO, London
1978.

Archer, B.H., de Vare, R. and Moore, B.H, Tourism in the
Coastal Strip of East Anglia 1976 , Quoted in English
Tourist Board,Planning for Tourism in England 1981.

Association of District Councils, Review of Local Authority
Assistance to Industry (Results of Survey), (ADC Circular
1980/136), 1980.

Association of Metropolitan Authorities, Priorities for
Progress. Local Government and Economic Recovery , 1978.

Association of Metropolitan Authorities, Investing in
Recovery. An Alternative View of the Economic Future ,
1981.

Association of Metropolitan Authorities, RSG Allocations for
Partnerships , 1982.

Ball, R.M., 'Spatial and Structural Characteristics of
Recent Unemployment Change: Some Policy Considerations',
Policy Review Section, Regional Studies, Vol. 17, No 2,
1983.

Bannock, G., The Smaller Business in Britain and Germany ,
Wilton House Publications, 1976.

Bannon, J., Privatisation of Cleansing Services in the
Wirral M.D.C. , Unpublished   Dissertation, Sheffield
City Polytechnic, Department of Public Sector
Administration, 1984.

Barbier, E., Earthworks: Environmental Approaches to
Employment Creation , Friends of the Earth, 1981

Barrett, S. and Boddy, M., Local Authority/Private Sector
Industrial Development Partnerships , Working Paper 18,
School for advanced Urban Studies, University of Bristol,
1981.

Binney, M. and Hanna, M., Preservation Pays , Save
Britains Heritage, London, 1978.

Birch, D., The Job Generation Process , MIT Program on
   Neighbourhood and Regional Change, Cambridge, Mass, 1979.
Bird, J., The Major Seaports of the United Kingdom ,
   Hutchinson, London, 1963.
Birmingham Metropolitan District Council, Inner City
   Partnership Programme 1980-1983 , 1979.
Birmingham Metropolitan District Council, Inner City
   Partnership Programme 1982-85 , 1981.
Boddy, M., 'Changing Public-Private Sector Relationships
   in the Industrial Development Process' in Young, K. and
   Mason, C. (eds), Urban Economic Development, Macmillan,
   London, 1983.
Boddy, M., Local Government and Industrial Development ,
   Univ of Bristol, School of Advanced Urban Studies -
   Occ Paper 7, 1982.
Boddy, M., 'Local Economic and Employment Strategies',
   in Boddy, M. and Fudge, C. (eds), Local Socialism?
   Macmillan, London, 1984.
Boddy, M. and Barrett, S., Local Government and the
   Industrial Development Process , Working Paper 6,
   School for Advanced Urban Studies University of Bristol,
   1980.
Boddy, M. and Fudge, C. (eds), Local Socialism? ,
   Macmillan, London, 1984.
Bolton, J.E., Small Firms , Report of the Committee Inquiry
   on Small Firms, Cmnd 4811, HMSO, 1971.
Botham, R., 'Local Authority Employment Subsidies', The
   Planner, Vol.69, No.5, 1983.
Botham, R., 'Employment Subsidies: A New Direction For
   Local Government Economic Initiatives', Regional Studies,
   Vol.18, No.1, 1984.
Bovaird, T., 'An Evaluation of Local Authority Employment
   Initiatives', Local Government Studies, Vol.7, No.4, 1981.
Bramley, G., Stewart, M. and Underwood, J., Local Economic
   Initiatives , School for Advanced Urban Studies, University
   of Bristol, Working Paper 1, 1978.
Bramley, G., Stewart, M., and Underwood, J., 'Local Economic
   Initiatives', Town Planning Review, Vol.50, No.2, 1979.
Briant, B., Local Government, Finance and Development.
   Finance for Development , Sheffield City Polytechnic, 1979.
British Tourist Authority, Legislation Affecting Tourism in
   the U.K. , B.T.A, London, 1981.
British Waterways Board and South Yorkshire County Council,
   Sheffield and South Yorkshire Navigation. Appraisal of
   the Improvement Proposals , 1977.
Bryden, J., Tourism and Development: A Case Study in the
   Commonwealth Caribbean , Cambridge University Press,
   Cambridge, 1973.

BSC Industry, Financial Incentives in the Opportunity Areas , 1984.

Burgess, A., 'Selling Places: Environmental Images for the Executive', Regional Studies, Vol.16, No.1, 1982.

Calouste Gulbenkian Foundation, Whose Business is Business? , 1981.

Calvert, H., A History of Hull , Phillimore, Chichester Sussex, 1978.

Cameron, G.C. and Clark, B.D., Industrial Movement and the Regional Problem , Social and Economic Studies, University of Glasgow, Occ Paper No.5, 1966.

Cameron, S.J. et al, Local Authority Aid to Industry: An Evaluation in Tyne and Wear , Department of the Environment, Inner Cities Research Programme, No.7, HMSO, 1982.

Cameron, S.J. and Dabinett, G.E., 'Employment Development and the Inner City', Planning Outlook, Vol.23, No.2, 1980.

Camina, M.M., Local Authorities and the Attraction of Industry , Pergamon Press, Oxford, 1974.

Catalano, A., A Review of UK Enterprise Zones , Centre for Environmental Studies, Paper 17, 1983.

Centre for Environmental Studies, Aspects of Structure Planning in Britain , CES R.P.20, 1975.

Chalkley, B.,'Redevelopment and the Small Firm: The Making of a Myth', The Planner, Vol.65, No.4, 1979.

Chalkley, B. and Perry, M., 'How Many Factories do we Need?', Town and Country Planning, Vol.53, No.2, 1984.

Chandler, J.A. and Yates, J.M., A Survey of Local Authority Pressure Group Action on behalf of the Local Economy , Unpublished, 1980.

Chandler, J.A. and Templeton, J.M., Made in Sheffield: Local Authority Action on behalf of a Declining Industry , Sheffield City Polytechnic, Department of Political Studies, Occasional Paper, EP/1/81, 1981.

City of Newcastle upon Tyne, Labour Resources in Newcastle , Undated.

Civic Catering Association, Management and Consultancy Report Policy Document , CCA, unpublished, 1977.

Cockerton, P., Gilmour-White, T., Pearce, J. and Whyatt, A., Workers' Co-operatives , Peoples Press, Aberdeen, 1980.

Collinge, C., Investing in the Local Economy: Business Finance and the Role of Local Government , Community Projects Foundation, London, 1983.

Committee on Municipal Savings Banks, Report , HMSO, Cmnd 3014, 1928.

Community Projects Foundation, Community Development: Towards a National Perspective. The Work of the Community Projects Foundation, 1978-1982 , 1982.

Confederation of British Industry, Enterprise into the Eighties , 1977.

Cooper, M.J., The Industrial Location Decision Making
Process , Unpublished PhD, University of Birmingham, 1974.

Cooper, M.J., The Industrial Location Decision Making
Process , Centre for Urban and Regional Studies, University
of Birmingham, Occasional Paper, No.34, 1975.

Cooper Report, Schools - Industry Link Schemes: A Study and
Recommendations , Neville Cooper, Director of Administration, Standard Telephone and Cable for Secretary of State
for Education, 1981.

Coopers Lybrand Associates, Streamlining the Cities. An
analysis of the costs involved in the Government proposals
for reorganising Government in the six Metropolitan
Counties and the GLC , Association of Metropolitan
Counties, 1984.

Cosgrove, I. and Jackson, R., The Geography of Recreation
and Leisure , Hutchinson, London, 1972.

Couch, C., 'Building for Sale in Inner Liverpool',
Chartered Surveyor, February, 1981.

Cousins, J., Curran, M. and Brown, R., Working in the
Inner City , Department of the Environment, Inner Cities
Research Programme,No.8, HMSO, 1982.

Cullingworth, J.B., Town and Country Planning in Britain
(6th Ed), George Allen and Unwin, London, 1976.

Cullingworth, J.B., Town and Country Planning in Britain
(8th Ed), George Allen and Unwin, London, 1982.

Cumberland Times and Star, (19/4/84)

Cumbria County Co-ordinating Committee, Minutes, 1973.

Dabinett, G. and Whisker, P., The Declaration of Industrial
Improvement Areas and the Provision of Advance Factories,
Loans and Grants by Local Authorities in Tyne and Wear
1974-79 , Department of Town and Country Planning,
University of Newcastle upon Tyne, Inner City Employment
Project, Working Paper, No.2, 1981.

Darley, G., 'Conservation in the Inner City: Old Buildings,
New Jobs?', Built Environment Quarterly, Vol.4, No.3, 1978.

Debenham, Tewson and Chinnocks, High Technology: Myths and
Realities , 1983.

Department of the Environment, Local Government and the
Industrial Strategy , Circular 71/77, 1977.

Department of the Environment, Inner City: Small Firms
Conference . Leeds, 1978.

Department of the Environment, Inner Urban Areas Act 1978 ,
Circular, 68/78, 1978.

Department of the Environment, Local Authority Assistance
to Industry and Commerce , 1982.

Donnison, D., Urban Policies: A New Approach , Fabian
Tract, 487, 1983.

Duffield, B.S., Tourism: A Tool for Regional Development ,
Leisure Studies Association Conference, Edinburgh, 1977,
Tourism and Recreation Research Unit, University of
Edinburgh, 1977.

Drudy, P.J., (ed), Regional and Rural Development ,
Alpha Academic, Chalfont St Giles, 1976.

Dumsday, J., 'Prizes Everyone has to Win', Town and Country
Planning, Vol.53, No.2, 1984.

Duleavy, P., Urban Political Analysis , Macmillan, London,
1980.

Dunleavy, P., 'The Limits to Local Government', in Boddy, M.
and Fudge, C. (eds), Local Socialism? Macmillan, London,
1984.

East Sussex County Council, County Structure Plans , 1980.

Edge , G., 'The Role of Enterprise Boards', The Planner,
Vol.69, No.5, 1983

English Tourist Board, A Study of Tourism in York ,
English Tourist Board, 1972.

English Tourist Board, Tourism Multipliers in Britain ,
English Tourist Board, 1976.

English Tourist Board, Investing in Tourism. Aid to Tourist
Projects in Englands Development Areas 1971-1976 , English
Tourist Board, 1977.

English Tourist Board, Planning for Tourism in England ,
English Tourist Board, 1981 a.

English Tourist Board, Scarborough District Tourism Study ,
English Tourist Board, 1981 b.

English Tourist Board, Tourism Enterprise by Local
Authorities , English Tourist Board, N.D.

Estall, R.C. and Buchanan, R.O., Industrial Activity and
Economic Geography , (3rd Ed), Hutchinson, London, 1973.

Eversley, D., 'Employment for the Inner City', Transactions
of the Institute of British Geographers, New Series,
Vol.5, No.2, 1980.

Fairley, J., 'Training Policy - The Local Perspective',
Policy Review Section, Regional Studies, Vol.17, No.2,
1983.

Falk, N., 'Growing New Firms: The Role of the Social
Entrepreneur', Built Environment Quarterly, Vol.4,
No.3, 1978.

Feinstein,C.H., (ed), York 1831 - 1981 , William Sessions,
York, 1981.

Firn, J. and Swales J., 'The Formation of New Manufacturing
Establishments in the Central Clydeside and West Midlands
Conerbations 1963-1972', Regional Studies, Vol.12, No.2,
1978.

Fogarty, M.P., Plan Your Own Industries, A Study of
Local and Regional Development Organisations ,
Basil Blackwell, Oxford, 1947.

Forsyth, D.J.C., U.S Investment in Scotland, Praeger, New York, 1972.

Fothergill, S. and Gudgin, G., The Job Generation Process in Britain, Centre for Environmental Studies, Research Series, 32, 1979.

Fothergill, S. and Gudgin, G., Unequal Growth: Urban and Regional Employment Change in the UK, Heinemann, London, 1982.

Fothergill, S. and Gudgin, G., 'Employment Prospects in the Thatcher Era', The Planner, Vol.69, No.5, 1983.

Goddard, J.B. and Thwaites, A.T., Technological Change and the Inner City, The Inner City in Context, 4, Social Science Research Council, 1980.

Goddard, J.B. and Thwaites, A.T., 'Science Parks in the Context of National, Regional and Local Technology Policy', The Planner, Vol.69, No.1, 1983.

Goodchild, B., The Application of Self-Help to Building Housing: A Critique of Self-Build and Urban Homesteading, Working Paper No.1, Department of Urban and Regional Studies, Sheffield City Polytechnic, 1981.

Gough, J., Noritt, D., Escott, K. and Leigh R., 'Local Authority Policies in Inner London - Monitoring the Responses of Manufacturing Firms', Local Government Studies, Vol.7, No.4, 1981.

Greater London Council, Minority Party Report: A Socialist Policy for the GLC, March 1981.

Greater London Council, Adult Training Strategy in London in the 1980's, 1983a.

Greater London Council, Small Firms and the London Industrial Strategy, 1983b.

Greater London Council, Industry and Employment; Mid Term Report, Economic Policy Group, Strategy Document, No.17, 1983c.

Greater London Council, Industry and Employment: The Mid Term Report, 1983d.

Greater London Council, 'Rates. Jobs and the GLC', Report by the Leader of the Council, 1983e.

Greater London Council, Jobs for a Change, GLC Economic Policy Group, Paper No.7, 1984.

Greater London Enterprise Board, Quarterly Report to the Industry and Employment Committee of the GLC, 1984.

Greater London Enterprise Board, GLEB Guidelines, Undated.

Green, D.H. and Walker, S., 'Small Firms', Town and Country Planning, Vol.49, No.8, 1980.

Green, H. and Foley, P., 'Making Homes for Small Firms', Town and Country Planning, Vol.52, No.1, 1983

Green, K. and Coombs, R., 'Local Authorities and New Technology - The Case of Tameside', Local Government Studies, Vol.7, No.4, 1981.

Gudgin, G., Moore, B. and Rhodes, J., 'Employment Problems in the Cities and Regions of the UK: Prospects for the 1980's', Cambridge Economic Policy Review, Vol.8, No.2, 1982.

Gulliver, S., 'The Role of the Scottish Development Agency', The Planner, Vol.69, No.5, 1983.

Hackney and Islington London Boroughs Inner City Partnership Programme 1979-1982 , 1978

Hampleton, R., 'Implementing Inner City Policy: Reflections from Experience', Policy and Politics, Vol.9, No.1, 1981.

Hammersmith and Fulham, Strategy for Employment and Economic Development, 1980.

Hampton, W., 'Democracy and Community', Oxford University Press, Oxford, 1970.

Hanna, M., 'Regional Tourism Multiplier Studies: Their fundings and use', in Duffield, B.S.,(ed), Tourism: A Tool for Regional Development , Tourism and Recreation Research Unit, University of Edinburgh, 1977.

Harris, D.F. and Taylor, F.J., The Service Sector: Its Changing Role as a Source of Employment , Centre for Environmental Studies, Research Series, 25, 1978.

Harrison, S., Local Plans and Employment Problems , Working Paper, Department of Town and Country Planning, Gloucestershire Institute of Higher Education, 1978.

Hayton, K., 'Employment Creation in Deprived Areas: The Local Authority Role in Promoting Community Business', Local Government Studies, Vol.9, No.6, 1983.

Henderson, R.A., 'The Location of Immigrant Industry within a UK Assisted Area', Progress in Planning, Vol.14, Part 2, 1980.

Hennock, E.P., Fit and Proper Persons , Edward Arnold, London, 1973.

Herring Son and Daw, 'Property and Technology. The Needs of Modern Industry', 1983.

HMSO, Transport Policy. A Consultation Document , Vol.1, 1976.

HMSO, Report of the Committee of Inquiry into Local Government Finance (Layfield Report) , 1976a.

HMSO, Regional IndustrialDevelopment , Cmnd 9111, 1984.

House of Commons Expenditure Committee (Trade and Industry Sub-Committee) Minutes of Evidence, 4/7/73, HMSO, 1973.

IBM/URBED, Creating Work Through Small Enterprise , IBM (UK) Ltd, Urban and Economic Development Group, 1977.

Jackson, B.G., 'Public Authority Costs of Tourism', in Duffield, B.S.(ed), Tourism: A Tool for Regional Development , Leisure Studies Association Conference, University of Edinburgh, 1977.

Johnson, N. and Cockran, A., Economic Policy Making by Local
Authorities in Britain and West Germany , George Allen and
Unwin, London, 1981.
Joint Docklands Action Group, Industrial Estates in
Docklands , 1977.
Jolley, P.D., A Consideration of the Extent to which
Central and Local Government Initiatives have and can
Aid the Development of Producer Co-operative Enterprise ,
Dissertation for Post-Graduate Diploma in Urban and
Regional Planning, Sheffield City Polytechnic, 1980.
JURUE (Joint Unit for Research on the Urban Evironment),
Local Authority Employment Initiatives , 1980.
Keeble, D., Industrial Location and Planning in the
United Kingdom , Methuen, London, 1976.
Keeble, D.E. and Hauser, D.P., 'Spatial Analysis of
Manufacturing Growth in Outer South East England
1960-1967 I Hypothesis', Regional Studies, Vol.5, No.4,
1971, and 'II Methods and Results', Regional Studies,
Vol.6, No.1, 1972.
Keith-Lucas, B. and Richards, P.G., A History of Local
Government in the Twentieth Century , George Allen
and Unwin, London, 1978.
Kitchen, T., 'Training Initiatives', The Planner, Vol.69,
No.5, 1983.
Lambeth Inner Area Study, Inner London: Policies for
Dispersal and Balance , Department of the Environment,
HMSO, 1977.
Langford, D.A., Direct Labour Organisations in the
Construction Industry , Gower, Aldershot,1982.
LATAC (Local Authorities Textile Action Committee),
The Textile Industry, The Effects of Decline and the
Need for Action , Oldham Metropolitan Borough Council, N.D.
LATAC (Local Authorities Textile Action Committee), News
Items, (Press Releases), Oldham Metropolitan BC, N.D.
Lawless, P., Urban Deprivation and Government Initiative ,
Faber and Faber, London, 1979.
Lawless, P., Britain's Inner Cities: Problems and Policies ,
Harper and Row, London, 1981.
Lawless, P., Inner Urban Intervention: The Evolution of
a Spatial Policy , Pion, London, Forthcoming, 1985.
Leeds Metropolitan District Council, Leeds Policy for
Industry , 1977.
Liverpool Metropolitan District Council, Liverpool Inner
City Partnership Programme 1979-1982 , 1978.
Lloyd, P.E., New Manufacturing Enterprises in Greater
Manchester and Merseyside , Report to the Department
of the Environment, 1980.
Local Economic Development Information Service, 'Industrial
Improvement Areas', Overview, No.B 11, 1982.

Local Economic Development Information Service, Newcastle Priority Area Teams , Initiative, A69, 1983.

Local Economic Development Information Service, Sheffield's Employment Department , 1984.

Local Government Research Unit, Flagstone Enterprises Limited , Paisley College of Technology, Local Government Unit, Working Paper, No.12, 1982.

Lomas, G.M., 'Local Government Under Siege, Social Consequences of Economic Change', Local Government Studies, Vol.7, No.4, 1981.

London Boroughs Association, Report on the Regeneration of Inner London , Housing and Works Committee, 1977.

London Borough of Southwark, Hope Sufferance Wharf , Nov, 1978.

London Borough of Wandsworth, Planning and Transport Committee Reports , 7223, 23 Sept, 1975, and 7331, 11 Nov, 1975.

London Industry and Employment Research Group, The Impact of Local Authorities on Manufacturing Firms: Recent Experience in London , Industry and Employment Studies, Occasional Paper, No.5, Middlesex Polytechnic, 1981.

London Voluntary Service Council, Employment Planning in London Boroughs , 1979.

Lyons, M., 'The 2p Rate and Powers for Economic Development', The Planner Vol.69, No.5, 1983.

MacEwen, A. and MacEwen, M., National Parks: Conservation or Cosmetics , George Allen and Unwin, London, 1982.

Manchester Metropolitan District, Employment and Unemployment in Manchester , 1981.

Manchester and Salford City Councils, Manchester/Salford Inner City Partnership New Life for the Inner Cities. The Inner Area Programme 1979/80 , 1979.

Manpower Services Commission, Sheffield and Rotherham Labour Market Study , 1980.

Manpower Services Commission, A New Training Initiative , 1981.

Markusen, A.R., 'High-Tech Jobs, Markets and Economic Development Prospects: Evidence from California', Built Environment, Vol.9, No.1, 1983.

Mason,C., 'Labour Market Policy' in Young, K. and Mason, C. (eds), Urban Economic Development. New Roles and Relationships, Macmillan, London, 1983.

Massey, D.B. and Meegan, R.A., The Anatomy of Job Loss , Methuen, London, 1982.

Matheson, A. and Wall, G., Tourism: Economic, Physical and Social Impacts , Longmans, Harlow,Essex, 1982.

Mawson, J., 'Changing Directions in Regional and Local Economic Policy: The West Midlands Experience', Planning Outlook, Vol.25, No.3, 1982.

Mawson, J., 'Local Authority Economic Policies in West Yorkshire 1974-1977, An Organisational Perspective', Centre for Urban and REgional Studies, University of Birmingham, Occasional Paper No.8, (New Series), 1983.

Mawson, J. and Miller, I., Agencies in Regional and Local Development , Conference, Regional Studies Association, Nov, 1982.

McDonald, I., 'Urban Improvement', The Royal Town Planning Institute, Summer School, 1979.

McIntosh, A. and Keddie, V., Industry and Employment in the City , Department of the Environment, Inner Cities Research, Programme No.1, HMSO, 1979.

McSweeney, B., 'Can Auditors put a Price on Democracy?', The Guardian, 25/4/84.

Middleton, A., Local Authorities and Economic Development , Centre for Urban and Regional Research, University of Glasgow, 1981.

Miller, J., Situation Vacant. The Social Consequences of Unemployment in a Welsh Town , Community Projects Foundation, 1982.

Minns, R. and Thornley, J., Local Government Economic Planning and the Provision of Risk Capital for Small Firms , Centre for Environmental Studies, Policy Series,6, 1978.

Morley, S., 'Positive Planning and Direct Development by Local Authorities', Town Planning Review, Vol.52, No.3, 1981.

Municipal Yearbook, The Municipal Yearbook , 1983.

Nabarro, R., and McDonald, I., 'The Urban Programme. Will it Really Help the Inner City?', The Planner, Vol.64, No.6, 1978.

Neale, R.S., Bath: A Social History 1680-1850 , Routledge and Keegan Paul, London, 1981.

Newcastle Metropolitan District, Economic Development Policy and Programme 1984/6 , 1983.

Newcastle and Gateshead Metropolitan District Councils, Cities of Newcastle and Gateshead Inner City Partnerships. Inner Area Programme , 1978.

Newnham, R., Community Enterprise. British Potential and American Experience , Occasional Papers, OP3, School of Planning Studies, University of Reading, 1980.

North Tyneside Metropolitan Borough Council, The Development Workshop , Report of the Chief Planning Officer, 1981.

Nottingham City Council, Nottingham Lace Market, Town Scheme , Advisory Handbook, 1976.

Oakeshott, R., 'Industrial Co-operatives: The Middle Way', Lloyds Bank Review, No.127, 1978.

Orwell, G., The Road to Wigan Pier , Penguin, Harmondsworth, 1974.

Pahl, R., 'Will The Inner City Problem Ever Go Away?',
The Royal Town Planning Institute Summer School, 1978.

Parry, K., Resorts of the Lancashire Coast , David and
Charles, Newton Abbot, 1983.

Peterson, D., City Limits , Chicago University Press,
Chicago, 1981.

Poole, K.P., The Local Government Service in England and
Wales , George Allen and Unwin, London, 1978.

Ratcliffe, J., An Introduction to Urban Land Administration ,
The Estates Gazette Limited, London, 1978.

Regional Studies, 'The Future of Regional Planning and Policy
in the UK: The Findings of the R.S.A. Inquiry', Regional
Studies, Vol.18, No.2, 1984.

Rigge, M. and Young, M., Workers Co-operatives and Their
Environment Comparative Analysis with a View to Job
Creation , Programme of Research and Actions on The
Development of The Labour Market, The Commission of the
European Communities, 1982.

Righter, R., Save Our Cities , Calouste Gulbenkian Foundation, 1977.

Robinson, F., Local Authority Economic Initiatives: A
Review , Centre for Environmental Studies, Occasional
Paper, 10, 1979.

Robinson, F. and Sadler, D., Return to Consett , A Special
Report for BBC North East, Centre for Urban and Regional
Development Studies, University of Newcastle upon Tyne,
1984.

Robson, W.A., The Development of Local Government ,
George Allen and Unwin, London, (3rd Edition), 1954.

Rogers, P.B. and Smith, C.R., 'The Local Authority's Role
in Economic Development; the Tyne and Wear Act 1976',
Regional Studies, Vol.11, No.3, 1977.

Sant, M., (ed), Regional Policy and Planning in Europe ,
Saxon House, Farnborough, 1974.

Sant, M., Industrial Movement and Regional Development,
The British Case, Pergamon Press, Oxford, 1975.

Saunders, P., Urban Politics: A Sociological Interpretation ,
Hutchinson, London, 1979.

Saunders, P., Social Theory and the Urban Question ,
Hutchinson, London, 1981.

Saunders, P., 'Rethinking Local Politics', in Boddy, M.
and Fudge, C. (eds), Local Socialism? Macmillan, London,
1984.

Saxenian, A., 'The Genesis of Silicon Valley', Built
Environment, Vol.9, No.1, 1983.

Schools Council Industry Project, SCIP News 1 , 1981.

Scott, A.J., 'Locational Patterns and Dynamics of Industrial
Activity in the Modern Metroplis', Urban Studies, Vol.19,
No.2, 1982.

Scottish Development Agency, Focus on Technology ,
Report 83, 1983.
Self, P., 'Unemployment and Local Action', Town and Country
Planning, Vol.52, No.1, 1983.
Shaw, G.B.,The Commonsense of Municipal Trading , The Fabian
Socialist Series, No.5, London, 1908.
Sheffield Metropolitan District Council, Industrial Rates in
Sheffield , Social Strategy Steering Group, 1981a.
Sheffield Metropolitan District Council, An Outline Plan for
the First Year , Employment Department, 1981b.
Sheffield Metropolitan District Council, Employment
Department: An Initial Outline , 1982.
Sheffield Metropolitan District Council, Urban Programme
1983-86 , City of Sheffield, 1983.
Sheffield Metropolitan District Council, Employment
Department: Review of the Work in the First Year , 1983b.
Sheffield Metropolitan District Council, The Impact of
Sheffield Council Spending on the Local Economy ,
Employment Programme Committee, (16/11/83), 1983.
Sheffield Metropolitan District Council, Employment
Research and Resources Unit Report 1982-1984 ,1984a.
Sheffield Metropolitan District Council, Positive Action
Project: Women Workers in the Local Authority ,
Employment Department, 1984b.
Sheffield Metropolitan District Council, Leaders Report
on the Consequences of "Streamlining the Cities" , 1984c.
Sheffield Metropolitan District Council, Contracting
Industry: Contract Compliance and the Building Industry ,
Employment Department, Information Pack, 1984d.
Sheffield Metropolitan District Council, Steel in Crisis ,
nd.
Shelter, Build Homes, Build Hope , 1981.
Smith, C., 'Local Authorities and Economic Development',
Planning Outlook, Vol.23, No.2, 1980.
South Yorkshire County Council, County Environment Study ,
1978.
South Yorkshire County Council, Structure Plan. Written
Statement , 1978.
South Yorkshire County Council, Corporate and Financial
Plan , Employment and Development Sub-Committee, 1978.
South Yorkshire County Council, An Economic Strategy for
the County Council , Employment and Economic Development
Sub-Committee, 1981.
Spooner, S., The Politics of Partnership , Planning Studies
No.6, The Polytechnic of Central London, School of
Environment, Planning Unit, 1980.
Stewart, M., 'Inner City Employment and the Built Stock',
Built Environment Quarterly, Vol.4, No.3, 1978.

Stonier, T., 'The Third Industrial Revolution: Micro-
  processors and Robots', The Royal Town Planning
  Institute, Summer School, 1980.
Storey, D., 'New Firm Formation Employment Change and the
  Small Firm: The Case of Cleveland County', Urban Studies,
  Vol.18, No.4, 1981.
Storey, D.J., 'Local Employment Initiatives in North East
  England: Evaluation and Assessment Problems', in Young, K.
  and Mason, C.(eds), Urban Economic Development ,
  MacMillan, London, 1983.
Storey, D.J. and Robinson, J.F.F., Local Authorities and the
  Attraction of Industry: The Case of Cleveland County
  Council , Centre for Urban and Regional Development,
  Discussion Paper 29, Newcastle upon Tyne University, 1981.
Stratford on Avon District Council, Report of the Tourism
  Steering Group , 1978.
Strathclyde Regional Council, Transport Policies and
  Programmes, 1980-85 , 1980.
Struthers, W.A.D. and Williamson, C.B., 'Local Economic
  Development: Integrated Policy Planning and Implementation
  in Merseyside', Town Planning Review, Vol.50, No.2, 1974.
Swain, A., 'New Homes in the Inner Cities', Municipal and
  Public Services Journal, 7/12/79.
Tayler, M., 'Industrial Improvement Areas', The Planner,
  Vol.68, No.3, 1982.
Taylor, A., 'Market Gap: A Route for Local Enterprise',
  Town and Country Planning , Vol.51, No.2, 1982.
Taylor, A., 'The Expansion of Worker Co-operatives: The
  Role of Local Authorities', Regional Studies, Vol.17,
  No.4, 1983.
Taylor, A., 'New Jobs in "Chips with Everything" ', Town and
  Country Planning, Vol.53, No.2, 1984.
Taylor, A., 'Making the Most of Workers Co-ops: The Local
  Agency Approach', Socialist Environment and Resources
  Association, n.d.
Taylor, T., 'High Technology Industry and the Development
  of Science Parks', Built Environment, Vol.9, No.1, 1983
Templeton, J., Education Policies and the Local Authority ,
  Sheffield City Polytechnic, n.d.
The Labour Party, Workers' Co-operatives , 1980.
The Royal Town Planning Institute, Employment Planning , 1979.
The Royal Town Planning Institute, Renewal of Older Housing
  Areas in the 1980's, A Policy Paper Prepared by the
  Housing Working Party, 1981.
The Treasury, Economic Progress Report , No.107, 1979.
Thwaites, A.T., 'Some Evidence of Regional Variations in the
  Introduction and Diffusion of Industrial Products and
  Processes Within British Manufacturing Industry', Regional
  Studies, Vol.16, No.5, 1982.

Tiebout, C.M., 'A Pure Theory of Local Public Expenditure',
Journal of Political Economy, Vol.64, 1956.

Titley, G., 'The Development of Worker Co-operatives',
The Planner, Vol.69, No.5, 1983.

Topham, S., Problems in the Re-Use of Industrial Buildings ,
Joint Unit for Research on the Urban Environment, Research
Note,14, 1978.

Town Planning Review, 'Industrial Improvement Areas. An
Editorial', Town Planning Review, Vol.49, No.2, 1978.

Townroe, P.M., Industrial Location Decisions , Centre for
Urban and Regional Studies, University of Birmingham,
Occasional Paper, No.15, 1971.

Townroe, P.M., Planning Industrial Location , Leonard
Hill Books, London, 1976.

Tressell,R., The Ragged Trousered Philanthropist ,
Panther, London, 1965.

Tym and Partners, Time for Industry , HMSO, London, 1979.

Tym, R. and Partners, Monitoring Enterprise Zones ,
Year Three Report, 1984.

Tyne and Wear County Council, Three Year Rolling Programme
of Economic Development Work , 1983.

Veal, A.J., Towards a Strategy of Tourism in the Heart
of England , West Midlands Tourist Board, 1975.

Wallwork, Derelict Land , David and Charles, Newton Abbot,
1974.

Wandsworth Industry Schools Project, A Report of the
First 3½ Years of WISP , 1981.

Wandsworth London Borough, Employment in Wandsworth , 1972.

Wandsworth London Borough, Prosperity or Slump? , 1976.

Wandsworth London Borough, Wandsworth Borough Plan , 1980.

Wannop, U.A., 'Strategic Planning and the Area Development
Projects of the Scottish Development Agency', Regional
Studies, Vol.18, No.1, 1984.

Watkins, D., Industrial Common Ownership , Fabian Tract, 455,
1978.

West Glamorgan County Council, Report of the County Clerk ,
Policy and Resources Committee, (Industrial Promotion
Sub-Committee), 1979.

West Midlands County Council, County Structure Plan.
Report of Survey Employment , 1978.

West Midlands County Council, 'Economic Development and
Policy Progress Report', March, 1983.

West Midlands County Council, Streamlining the Cities ,
Response of the Economic Development Committee, 1984.

White, J., A Review of Tourism in Structure Plans ,
Centre for Urban and Regional Studies, Birmingham, 1981.

White, P., An Appraisal: Some Comparisons of Efficiency.
South Yorkshire Public Transport Policies , Conference
Transcripts, Sheffield City Polytechnic, Department of
Urban and Regional Studies, 1980.

Whyatt, A., 'Developments in the Structure and Organisation of the Co-operative Movement: Some Policy Considerations', Regional Studies, Vol.17, No.4, 1983.

Williams, H., Bozeat, N., Cook, A. and Hardy, B., Industrial Renewal in the Inner City , Department of the Environment Inner Cities Research Programme, No.2, HMSO, 1980.

Williams, J.F.D., A Review of Science Parks and High Technology Developments , Drivas Jonas, 1982.

Willis, K.G. and Whisker, P.M., 'Economic Assessment of Local Authority Aid to Industry', Planning Outlook, Vol.23, No.2, 1980.

Willis, R., Portrait of York , Robert Hale, London, 1972.

Wilson The Rt Hon Sir Harold, The Financing of Small Firms , Interim Report of the Committee to Review the Functioning of Financial Institutions, Cmnd 7503, HMSO, 1979.

Woodward, R., Foster, N.R. and Patel, S., Trends in the Sheffield Local Labour Market in the 1970's. Some Comments on the Implications for School Leavers and for Education Industry Liaison , Sheffield City Polytechnic, Department of Economics and Business Studies, March, 1980.

Yates, J.M., Local Authority Employment Creation through the promotion of Tourism , Sheffield City Polytechnic, Department of Political Studies, Occasional Paper, EP/1/82, 1982.

York District Council, Economic Development Strategy Report , 1983.

Young, K., Mason, C. and Mills, E., Urban Governments and Economic Change , Social Science Research Council, The Inner City in Context, No.11, 1980.

Index

Glasgow: 50, 56, 218;
  District Council 23, 41;
  eastern area renewal
  project 219; underground
  railway 83
Goodwill Incorporated 121
Grants and loans: 113, 124,
  126, 129, 155, 248; to
  community projects 120,
  121; to co-operatives 116;
  to industrial improvement
  areas 102; to small businesses 129, 261; from urban
  aid 120, 122
Greater London Council: 5, 25,
  31, 139, 193, 196, 197, 226,
  257, 259, 260, 262; abolition of 168-169, 232, 262;
  and attraction of industry
  46, 48, 50, 53; contract
  compliance 165-167;
  economic development group
  193, 227; help to Trade
  Unions 147; housing 78, 79;
  Labour Party manifesto
  (1981) 27, 31, 32-33, 152,
  181, 203; municipalisation
  178, 181-182; organisation
  193; political campaigning
  150-151; popular planning
  257, 259; racial and sexual
  equality 152; rates 158-
  159; and small firms 131;
  tourism 60, 71; training
  222; transport policies 83,
  181
Greater London Enterprise
  Board 21, 33, 178, 193, 230,
  231, 246, 259, 262
Greater London Training Board
  204, 229
Greater Manchester 142, 217
Greater Manchester County
  Council 142, 144, 174
Guest Keen and Nettlefolds
  147, 150

Hackney 83; London Borough of
  22, 139, 151, 258, 262

Halls of Residence 69
Halifax Borough Council 60
Hammersmith and Fulham, London
  Borough of 28, 107, 181, 205
Harrogate 55, 56, 62; conference
  promotion 69-70
Health and Safety at Work Act
  166
Health Resorts and Watering
  Places Act 1921 13, 67
Heriot-Watt, University of 110
Heritage Coasts 58
Highlands and Islands Develop-
  ment Board 202
Highways Act (1862) 4
Historic Buildings and Monu-
  ments Council 59
Hotels 63-64, 69
Housing 7, 76, 77-81, 108, 200-
  201; renovation 80
Housing Act (1925) 7
Housing Act (1980) 78
Housing and Town Planning Act
  (1909) 7
Housing and Town Planning Act
  (1919) 7
Howard, Ebeneezer 11
Humber Bridge 45

I.T.E.C. 211
Industrial and Commercial
  Finance Corporation 126
Industrial and Commercial
  Improvement Areas 97-103
Industrial and Common Ownership
  Act (1976) 115, 116
Industrial Common Ownership
  Finance 115-116
Industrial democracy 114
Industrial Development
  Certificates 16, 136
Industrial Development Officers
  18, 19, 21, 22, 23, 24, 27,
  38-39, 40-44, 138, 153, 190,
  192, 196, 256
Industrial Estates 14, 22, 45,
  95, 112-113

Industrial premises and units 21, 44, 50, 92-93, 96-104, 111, 121, 128, 159, 247; improvement of 96-103, 144-145, 230

Industrial sites 44, 50, 90-92; management of 91

Industrial Training Act (1964) 201

Industrial Training Boards 201

Industry Act (1972) 220

Infra-structure improvements 20, 38, 45-46, 76-88, 99; for tourism 63-66

Inner City Intervention 223-224

Inner City Partnership Finance 121, 205, 273

Inner London Education Authority 210, 222

Inner Urban Areas Act (1978) 60, 98, 102, 103, 116, 188, 224, 226

Innovation Centres 109-110

Investment 239, 241; in industrial units 94-95, 239

Iron and Steel industry 148-150, 155, 176, 260

Isle of Wight Tourist Board 56

Italy 114, 119

Jarrow Hunger March 14, 135

Job Sharing 109, 162, 199

Key worker housing 18, 38, 46, 77-78, 201

Kingston upon Hull 23

Kingston upon Hull telephone service 10, 176

Kodak Ltd 147

Labour controlled authorities 148, 183, 245, 256

Labour governments: 263; of 1945-1951 15, 16, 29-30, 184, 265; of 1974-1979 84

Labour Party 11, 15, 17. 29-31, 118, 155, 196, 264; and municipalisation 11, 183, 184, 260

Lady Margaret Hall Settlement 121

Lake District 65, 73

Lambeth London Borough of 200

Lambeth Industrial Enterprises 121

Lancashire: 135, 142; County Council 142

Lancashire Enterprise Board 230

Land Development and Purchase 225, 247, 249

Land Reclamation 60-61, 86, 99

Layfield Report 158

Leeds: 127, 129, 163; Metropolitan District of 164, 256

Leicestershire County Council 129

Letchworth 14

Liaison Committees 191-192

Liberal Party 17, 135, 155

Listed Buildings 58-59

Liverpool: 28, 62, 175, 185; docklands 175, 223; Metropolitan District Council 161, 258; environment 85, housing 79, 161; industrial premises 128; rates 168; roads 81

Livingstone, Ken 263

Loans: see Grants and loans

Local Acts of Parliament 226, 261

Local Authorities as interest groups 108, 134-137, 140-156, 267

Local Authorities as emloyers 152, 160-167, 250

Local Authorities (Goods and Services) Act (1970) 226

Local Authorities (Land) Act 1963 90, 224

Local Authorities (Publicity) Act 1931 13, 39

Local Authority Textile Action Committee 142-143

Local Employment Act (1972) 220